Principles and Prac Working with Pupil Special Educational Needs and Disability

Providing insight into current research, and comprehensive guidance on recent legislation and policy, this key text offers anyone working or preparing to work with children with Special Educational Needs and Disability (SEND) essential academic and theoretical understanding to underpin and inform existing and future practice.

Exploring prime areas in which professionals work directly with children with SEND, chapters broach current issues and debates relating to practice, and examine recent advances in research, policy and legislation in areas including education, health and social care. This interdisciplinary approach, coupled with case studies, points for reflection and clearly signposted activities throughout, gives readers the opportunity to develop a thorough understanding of the complexities surrounding SEND and enables them to relate these to their own practice. Packed with practical tips and examples of best practice, topics discussed include:

- approaches to inclusion, integration and segregation

- competing discourses surrounding SEND and their impacts on children, families and professionals

- safeguarding and the voice of the child

- multi-agency work and the changing role of the SEND practitioner

- working in partnership with parents and families

- research and practice in relation to issues such as Autism Spectrum Disorder (ASD), Chromosomal and Gestational Diversity, Attention Deficit Hyperactivity Disorder (ADHD) and Profound and Multiple Learning Disabilities and Difficulties (PMLD).

Demystifying changes to policy, exploring legislation and identifying best practices, this invaluable resource will support students, SEND practitioners and professionals to develop and enhance practice with children with SEND.

Trevor Cotterill is Programme Leader for the FdA SEND and the BA (Hons) SEND at the University of Derby, UK.

Principles and Practices of Working with Pupils with Special Educational Needs and Disability

A Student Guide

Trevor Cotterill

Routledge
Taylor & Francis Group

LONDON AND NEW YORK

First published 2019
by Routledge
2 Park Square, Milton Park, Abingdon, Oxon OX14 4RN

and by Routledge
52 Vanderbilt Avenue, New York, NY 10017

Routledge is an imprint of the Taylor & Francis Group, an informa business

British Library Cataloguing-in-Publication Data
A catalogue record for this book is available from the British Library

Library of Congress Cataloging-in-Publication Data
A catalog record has been requested for this book

ISBN: 978-1-138-57008-5 (hbk)
ISBN: 978-1-138-57009-2 (pbk)
ISBN: 978-0-203-70383-0 (ebk)

Typeset in Melior
by codeMantra

Table of Contents

Introduction   1

1 The SEND professional   6

2 Safeguarding and Child Protection   25

3 The changing role of the SEND practitioner   41

4 Working with families in the SEND context   60

5 Inclusivity, models and discourses   76

6 Introducing developmental diversities   94

7 Profound and multiple learning disabilities and difficulties   115

8 Autism spectrum disorder   131

9 Attention disorders (ADD and ADHD)   152

10 Dyslexia   170

11 Understanding and managing speech, language and
    communication difficulties   192

12 Chromosomal and gestational diversity   212

Index   235

Introduction

Working in the area of Special Educational Needs and Disability can be one of the most rewarding careers we can follow, but it is also one which has seen a rapidly changing agenda. The aims of this book are to explore this ever-changing landscape, focussing on policy, practice and research to support Special Educational Needs and Disability (SEND) practitioners. The book is aimed at supporting both students about to enter the field and existing practitioners who are looking for a resource to support their everyday practice.

The book follows an interdisciplinary approach and is divided into self-contained chapters focussing on a specific issue, such as Autism Spectrum Disorder, Dyslexia or Profound and Multiple Learning Difficulties or Disabilities, or an area such as Safeguarding, Practices and Debates surrounding Inclusion, Working with Families, or key policies and legislation in the area. When talking to practitioners such as teachers, teaching assistants, support staff and initial teacher training students, I am always heartened by their professionalism in, passion for and commitment to working with pupils, their families and each other.

I hope that this book will be beneficial for students in courses such as undergraduate and foundation degrees in SEND, initial teacher training, or supporting courses in education or health and social care. A key objective of this book is to support existing practitioners in understanding the issues and debates in the field of SEND surrounding theoretical and research evidence, discourses and models of disability, as well as pedagogical strategies. It can be used alongside course books or other texts that explore the issues raised in this book in more depth. This not only is an introduction to issues related to the area, but can also provide readers with key information in each of the chapters. As well as providing an academic focus, each chapter identifies case studies, points for reflection and clearly signposted activities throughout, gives readers the opportunity to develop a thorough understanding of the complexities surrounding SEND and enables them to relate these to their own practice. In each chapter, the 'Pause for Reflection' icon allows the reader to step back and reflect on their own thoughts about a specific point raised, or their own practice. The 'Activity' icon provides opportunities for the reader to carry out further research or consolidate and develop the information provided, in respect to both the background information and pedagogical strategies.

Chapter 1 The SEND professional

This chapter reviews key legislation and policies, which are enshrined within the practice of supporting both practitioners and pupils. Commencing with the Warnock Report and charting the way in which society and the understanding of how best to support individuals with SEND have changed in the previous 40 years, the Chapter discusses the impact of these on professional practice, reviews the role of Ofsted in the inspection of professional practice, with particular reference to the outcomes for SEND pupils and analyses the importance of the SEND Code of Practice (2015).

Chapter 2 Safeguarding and Child Protection

This chapter examines the importance of safeguarding and child protection within the context education in particular. It outlines key legislation and statutory guidance in the area of safeguarding and child protection and relates these to the area of SEND. The role of Ofsted in inspecting safeguarding and child protection, the importance of information sharing and the multi-agency approach are also explored. The importance of the voice of the child in this area is identified and the chapter concludes with an introduction to the Prevent strategy as it relates to safeguarding.

Chapter 3 The changing role of the SEND practitioner

Special Educational Needs and Disability Practitioners in the UK have a key role to play in preparing SEND children and young people to take their place in society and in the world of work. There are a number of specialist and support professionals working in this area, including the teaching assistant, the Special Educational Needs Co-ordinator (SENCO), the teacher, the Inclusion Manager, Behaviour Support Manager, and Educational Psychologist. A key aspect of the changing role of the SEND practitioner is that professionals work within a multi-agency framework. As such multi-agency working is seen to provide improved responses for children and young adults through better communication and information sharing so that a higher quality safeguarding response can be made. This chapter explores how multi-agency practice is at the centre of the changing role of the SEND practitioner and examines the roles that a SENCO and a Teaching Assistant carry out within the SEND context.

Chapter 4 Working with families in the SEND context

This chapter explores the complexity of working with families in the SEND context and how policies and legislation have supported the move towards families' having of voice in how their child is supported. It both focusses on the theoretical underpinning of the professional/family relationship and outlines some of the practical applications arising from this. It emphasises the critical role that families play in the education of their children living with SEND, including how to engage hard-to-reach parents. The use of critical incidences and communication with families are analysed, alongside the use of models and power relations in the area.

Chapter 5 Inclusivity, models and discourses

Nothing is debated more in education than the issue of where pupils with additional needs should be educated. The complex nature of SEND, with its categories of need, language used and competing models identifying the causes of disability and how these impact children and young people, their families and practitioners adds to the debate. This chapter examines some of these theoretical and practical issues surrounding the complexities of working within the area of SEND, including the uses of the terms inclusion, integration and segregation and the corresponding strategies associated with these. It focusses on the notion of the Quality First teaching approach to SEND, and how competing discourses arising from the medical, social and biopsychosocial models of disability, the "Dilemma of Difference" and labelling underpin practice.

Chapter 6 Introducing developmental diversities

In whichever SEND context you are likely to be working, there is a fundamental need to be conversant with a range of perspectives, research and theoretical explanations for human growth, development and behaviour. This chapter examines the frameworks of biology, sociology and psychology and a range of theories spanning the stages in life relevant to SEND. It identifies issues such as the nature or nurture debate in relation to SEND, the notion of disability and impairment with respect to development and discusses attachment theory and the impact that early experience has on the process of attachment. It outlines the theories of development proposed by Erikson, Piaget, Vygotsky and Bruner in relation to the inclusive classroom.

Chapter 7 Profound and multiple learning disabilities and difficulties

Pupils with profound and multiple learning disabilities/difficulties (PMLD) have complex learning needs. In addition to very severe learning difficulties, pupils have other significant difficulties such as physical disabilities, sensory impairment or a severe medical condition. Pupils require a high level of adult support, both for their learning needs and for their personal care. They are likely to need sensory stimulation and a curriculum broken down into very small steps. Some pupils communicate by gesture, eye pointing or symbols and others by very simple language. Although the chapter cannot cover such a wide and diverse spectrum of categories under the umbrella of PMLD, it provides an overview of the historical perspective of PMLD as well as identifying where PMLD lies within the SEND Code of Practice (2015). It discusses the aetiology of PMLD, describes Rett syndrome as an example of a Profound and Multiple Learning Disability/Difficulty and reviews a number of teaching, learning and assessment methods for practitioners working with PMLD pupils.

Chapter 8 Autism spectrum disorder

The behaviours that we see in the classroom by pupils with Autism Spectrum Disorder are a result of complex and interacting factors, and using evidence from research, along with case studies, this chapter offers suggestions which practitioners could use within their context to support such individuals. It seeks to get the reader to reflect upon their own views and practices around such issues as the classification and diagnosis of autism, using research findings to evaluate the standing of the role of genetics, neurobiology, environmental and risk factors on the development of autism. It also discusses cognitive theories relating to autism, such as Theory of Mind, Weak Central Coherence and Executive Dysfunction. In relation to practice, it seeks to outline the General and Unique Differences approach to Special Educational Needs (SEN) and autism and the use of Social, (or Narrative) Stories, Comic Strip Conversations, Power Cards and Token Economy Strategies, in working with pupils with Autism Spectrum Disorder (ASD).

Chapter 9 Attention disorders (ADD, ADHD)

Attention deficit hyperactivity disorder (ADHD) is a neurodevelopmental disorder present from childhood involving distractibility, impulsivity and excessive motor activity often leading to academic failure and social difficulties, or a syndrome characterised by a group of symptoms, which include hyperactivity, poor attention and impulsivity. Using evidence from research, along with case studies and suggestions for strategies designed to support individuals with ASD, this chapter seeks to develop your understanding of the aetiology and the cognitive and behavioural impact on an individual living with attention disorder. It defines the terms Attention Deficit Hyperactivity Disorder (ADHD), Hyperkinetic Disorder and ADD (Attention Disorder) and the two approaches in the classification of ADHD (Diagnostic and Statistical Manual of Mental Disorders (DSM-V) and International Classification of Diseases (ICD-11). Using research findings, it evaluates the standing of the role of genetics, neurobiology and neurotransmitters, in relation to ADHD. It evaluates the suggestion that ADHD is a social construct and outlines examples of pedagogical strategies to address Inattentiveness, Hyperactivity and Impulsivity.

Chapter 10 Dyslexia

There are multiple definitions related to this learning difficulty, so dyslexia can be simply defined as a neurobiological impairment within the brain, which causes an individual to struggle more than their peers in reading, spelling and writing (Mather and Wendling, 2012). This, however, does not mean the individual struggles to learn, but, due to a lack of reading experience, it could potentially limit their vocabulary throughout their life. In addition to this, the brain receives information and cognitively processes this differently compared to someone who does not live with the learning difficulty. This chapter examines the notion of viewing dyslexia as a difficulty or difference in cognitive processing, and the characteristics, classification and diagnosis of dyslexia. It summarises the biological factors associated with dyslexia, including the role of genetics and neurobiology and introduces contrasting views about the nature and impact of dyslexia on pupils. It finally reviews a range of classroom strategies aimed at supporting the characteristics associated with dyslexia.

Chapter 11 Understanding and managing speech, language and communication difficulties

Speech, Language and Communication skills are crucial in the development of children and young people, and individuals with Speech, Language and Communication Needs (SLCN) often exhibit either language delays or disorders. This chapter aims to introduce you to issues surrounding Speech, Language and Communication Development, the impact that this has on an individual and suggestions as to possible supporting strategies. Using evidence from research, along with case studies and questions for reflection, it examines approaches in our understanding of language delay and language disorder and the social and cognitive impact of language delay and language disorder, and suggests possible supporting strategies for individuals experiencing issues with SLCN.

Chapter 12 Chromosomal and gestational diversity

The numbers of pupils seen in inclusive classrooms with chromosomal and gestational issues have risen in inclusive classrooms over the past few years. This chapter examines the causes, characteristics and strategies to support individuals with Fragile X syndrome, Down's syndrome, Cri-du-chat syndrome and foetal alcohol syndrome. It describes the causes and features of these four syndromes, discusses the moral and ethical dilemma associated with prenatal testing for Down's syndrome and outlines classroom support strategies for pupils with these issues.

The SEND professional

Introduction

Anyone working in the Special Educational Needs and Disability (SEND) context will no doubt be familiar with the legislation and range of policies which derive from these and are then used to underpin practice. This chapter starts by reviewing key legislation and policies which are enshrined within the practice of supporting both practitioners and pupils. Commencing with the Warnock Report and charting the way in which society and the understanding of how best to support individuals with SEND have changed in the previous 40 years, this chapter aims to:

■ identify and outline some of the key reports, acts and codes of practice relevant to the area of SEND

■ describe the impact that these had on the professional practice

■ review the role of Ofsted in the inspection of professional practice, with particular reference to outcomes for SEND pupils and local area SEND inspections

■ analyse the importance of the SEND Code of Practice (2015) and examine the implications of differing contexts, the importance of the local offer and the implications of the Graduated Response and Education, Health and Care Plans (EHCP) deriving from the SEND Code of Practice.

The following section focusses on some of the key reports, acts and codes of practice, which have had an impact of our perception of SEND over the past 40 years. It is not an exhaustive list but outlines the key recommendations or findings as they relate to policy and practice. Chapter 2 outlines legislation and acts specifically aimed at safeguarding.

Pause for reflection

A colleague of yours who does not work in the area of SEND asks you the question: 'How have views concerning the education of pupils with SEND changed over the past 40 years?'

■ What would your response be?

 Activity

Read the following outlines and for each of the key reports, acts and codes of practice focus on the following:

■ Which political parties were in power at that particular time?

■ What cultural and social factors might have influenced the outcomes?

■ Which models of disability and discourses were in evidence?

Warnock Report (1978)

The Warnock Report (1978) introduced the idea of special educational needs (SEN), 'statements' of SEN and an 'integrative' – which later became known as inclusive – approach, based on common educational goals for all children regardless of their abilities or disabilities, namely independence, enjoyment and understanding. The Report of the Committee of Enquiry into the Education of Handicapped Children and Young People chaired by Mary (later Baroness) Warnock stated that there was a clear obligation to educate all children, including those with severe disabilities. The Warnock Committee introduced the term 'special education needs' to replace the term 'handicapped' and was a move anyway from placing the child with a disability in a category of need (Tutt and Williams, 2015). SEN statements were proposed and it suggested that as long as an individual's needs could be met in a mainstream school, this should always be the first choice for children with SEN, noting that too many children were being sent to special schools when this was not always necessary. Its wide scope of reference included categorisations of SEND; education in mainstream, special, independent, residential and hospital schools; relationships between families, health and social services; and the roles of colleges, universities and teacher training.

In the terms of reference, the Committee aimed to consider the most effective use of resources and to prepare young people with disabilities for entry into employment. The committee responded by setting out a coherent case for improving the quality of special education and for forms of schooling that embodied social acceptance. The report asserted the hard-won rights of those with SEND to have the usual choices of association, movement and activity, from working and contributing materially to the community, to travelling without fuss on public transport and having a social life and a love life. There exists, therefore, a clear obligation to educate the most severely disabled for no other reason than that they are human (Warnock Report, 1978). We were moving rapidly away from the idea of education as an intrinsic good to which all were entitled, towards the idea of education as a means of producing an improved economy (Warnock, Norwich and Terzi, 2010).

 Activity

Read the following article 'Warnock U-turn on special schools' from the Telegraph, 2005, in which Baroness Warnock revisits the notion of inclusive education. This can be accessed online via the Telegraph website (Telegraph, 2018).

■ What are her views in 2005 concerning inclusion and why does she now admit to a 'disastrous legacy' of problem children in mainstream teaching?

Education Act (1981)

The act which progressed the Warnock Report into legislation came into force on 1 April 1983 and stated that a child has SEN if he has a learning difficulty which calls for special educational provision to be made for him. (This was also echoed in the 1996 Education Act and 2014 Children and Families Act.) It emphasised mainstream, but with caveats, and outlined the statementing process. The 11 categories of handicap were replaced and defined SEN within an umbrella of the continuum of difficulties. The act outlined assessment procedures for parents, teachers and other professionals and statements of SEN for children with severe and/or complex needs, and introduced support plans for children regarding educational provisions. However, the aims of the original Warnock Report proved incredibly difficult to achieve despite the 1981 legislation (Legislation.gov.uk., 1981).

SEND Code of Practice (1994)

The SEND Code of Practice first came into effect in 1994, and this policy established a framework of addressing and meeting the needs of children with SEN and disabilities. The code gave practical guidance on how to identify and assess children with SEN and called upon Governments to adopt the principle of inclusive education and outlined the statutory role of the SEN Co-ordinator (SENCO). This code outlined practical guidance on how to implement the Education Act of 1993, regarding the legislative duties of governing bodies, Local Education Authorities (LEAs) and schools concerning provision for children with SEN (Department for Education, 1994).

Education Act (1996)

The purpose of this Act was to consolidate the Education Act of 1944. It defined SEN as a learning difficulty, which requires special educational provision to be made, and this provision is more than what the average child requires. It also clarifies that the learning difficulty must be significantly greater than others of the same age. It stated that children with SEN should be educated in a mainstream setting as long as they are receiving the educational support that they need and that this does not interfere with the education of others (Legislation.gov.uk., 1996).

Green Paper: excellence for all children meeting SEN (1997)

In this paper, the Labour Government gave public support to the UN statement on Special Needs Education 1994, which calls on governments to adopt the principle of inclusive education and implies a progressive extension of the capacity of mainstream schools to provide for children with a wide range of needs. It identified the difficulties of early intervention and suggested how appropriated intervention would be made for children with SEN at the start of their education (Gov.uk., 1997).

The Special Educational Needs and Disability Act (2001)

The Special Educational Needs and Disability Act (2001) provided further provision against discrimination towards students at any level of education on the grounds of disability. In order to avoid discrimination of disabled people, all education providers were required to make reasonable adjustments for students with disabilities to ensure that they are offered the same choice and opportunities as the rest of society. The reasonable adjustments that are required may include: physical changes of a building, delivering classes in alternative ways and providing materials in other formats. This act also gave children with disabilities a stronger right to mainstream education and, if parents wanted a mainstream place for their child, everything possible should be done to provide it (Legislation. gov.uk., 2001).

Removing barriers to achievement (2004)

The DfES SEN Strategy had the aim to improve access to education for children with disabilities in order to help them reach their potential and it aimed to personalise learning for all children. Another aim was to raise the standards of teaching and set out a clear plan for improvements with children and their parents; in doing so, this would also raise the achievement of individuals with SEND. This policy also called for services affecting children with SEN to become more integrated; it wanted to make education more innovative and responsive to cater for individuals' needs, with the hope that this would reduce the reliance on separate services for SEN support.

It aimed to drive the inclusion agenda forward by suggesting that policies based on mainstream schooling with inclusive practices, where achievement is measured against the norm, creates an educational environment for children with SEN being disadvantaged and marginalised. Educational targets for SEN pupils should thus be realistically attainable and accessible to ensure a truly inclusive ethos. Furthermore, in terms of guidance given to local authorities, the SEN Strategy specifically says that the proportion of children educated in special schools should fall over time as mainstream schools grow in their skills and capacity to meet a wider range of needs with children with less significant needs. However, a small number of children have such severe and complex needs that they will continue to require special provision; and the desired goal for local authorities to reduce reliance on statements (Department for Education and Skills, 2004).

Education select committee report on SEN (2006)

The purpose of this report was to examine where the SEN system is failing in order to consider how the government could improve outcomes for all children with SEN. Therefore, they wanted to set out a clear policy of inclusion. One suggestion put towards the government was to develop a child-centred approach in terms of the statementing process; it stressed a multi-agency approach throughout an individual's life. It also highlighted that the closure of many special schools was an issue for many children with special educational needs and disabilities, and so it suggested how progress could be made in order to provide individuals with high-quality education that could meet their needs. The Committee highlighted the difficulties experienced by parents of children with SEND whereby the system fails to support their needs. It noted confusion over the changing definition of 'inclusion' in government policies, which had directly impacted special schools by closures, forcing inclusion in mainstream schools. At times, this had been against the best interests of the child and a distressing experience and concluded that the government needed to give greater priority to understanding the continuing correlation between children with SEN and exclusions, low attainment, not being education, employment or training figures and crime (Gov.uk., 2006).

Lamb inquiry (2009)

The inquiry was led by Brian Lamb, the chair of the Special Educational Consortium, to explore how parents felt about the SEN assessment process.

It was discovered that although some parents had positive experiences of the assessment process, many others experienced many problems. Therefore, the main aim of this enquiry was to improve communication with parents, giving them greater opportunity to access important information to support their children's needs. Therefore, the enquiry made 51 recommendations to the government with an implementation plan; this focusses on improving skills and practices as well as encouraging much more engagement with parents. It recognised a national shortfall in information being available to parents of children with SEN concerning available support and provisions and suggested that parents, who know their child well to act as a trusted advocate, needed access to clear, easy-to-understand information, which aids them with their child's needs (Lamb, 2009).

Green Paper: support and aspiration (2011)

The key aims of this paper were about providing better life outcomes for children and young people with SEND. The paper suggested that this should be done through applying a new approach to identifying SEN and giving parents direct funding for support. One of the main ideas was to place children and their families at the centre of decisions that affected them and the paper unified a SEN classification. The aim of the paper was to give children the best chance to successes by spotting any problems early. It acknowledged and developed significant regulations concerning the role of SENCOs within the five areas covered by the Green Paper: early identification and assessment; giving parents control; learning and achieving; and preparing for adulthood and collaboration for families (DfE, 2011).

Children and Families Act (2014)

In terms of SEN, the aim of this act was for children and their parents to participate in decision-making, giving them greater control over their support. It also called for early identification of children's needs in order to provide early intervention to support them. The act states that a child has SEN if they have a learning difficulty with calls for special educational provision to be made. This Act also changed the law to give greater protection for vulnerable children as well as improve services for them and support their families. Statements of SEN were replaced by Education, Health and Care Plans (EHCP) with personal budgets being created for parents and young people to self-manage support packages. Local authorities were legislated to provide information to parents and young people regarding available services in local area and the Act paved the way for individuals with SEND being supported from birth to age 25, while in education or training (Legislation.gov.uk., 2014).

Special educational needs and disability Code of Practice: 0–25 years (2015)

The SEND Code of Practice (2015) created a single assessment process which better involved children and their parents. It also replaced statements with EHC plans, first introduced in 2014 in order to bring services together. As a part of this plan, personal budgets are offered to families and it also referred to One Page Profiles as part of the personalisation agenda. It called for early identification of children with SEN, and increases choice, opportunity and control for parents. Within the code, four broad areas of SEN were identified: communication and interaction difficulties; cognition and learning needs; social, emotional and mental health difficulties; and sensory and physical needs. It provides practical guidance regarding implementing the duties, policies and procedures in Part 3 of the Children and Families Bill. It highlights the transfer of decision-making rights from the parent to child at age 16; school support should be allocated on an Assess, Plan, Do and Review basis; this would be outlined in new EHCPs regarding the type of SEN provision required, how and who delivers it. It also amended the reported category of 'behaviour, emotional and social development' to 'social, emotional and mental health' and that pupils have SEN where their learning difficulty/disability calls for special provision different from or additional to that normally available (Department for Education, 2015).

Ofsted framework for SEND

Ofsted inspects educational settings to improve practice. There is a requirement to show that all pupils are making progress. When making their judgements inspectors must consider pupils with SEND and the extent to which the education provided meets their needs. During an Ofsted inspection, the focus will be on the vulnerable pupils and the pupils who are underachieving or not making expected progress. Ofsted does not make a separate judgement about schools' SEN provision. Instead, SEN provision is inspected as part of the whole-school inspection. Paragraph 146 of Ofsted's School Inspection Handbook (Gov.uk., 2018a) says that before making their final judgement on a school's overall effectiveness, inspectors must evaluate the extent to which the education provided by the school meets the needs of the range of pupils at the school, including pupils with disabilities and pupils with SEN.

The SEND Policy and other relevant policies (for example, behaviour policy, equality policy, accessibility plan) are key to good practice. Parent friendly information must be available through the SEND Local Offer (School Information Report) on the school/college/setting website. Being prepared is an ongoing process and the whole school, supported by the senior leadership, needs to be part of this. Setting time to meet regularly with senior leadership enables SENCOs to be more effective when monitoring and evaluating SEND provision and this, in turn, helps the whole school to support the progress of the more vulnerable pupils. There are opportunities too for analysis of others' views of SEND Provision, for example, whole staff professional development audits and parent questionnaires.

Gathering evidence to demonstrate success is helpful and it can be collected at planned times by all staff as part of whole-school improvement processes. Examples of evidence are: case studies, samples of work, minutes from work scrutiny sessions, attendance data, formative and summative assessments, minutes from support agency meetings and letters from pleased parents. Ensure that the evidence is well organised and easily accessible.

There is a range of evidence that could be used as a portfolio evaluating the school's effectiveness, including data analysis showing progress according to age and prior attainment; evidence of the Graduated Approach: Assess-Plan-Do-Review; evidence that shows there are good identification processes for pupils with SEND, which are moderated by the senior leadership; and analysis of behaviour and attendance data in relation to SEND pupils – including punctuality, exclusions, bullying and evidence that all staff make effective use of assessments to develop positive behaviour and learning opportunities with high expectations, which enable all SEND pupils to achieve among others.

 Activity

Ofsted would also look for some form of self-evaluation of SEND provision.

Using the following questions, how would you evaluate your own organisation's provision?

- Do all staff and pupils have high expectations for the achievement of all SEND pupils?

- Can good or better teaching and learning for all our SEND pupils at all times be demonstrated?

- Is provision based on a careful analysis of need?

- Is an individual's progress closely monitored?

- Is there a whole school approach to improving general provision as part of a Graduated Approach to SEND rather than just increasing additional provision?

- Do SEND pupils become independent and resilient learners?

Effectiveness of leadership and management

Inspectors will report on the achievement of pupils who have SEN and/or disabilities and leadership and management are likely to be judged 'inadequate' if leaders are not doing enough to tackle poor teaching, learning and assessment, which significantly impairs the progress of pupils, especially those who are disadvantaged, or who have SEN and/or disabilities.

The outcomes of disabled pupils and those who have SEN

Inspectors will consider the progress of disabled pupils and those with SEN in relation to the progress of all pupils nationally with similar starting points. Inspectors will examine the impact of funded support for them on closing any gaps in progress and attainment. The expectation is that the identification of SEN leads to additional or different arrangements being made and a consequent improvement in progress. For groups of pupils whose cognitive ability is such that their attainment is unlikely ever to rise above 'low,' the judgement on outcomes will be based on an evaluation of the pupils' learning and progress relative to their starting points at particular ages and any assessment measures the school holds. Evaluations should not take into account their attainment compared with that of all other pupils.

The progress across the curriculum of disadvantaged pupils, disabled pupils and those with SEN currently on roll matches or is improving towards that of other pupils with the same starting points. For pupils generally, and specifically for disadvantaged pupils and those who have SEN, progress is above average across nearly all subject areas. Pupils are exceptionally well prepared for the next stage of their education, training or employment (Gov.uk., 2018b). Grade descriptors for the outcomes for pupils are on pages 62–64 of the handbook.

Pupils with SEND are also mentioned in the grade descriptors for the effectiveness of Early Years provision, found on pages 67–69 of the inspection handbook. The descriptors for 'outstanding' Early Years provision include:

▓ Almost all children, including those who have SEN and/or disabilities, disadvantaged children and the most able, are making substantial and sustained progress in relation to their starting points. They are extremely well prepared academically, socially and emotionally for the next stage of their education.

Ofsted and the Quality Care Commission also undertake the inspection of local areas' effectiveness in identifying and meeting the needs of children and young people who have SEN and/or disabilities. These inspections will evaluate how effectively the local area meets its responsibilities, and not just the local authority. The local area includes the local authority, clinical commissioning groups, public health, National Health Service (NHS) England for specialist services, early year's settings, schools and further education providers. Inspectors will consider how effectively the local area identifies, meets the needs of and improves the outcomes of the wide range of different groups of children and young people who have SEN and/or disabilities as defined in the Children and Families Act (2014) and described in the SEND Code of Practice (2015) (DfE, 2015). The inspection focusses on the contribution of education, social care and health services to children and young people with SEN and/or disabilities.

Activity

The Annual Report of Her Majesty's Chief Inspector of Education, Children's Services and Skills 2016/17 to Parliament (Gov.uk., 2017) gave a number of observations from the first 30 local area SEND inspections:

1. That children and young people who were identified as needing SEND support but who were without an EHC plan did not benefit as consistently from a coordinated approach between education, health and care as those with a plan. Consequently, parents reported that getting an EHC plan was like a 'golden ticket' to better outcomes, even though an EHC plan was rightly not issued because the complexity of the child's need did not require it.

2. Many children who have SEND present very challenging behaviour. These children and young people can be particularly vulnerable to underachievement. The underlying causes of poor behaviour in children are not always evident, and therefore there is always a risk of misidentification.

3. The number of pupils who have SEND and were excluded was typically high. Nearly half of the local areas inspected were criticised for the poor attendance of the same group. Across the majority of local areas inspected, leaders did not have appropriate plans to deal with either issue. Some parents reported that they had been asked to keep their children at home because school leaders said that they could not meet their children's needs.

● What do you think may be the underlying reasons for such observations?

● If you were in charge of developing an action plan to overcome some of the issues identified, what would be your priorities?

Special educational needs and disability Code of Practice: 0–25 years (2015)

The Children and Families Act (2014) reformed legislation relating to children and young people with SEND and the SEND Code of Practice is statutory guidance for organisations that work with and support these individuals. It sets out duties, policies and procedures relating to Part 3 of the Children and Families Act 2014 and the associated regulations, and it applies to England. Bodies such as local authorities, school governing bodies (including non-maintained special schools), further education and sixth-form colleges, proprietors of academies (including free schools, university technical colleges and studio schools), Early Years providers in the maintained, private, voluntary and independent sectors, NHS trusts, NHS foundation trusts and local must have regard to the Code, which means that they must give consideration to what the Code says whenever they are making decisions – they cannot ignore it and need to be able to demonstrate in their arrangements for children and young people with SEND that they are fulfilling their statutory duty to have regard to the code.

The principle of the code is to ensure that children, their parents and young people are involved in discussions and decisions about their individual support and local provision, and have the information, advice and support they need to enable them to participate in such discussions and decisions. There also needs to be greater collaboration between education, health and social care services to provide support. The code supports the focus on inclusive practice and removal of barriers to education, but a key focus is that children, young people and parents involved in planning, commissioning and reviewing services have greater choice and control over their support.

Changes from the previous code of practice (2001) included: a single assessment process, which is more streamlined, better involves children, young people and families and is completed quickly; an EHCP which brings services together and is focussed on improving outcomes; and an offer of a personal budget for families with an EHCP (Gov.uk., 2012), which sought to:

▓ put children, and young people at the heart of the system;

▓ identify the need for close cooperation between all services;

▓ the early identification of children and young people with SEN;

▓ a clear and easy way to understand the 'local offer' of education;

▓ a coordinated assessment of needs for 0–25 years of EHC plans;

▓ a clear focus on outcomes for children and young people with EHC plans;

▓ increased choice, opportunity and control for parents and young people (DfE, 2012).

The local offer

Local authorities have a statutory duty to develop and publish a local offer setting out the support they expect to be available for local children and young people with SEND. It should set out the provision they expect to be available across education, health and social care for children and young people in their area and outside with SEND, including those who do not have EHC plans. The local offer is the name given to the range of services which are locally available for a child with SEN or disability. It captures the key services which are commissioned across health, social care and education. Each local authority will publish clear, comprehensive and accessible information about these services, including information on how they are accessed, eligibility criteria, etc. The local offer is more than just a list or directory of services, as the local authority and its partners should involve children and young people with SEND, parent carers and service providers in its development and review.

Activity

Two examples of Local Offers can be accessed online via the LA websites (Derbyshire County Council, 2018; Nottinghamshire County Council, 2018).

▨ What does the local offer look like from these two authorities?

▨ Are there any similarities and differences?

▨ Compare these to the local offer from your own local authority.

Differing contexts

Chapter 5 of the code refers to Early Years providers and sets out the actions that Early Years providers should take to meet their duties in relation to identifying and supporting children with SEND, whether or not they have an EHC plan. These include: focussing on high expectations and improved outcomes; having arrangements in place to identify and support children with SEND; reviewing children's development and progress and notifying parents; working in partnership with parents to establish and support the needs of children with SEND and adopting a graduated approach to SEND provision with four stages of action: assess, plan, do, review among others.

Chapter 6 of the code explains the actions that mainstream schools should take to meet their duties in relation to identifying and supporting children with SEND, whether or not they have an EHC plan. It focusses on the right of every child and young person to receive an education that enables them to make progress, so that they achieve their best, become confident and make successful transitions into adulthood. There is a range of requirements identified in this chapter including: monitoring the progress and development of all pupils; doing everything they can to meet pupils' SEN; ensuring that pupils with SEND engage in activities alongside their peers; making the quality of teaching and progress for pupils with SEND a core part of the school's performance management arrangements and professional development for teaching and support staff and designating a teacher (a SENCO) to be responsible for coordinating SEND. Other aspects covered include: equality and inclusion; curriculum; identifying SEN in schools; transition and the role of the SENCO in schools.

Chapter 7 of the code explains and provides guidance on the statutory duties of post-16 providers to identify, assess and provide support for young people with

SEND. These include the duty to cooperate with the local authority on arrangements for children and young people with SEND and to admit a young person if the institution is named in an EHC plan. Other sections focus on transition planning, ensuring that appropriately qualified staff provide the support needed and reviewing the effectiveness of support.

Activity

From the above contexts, identify the one in which you are currently working, aim to work or are on placement.

■ Review the relevant chapter from the code and identify how your organisation is meeting the statutory requirements.

■ Are there any duties that are not currently being undertaken?

■ Is there an action plan to address any shortcomings?

The graduated response

In the new SEND Code of Practice, the categories of School Action and School Action Plus have been replaced by a single category called SEN Support. Where a pupil is identified as having a SEN or disability, to enable the pupil to participate, learn and make progress, schools should act to remove barriers to learning and put effective special educational provision in place. SEN support should arise from a four-part cycle, known as the graduated approach, through which earlier decisions and actions are revisited, refined and revised, leading to a growing understanding of the pupil's needs and of what supports the pupil in making good progress and securing good outcomes. The four stages of the cycle are: Assess, Plan, Do and Review. In a spiral of support, the graduated approach draws on more personalised approaches, more frequent review and more specialist expertise in successive cycles in order to tailor interventions to meet the particular needs of children and young people.

In the Assess stage, teachers gain a growing understanding of a pupil's needs that they can identify quickly where a child is not making expected progress. Many schools use regular pupil progress meetings to identify this issue and for pupils identified as underachieving, further assessment may indicate the cause of their difficulties and suggest what might need to be done to enable them to get back on track. A range of assessment tools might support this process including standardised tests, screening assessments, questionnaires and observation schedules. In Early Years provision:

The early years practitioner works with the setting SENCO and the child's parents and:

- Brings together all the information

- Analyses the child's needs

This discussion will build on, and may be held at the same time as, the discussion with parents about their child's SEN and the decision to make special educational provision for them.

(SEND Code of Practice para 5.32)

In the Plan stage, teachers gain a growing understanding of what teaching approaches work and for pupils requiring support including high-quality class and/or subject teaching and targeted provision. Once the need for SEN support has been identified, the first step in responding to a pupil's identified needs is to ensure that high-quality teaching, differentiated for individual pupils, is in place. The SEND Code of Practice adds that additional intervention and support cannot compensate for a lack of good quality teaching. Targeted provision is provision that is additional to or different from that made for the majority of pupils in the school. Once again, the analysis done at the 'assess' stage of the graduated approach will help to pinpoint the kind of provision that is likely to be most effective in meeting the pupil's needs. The class and/or subject teacher remains directly responsible and accountable for all pupils in their class, whether pupils are receiving targeted support within or outside the classroom. In Early Years provision:

Where the broad approach to SEN Support has been agreed, the practitioner and the SENCO should agree, in consultation with the parent:

- The outcomes they are seeking for the child

- The interventions and support to be put in place

- The expected impact on progress, development, behaviour

- Date for review

Plans should:

- Consider the views of the child

- Select the interventions and support to meet the outcomes identified

- Base interventions and support on reliable evidence of effectiveness

- Be delivered by practitioners with relevant skills and knowledge

- Identify and address any related staff development needs

(SEND Code of Practice para 5.40)

In the Do stage, teachers gain a growing understanding of effective support and work closely with teaching assistants or other specialist staff to plan and assess the impact of targeted interventions. The role of the teacher is to be responsible for working with the child on a daily basis and even if teaching occurs away from the main class, they still retain responsibility for the pupil. The SENCO should support the class or subject teacher in the further assessment of the pupil and advising on the effective implementation of the support. In Early Years provision:

The practitioner, usually the child's key person:

■ Remains responsible for working with child on daily basis

■ Implements the agreed interventions or programmes

The SENCO supports the key person in:

■ Assessing the child's response to action taken

■ Problem solving

■ Advising on effective implementation

(SEND Code of Practice para 5.42)

In the Review stage, teachers review the pupils' progress, formally and informally and, if appropriate, make changes to teaching approaches and other provision. The Code states that progress towards meeting planned outcomes should be tracked and reviewed at least once a term and the outcomes of the review should feed directly into the next planning phase of the graduated approach. There must also be a way to engage and involve parents and carers at the centre of planning and reviewing of provision. In Early Years provision:

On the agreed date, the practitioner and SENCO working with the child's parents, and considering the child's views, should:

■ Review the effectiveness of the support

■ Review the impact of the support on the child's progress

■ Evaluate the impact and quality of support

In the light of child's progress, they agree:

■ Any changes to the outcomes

■ Any changes to the support and

■ Next steps

(SEND Code of Practice para 5.43)

✏ **Activity**

Use a grid, similar to the one below, to plan a graduated response for

Name of child: Date: Class:

Date	Assessed/identified needs	Support in place	Date	Impact of intervention	Actions or changes to be made

▨ Focus upon one area of need from the following: communication and interaction; cognition and learning; social, emotional and mental health; and sensory and/or physical needs. Suggest examples of the intervention and specific support recommendations you could use with the pupils you work with, under the following headings:

A. Universal: All pupils

B. Targeted: Some pupils

C. Specialist: A few pupils

EHC plans

Like a statement, an EHC plan is a statutory document: a local authority must secure the specified special educational provision for the child or young person. If the plan specifies healthcare provision, the responsible commissioning body must arrange the specified healthcare provision for the child or young person. The coordinated assessment and EHC planning process should promote a 'tell us once' approach to sharing information wherever possible; put children, families and young people at the centre of the process; have effective coordination between EHC services, with joint agreement on key outcomes and include consideration of a step down process for children/young people who do not have plan following assessment or who do not meet the criteria for an assessment. There is potentially a range of individuals who could contribute to EHC plans including the child or young person themselves, parents and family, the school, community paediatricians, therapists, nurses, educational psychologist, etc. A key aspect is that it should involve the child/young person and their family and who should experience well-coordinated assessment and planning leading to timely, well-informed decisions. Local authorities must consult the child and the child's parent or the young person throughout the process of assessment and production of an EHC plan.

The plan captures:

- the child or young person's SEN and any health and social care needs;
- the services which the relevant commissioners intend to secure;
- the outcomes which they will aim to deliver, based on the child or young person's needs and aspirations.

 Activity

EHC plans should be clear, concise, readable and accessible to parents, children, young people and practitioners and be agreed locally. EHC plans are divided into a number of sections:

A. Views and aspirations

B. SEN needs

C. Health needs

D. Social care needs

E. Outcomes

F. SEN provision

G. Health provision

H. Social care provision

I. Placement

J. Personal budget

K. Advice and information

The Council for Disabled Children have produced examples of good practice in EHC plans. They can be accessed online via the council website (Council for Disabled Children, 2018).

- Review the examples of good practice they advocate. How are they similar or different to the ones you have seen within your practice?

Summary

As practitioners working in the area of SEND, we are minded to take account of the legislation, acts and policies which underpin our practice. We have come a long way from the time that pupils with SEND were identified based on a medical model of 'defects,' rather than potential. In the 1970s, attitudes to special education in general started to change and the teaching of children with learning difficulties in mainstream schools, with a focus on the message of inclusion, became prominent. The 1993 Education Act obliged schools to provide for children with SEND and all schools had to publish their SEND policies and name a SENCO. The SENCO would put things in place and provide support for all pupils that have statements of SEN. In September 2014, the new SEND Code of Practice was put into action, and this was the biggest shake-up to the system in over 30 years. Instead of giving a child a statement, the child would be given an EHC plan, which covers people from birth up to 25 years of age. The voice of the child/young person and their family was beginning to be heard and heralded the era of consultation about the support needs and a personalised approach to education.

References

Council for Disabled Children (2018). *Education, health and care plans: Examples of good practice.* Available online at: https://councilfordisabledchildren.org.uk/help-resources/resources/education-health-and-care-plans-examples-good-practice (Accessed 19/06/2018).

Department for Education (1994). *Code of practice on the identification and assessment of special educational needs.* London: DFE.

Department for Education (2011). *Support and aspiration: A new approach to special educational needs and disability.* London: The Stationery Office.

Department for Education (2015). *Special educational needs and disability code of practice: 0 to 25 years.* Department for Education.

Department for Education and Skills (2004). *Removing barriers to achievement – the government's strategy for special educational needs.* [online] Nottingham: Department for Education, 5. Available online at: www.bexley.gov.uk/CHttpHandler.ashx?id=683&p=0 (Accessed 07/07/2017).

Derbyshire County Council (2018). *Local offer.* Available online at: www.nottshelpyourself.org.uk/kb5/nottinghamshire/directory/localoffer.page?directorychannel=10 (Accessed 05/03/2018).

Gov.uk. (1997). *Excellence for all children: Meeting special educational needs consultation results: e-consultations: Department for education.* Available online at: https://education.gov.uk/consultations/index.cfm?action=conResults&consultationId=1109&external=n&menu=3 (Accessed 19/05/2018).

Gov.uk. (2012). *Special educational needs support: Families to be given personal budgets.* Available online at: www.gov.uk/government/news/special-educational-needs-support-families-to-be-given-personal-budgets (Accessed 19/05/2018).

Gov.uk. (2017). *Ofsted annual report 2017.* Available online at: https://assets.publishing.service.gov.uk/government/uploads/system/uploads/attachment_data/file/666871/Ofsted_Annual_Report_2016-17_Accessible.pdf (Accessed 12/06/2018).

Gov.uk. (2018a). *School inspection handbook 2015.* Available online at: www.gov.uk/government/publications/school-inspection-handbook-from-september-2015 (Accessed 10/07/2018).

Gov.uk. (2018b). *Government response to the education and skills committee report on special educational needs* (October 2006). Available online at: www.gov.uk/government/uploads/system/uploads/attachment_data/file/335253/GovResponse-EducationSkills-SelectCommittee-SEN.pdf (Accessed 07/07/2018).

Lamb, B. (2009). *Lamb inquiry special educational needs and parental confidence.* Annesley: DCSF Publications.

Legislation.gov.uk. (1996). *Education Act 1996.* Available online at: www.legislation.gov.uk/ukpga/1996/60/enacted (Accessed 19/05/2018).

Legislation.gov.uk. (2001). *Special Educational Needs and Disability Act 2001.* Available online at: www.legislation.gov.uk/ukpga/2001/10/section/1 (Accessed 10/04/2018).

Legislation.gov.uk. (2014). *Children and Families Act 2014.* Available online at: www.legislation.gov.uk/ukpga/2014/6/contents/enacted (Accessed 10/07/2018).

Nottinghamshire County Council (2018). *Local offer.* Available online at: http://localoffer.derbyshire.gov.uk (Accessed 05/03/2018).

Telegraph (2018). *Warnock U-turn on special schools.* Available online at: www.telegraph.co.uk/news/uknews/1491679/Warnock-U-turn-on-special-schools.html (Accessed 12/07/2019).

Tutt, R. and Williams, P. (2015). *The SEND code of practice 0–25 years.* 1st ed. London: SAGE Publications Ltd.

Warnock, M. (1978). *House of commons - education and skills - third report. Publications.parliament.uk.* Available online at: www.publications.parliament.uk/pa/cm200506/cmselect/cmeduski/478/47805.htm (Accessed 12/07/2018).

Warnock, M., Norwich, B. and Terzi, L. (2010). *Special educational needs.* London: Continuum.

2 Safeguarding and Child Protection

Introduction

The importance of Safeguarding and Child Protection in education cannot be underestimated. It is a topic which permeates our society, whether it is thinking about protecting children online, playing in the park or protecting children from harm. This chapter explores the importance of safeguarding and protecting pupils within the classroom and it aims to:

- define the term "safeguarding"
- identify legislation and statutory guidance in the area of Safeguarding and Child Protection
- ascertain if there are any differences in safeguarding children with SEND
- examine the school culture around safeguarding, including the training of staff
- review the role of Office for Standards in Education, Children's Services and Skills (Ofsted) in inspecting Safeguarding and Child Protection
- outline the importance of information sharing and the multi-agency approach
- recognise the importance of the voice of the child in this area
- introduce the Prevent strategy as it relates to safeguarding.

What is safeguarding?

Safeguarding is the process of protecting children maltreatment, preventing the impairment of their health or development, ensuring they grow up in a setting that is continuously providing safe and effective care and also taking the necessary steps that enables all children to have the best outcome possible. Child protection also falls under the terms of safeguarding children and involves the promotion of welfare and relates to protecting children who are suffering or are likely to suffer from harm. Safeguarding children is not a new concept, in 1889 one of the first Acts was passed making cruelty to children illegal (The Children's Charter). Safeguarding is a comprehensive term that constitutes the action taken to promote the welfare of children and to protect them from harm.

Working Together to Safeguard Children (2015) defines safeguarding as:

> protecting children from maltreatment; preventing impairment of children's health or development; ensuring that children grow up in circumstance consistent with the provision of safe and effect care; and taking action to enable all children to have the best outcomes
>
> (Gov.uk., 2015a, 5)

The Children Act (1989) started the notion of safeguarding by providing a thorough framework for the care and protection of children (Legislation.gov.uk., 1989), followed by the Children Act (2004), which called for a distribution of duty on local authorities and their partners (for example, health service providers, police and youth justice system) to make necessary arrangements to safeguard and promote the well-being of children and young people. This led to the setting up of the Local Safeguarding Children Boards (LSCBs) to coordinate such multi-agency work and provide a platform for early concerns to be shared. This is included in the Education Act (2002), which mandates school governing bodies, local education authorities and further education institutes to make arrangements to safeguard and promote the welfare of children and young people (Parliament of the United Kingdom, 2002).

In 2015, Working Together to Safeguard Children became a key statutory guidance for anyone who works in England with children. The guidance is set out to help professionals understand what they can expect from one another and what they can do to safeguard children. It focusses on core legal requirements, clearly identifying what organisations and individuals should do to keep children safe. It sets out in detail how individuals and organisations should work together to conduct assessments based on positive outcomes for children (Gov.uk. 2015a). It accentuates that safeguarding should be child-centred whereby services should be based on a clear understanding of needs and views of children and that it is the responsibility of everyone to play their full part for services to be effective. An indispensable document that schools should look to guide their practice is Keeping Children Safe in Education (2016), updated 2018 (Gov.uk., 2018b). which identifies three mandatory aspects of safeguarding in schools, a safeguarding policy that sets our clear expectations and processes; high-quality training that ensures staff know what to do and a clear safeguarding ethos.

Governing bodies are vital in the role of managing and safeguarding children in schools, and it is mandatory that all schools should have a senior board level-lead to take responsibility in directing the organisation's safeguarding arrangements. Head teachers must provide a calm, safe and well-ordered environment for all staff and pupils as well as focussing on safeguarding pupils and developing their exemplary behaviour in the school and the wider community. Organisations should have in place a Designated Safeguarding Lead (DSL) for safeguarding and be given sufficient time, supervision, funding and support to fulfil their responsibilities effectively. The DSL also must liaise with the local authority and work with other agencies in line with Working Together to Safeguard Children (2015) (Gov. uk. 2015a). Where there are serious needs or child protection concerns, referrals should be made to Children's Social Care.

Therefore, every school should have a DSL who is responsible for assuring that all safeguarding issues raised are effectively responded to, documented and referred to the appropriate agency. It should be read together with What to do if You're Worried a Child is Being Abused (2015) that is produced to help anyone identify child abuse and neglect and how to take appropriate response (Gov.uk., 2015b). Advice for practitioners providing safeguarding services to children, young people, parents and carers (2018) is another document that aims to help practitioners and agencies decide when and how to share personal information legally and professionally (Gov.uk., 2018a).

 Activity

Safeguarding and Child Protection
Key aspects of such a child protection policy might include:

1. Ensuring that children feel safe, secure and listened to

2. Staff/volunteers are encouraged to talk about concerns

3. Safeguarding issues are explored as part of the curriculum

4. Reference to the Statutory Framework

5. Legal responsibilities and duties

6. Duty to share information

7. Roles and responsibilities

8. Designated person(s)

9. Practical advice

10. Identifying signs and symptoms of abuse

11. What to do about concerns

12. Dealing with disclosures

13. Physical intervention

14. Intimate care

15. Changing for PE and swimming

16. 1:1 Working

17. Record-keeping

18. Confidentiality

19. Procedure for dealing with complaints and allegations about staff

20. Safer recruitment

21. Whistle-blowing

- Examine the Safeguarding and Child Protection Policy from your own context and identify how many of the statements above are evidenced.

To ensure that the policy is effective on a day-to-day basis, it is important that a recording system is in place. The components of such a policy might include the following:

1. Concern form, including body chart

2. Referral forms

3. School report template

4. Chronology forms

5. Observation statements

6. Postcards and posters reminding staff what to do if they have concerns

7. Training register

8. Child protection register

9. Single central record

10. List of important contacts and telephone number

- Again, examine the Child Protection Policy from your own context and identify how many of the statements above are evidenced.

Safeguarding and SEND

Children with a diagnosis of SEND have been proven to be more at risk of abuse. A study carried out by Sullivan and Knutson (2000) showed that, out of 40,000 children in an American city, disabled children were 3.4 times more likely to experience some type of abuse. Risk factors as to why SEND children have an increased likelihood of experiencing abuse have been divided into three categories by the National Working Group on Child Protection and Disability in England (2003) (NSPCC, 2018). They highlighted attitudes such as not fully understanding the whole impact abuse can have on disabled children. For example, a child who relies on signs and symbols to communicate may not know the necessary signs or have access to the symbols to express that they are being abused.

According to the Equality Act, (2010) a child with SEND should be viewed as a child before viewing the label of SEND and, for this reason, safeguarding for children with SEND is essentially the same as for children without SEND (Legislation.gov.uk., 2010). In fact, particular attention and additional action should be taken to promote high standards of practice and greater level of awareness because children and young people with SEND are more vulnerable to abuse and neglect due to the limitations in their physical, sensory, cognitive and/or communication needs. Research has shown that children and young people with SEND are at a significantly greater risk of all types of abuse than their typical peers, with 20.4 per cent of them experiencing physical violence, 13.7 per cent sexual violence, 18 per cent emotional abuse and 9.5 per cent encountering neglect (Jones et al., 2012).

In addition, it is suggested that the greater the severity of SEND, the greater the risk of maltreatment because of the created vulnerability and negative impressions that their SEND pose (Hershkowitz, Lamb and Horowitz, 2007). Thus, it is possible that they are likely to experience multiple kinds of abuse and multiple episodes of abuse, and yet, investigations reveal that children and young people with SEND are inadequately represented in safeguarding systems and go away unnoticed simply because of their circumstances (Higgins and McCabe, 2001).

 Activity

The Department for Education (2016) published *Keeping Children Safe in Education*, updated 2018, (Gov.uk., 2018) which identifies a range of issues relating to safeguarding for those working in schools and other educational settings to be aware of, including bullying and cyberbullying, children missing from education, mental health and gender-based violence/violence against women and girls.

The statuary guidance can be located online.

At first glance, it may appear that these do not necessarily relate to children with SEND; however, they certainly can do.

▓ Take two or three of the areas from p12 of the document and complete the table below:

Issue	Concerns for the school, parents and the individual	How might the concerns be specifically related to someone with SEND?
e.g. sexting		

Whole-school culture

To apply the principles of an effective safeguarding system in schools, the school ethos and culture is paramount. The school should not only talk and write about safeguarding in their mottos, visions and policies, but the idea has to be accepted and become part of the living existence of the school (Mclaughlin, 2005). Besides ensuring that staff are Disclosure and Barring Service-checked and safe to work with children, the school should also look at developing a notion of prevention instead of reaction with regard to safeguarding issues. This would mean that students are taught about personal safety skills including relationship and sex education to raise their awareness and capacity to see help and that practitioners are able to whistle blow any concerns they have actively before problems arise (Briggs, 2006). In pushing for such an environment, the school and staff must be able to balance risk and protection especially when working with children with SEND. This is because by eliminating all risk in the environment and devising procedures that protect at a superficial level can restrict opportunities and disempower students to feel a loss of dignity and control. It is trickier with children with SEND because sometimes restraining the child is a way to protect them. For example, a physically impaired child should be wheelchair bound at all times as he is not safe to move around on his own. Hence, the school should create a culture of empowerment that creates opportunities for growth within a secure structure of risk management.

Appropriate training for all staff

Staff training is a crucial enabler of effective safeguarding. In fact, high-quality training can ensure that staff know and respect the rights of children, be able to identify signs of abuse and neglect and respond to them appropriately (Cooke and Standen, 2002). Bandele (2009) adds on that safeguarding training is important to increase the levels of knowledge and confidence in safeguarding for the day-to-day work that is expected of them. It also encompasses the skills to document clear, factual and up-to-date records, which demonstrates justification of decision-making with objective evidence (Hobart, Frankel and Walker, 2009). In addition, there is also a need for specialist training that focusses specifically on safeguarding issues and children with SEND (Miller and Brown, 2014), for example, the acquisition of skills to communicate with children with SEND, to understand their nature of vulnerability and to carry out assessment of their needs accordingly. Schools should also ensure that all trainee teachers, at the start of their training in each school, are provided with the following:

- the child protection policy

- the staff behaviour policy (sometimes called a code of conduct)

- information about the role of the DSL

- a copy of *Keeping Children Safe in Education*.

Working Together to Safeguard Children (Gov.uk., 2015a) states that all staff working with children must be given sufficient training, supervision and support in safeguarding. The guide necessitates an induction into safeguarding, along with regular reviews to ensure that staff are improving in their safeguarding responsibilities. Policy states that safeguarding is everyone's responsibility and that all professionals who come into contact with children and vulnerable people should be trained to safeguard, keeping the best interests of the vulnerable individual at heart. In addition to this, policy dictates that there should be a DSL in all schools, whose responsibility is to support their fellow professionals in recognising children's needs with relation to safeguarding and child protection.

International studies have shown that, despite these government recommendations, teaching staff are often insufficiently trained in safeguarding, many being unaware of the school's safeguarding policies and practice (Buckley and McGarry, 2011; Bergström, Eidevald and Westberg-Broström, 2016). Furthermore, staff who are given a greater safeguarding responsibility such as the DSLs are often given insufficient training and time to fulfil their responsibility, with many only receiving the statutory safeguarding training and some being full-time teachers or head teachers (Richards, 2018). Without being provided with extra time and training, these professionals will not be able to fulfil their role as successfully as possible If the DSL is a teacher/head teacher with a full timetable, they will not have the time to ensure effective safeguarding practice and deliver training to other staff. For this reason, appropriate time and training should be given to all staff from the top down in order to maximise the effectiveness of safeguarding provisions in the school (Richards, 2018).

The Teacher's Standards (2011) outlines how practitioners involved in work with children and young people are given the authorisation for prevention, intervention and proactive work with children and their families regarding a responsibility to recognise and respond to indicators and concerns that one of their pupils may be suffering abuse, such as emotional, physical and sexual, and/or neglect (Lindon and Webb, 2016). These standards define the minimum level of practice expected of teachers (DfE, 2011) and were developed to 'raise the bar for teaching' (Sellgren, 2011, 1) and teachers are expected to demonstrate consistently high standards of personal and professional conduct inside and outside the school premises (Batty and Metcalfe, 2018) by safeguarding pupils' well-being.

 Activity

An important area is how initial teacher trainees are given training in safeguarding.

- From a range of initial teacher training organisations such as a university and Schools Direct, find out how safeguarding is taught as part of the curriculum.

- What training did you have during a relevant course in the role you occupy now?

The role of Ofsted

The Ofsted uses the definitions of the term 'safeguarding' from statutory guidance. Safeguarding children is defined as:

■ protecting children from maltreatment

■ preventing impairment of children's health or development

■ ensuring that children are growing up in circumstances consistent with the provision of safe and effective care

■ taking action to enable all children to have the best outcomes (Ofsted, 2016).

The way to evaluate that schools have ensured that all appropriate and expected steps have been taken to guarantee and promote the safety of children is through inspection and regulation. Ofsted is in charge of assessing and monitoring the effectiveness of safeguarding arrangements in schools and the timeliness of response to any safeguarding concerns that are raised.

With the introduction of the Common Inspection Framework in 2015, safeguarding in education has a much stronger emphasis than it ever has done before, with Ofsted focussing on how well schools have embedded a culture of vigilance into their practices. The careful monitoring of safeguarding in schools is important in ensuring that children are kept safe and that serious cases are prevented. Laming (2003) advises a clear line of accountability within and between services, for example, staff are monitored by the DSL and deputy safeguard lead, who, in turn, are monitored.

The Common Inspection Framework (2016) made some revisions from previous publication including references to 'safeguarding policies' being replaced with 'child protection policies' to fit with statutory guidance. Ofsted have updated and republished their guidance to inspectors on 'Inspecting Safeguarding in early years, education and skills'. These changes have been made to reflect the changes to the latest version of *Keeping Children Safe in Education* and include new references to safeguarding children who have special educational needs and/or disabilities in paragraphs 11 and 18. Ofsted (2016) states that a culture of vigilance should be created in schools, where children's welfare is promoted, and safeguarding concerns are dealt with in a timely and effective manner. It is the responsibility of Ofsted to evaluate the success of the safeguarding arrangements that have been implemented in schools, looking for the signs of successful safeguarding practice set out in sections 4 and 5 of 'Inspecting safeguarding in early years, education and skills settings'.

Key indicators of successful practice include a relationship of trust in which children feel that they are being listened to, clear and effective training arrangements for staff and the quality of multi-agency work. Key areas that Ofsted inspectors will be looking for evidence include:

■ the creation of a positive culture backed up by staff training at every level

■ the effectiveness of safer recruitment, vetting and safeguarding policies and procedures

■ staff awareness of signs of harm from within the family and wider community

■ the response to safeguarding concerns

■ the quality of the school contribution to multi-agency plans for the child.

Specifically, they would seek evidence for policies such as those for behaviour, health and safety, child protection, etc. It is important to note that there is a limiting judgement to safeguarding. If a school is found to be inadequate in the judgement 'the effectiveness of safeguarding procedures', then the overall effectiveness of the school is also likely to be judged to be inadequate.

 Activity

'School X is performing significantly less well than in all the circumstances it could reasonably be expected to perform. The school is, therefore, given a notice to improve. Significant improvement is required in relation to the application of safeguarding procedures as part of the staff recruitment process. Although School X provides a satisfactory education for the pupils, its overall effectiveness is inadequate because its leaders have failed to ensure that all government requirements relating to the safeguarding of pupils are followed. Consequently, care, guidance and support, and governance, are inadequate. Significant improvement is required in relation to its safeguarding procedures'.

What do you think that the school had not been doing (or doing) with respect to safeguarding pupils?

Information sharing and the multi-agency approach

Children with SEND are generally recognised as being the most challenging to support and teach, with most requiring skilful and attentive management. This is because they have complex needs that overlap education, health and care issues. Therefore, effective safeguarding also calls for the collaborations between professionals and agencies. Ferguson (2009) resonates that safeguarding is a part of the continuum of care provided by a range of practitioners who come in contact with children and families and are best placed to identify issues of concern. The variety of professionals and their responsibility towards safeguarding will enable a holistic assessment based on all available information, which can allow the cross-checking and conveying of clear and sufficient information. This is because no single professional can have a full picture of a child's needs and circumstances and if children and families are to receive help promptly, everyone who comes in contact with them has a role to play in identifying concerns, sharing information and taking prompt action.

It is also highlighted in the Multi Agency Working and Information Sharing Project: Final Report (2014) that interagency collaborations are needed to secure improved safeguarding outcomes as it ensures a more accurate assessment of risk and need and greater efficiencies in processes and resources (Home Office, 2014). Therefore, schools need to have a regulatory system that works smoothly to share information legally and professionally.

Working Together to Safeguard Children (Gov.uk., 2015) highlights the importance of a clear information-sharing process between agencies and the LSCB. The idea of an LSCB was first suggested in Every Child Matters framework (Gov.uk., 2003), which, following the serious case review of Victoria Climbié, proposed many necessary changes to the services in place to safeguard vulnerable people. Since this initiative, the idea of professionals working together in a multi-agency approach has been given a much higher standing, with the SEND code of practice stating that it is essential (DfE, 2015). The benefits of multi-agency working for education professionals was identified by Pettitt (2003) in stating that working collaboratively strengthened the support that CAMHS were able to provide in schools. Furthermore, Stewart-Brown and Edmunds (2003) highlight the benefit that teachers gain from an effective multi-agency approach, as they are able to access specialised support and resources, which, in turn, raised pupil attainment levels and can be helpful in ensuring that all students reach their potential (Forbes, 2007).

A significant issue with the structure of children's services prior to the introduction of multi-agency approaches was that children were falling through the net as agencies were not sharing information effectively and there was a lack of awareness of responsibility (Roaf, 2002; Walker, 2018). In order to combat this, there needs to be a 'culture of vigilance' in schools, which includes school staff working effectively with other external agencies to support pupils who are at risk of harm. Government legislation around safeguarding also encourages a fool proof approach to information sharing, placing a responsibility on all agencies to see past professional boundaries, collaborate and share information in order to keep children safe.

Unfortunately, however, despite the extensive and clear guidance, agencies continue to fail to work together and share information effectively to safeguard children. The inquiry into the death of four-year-old Daniel Pelka identified the failure of schools and social services to share information, despite their professional obligations (Rogers, 2013). Baginsky (2014) identified that teachers have an unrealistic expectation of the role and responsibility of social workers, expecting them to be the key professional involved in safeguarding children and therefore thinking that, just by making a referral, they as teachers have fulfilled their responsibility (Baginsky, Driscoll and Manthorpe, 2015).

Activity

Multi-agency working was discussed in Chapter 3 on the Changing Role of the SEND Practitioner.

▓ What agencies do you think are involved in Safeguarding and Child Protection?

▓ How is the multi-agency approach coordinated?

The child's voice

Studies have shown that the failings in safeguarding systems are often the result of losing sight of the needs and voice of the child (DCSF, 2005). Therefore, the focus should be on the child to ensure that his/her best interest is considered at all times. To do this, it is recommended to develop a relationship with the child to gather information about his/her needs, situation, wishes and feelings. Featherstone and Evans (2004) concluded that a societal context is required so that children feel they are listened to, respected as participants of society and acknowledged in their decision-making. This would also mean that the child should be provided with honest and accurate information about what is happening so that they can make an informed decision about the possible support they need (Cleaver, Walker and Meadows, 2004). However, this may not be easy for children with SEND as some might not have the capacity to communicate, understand and make the best decisions for themselves. If finding an appropriate method of communication is impeded, it is important for practitioners to understand the child's existing support network, establish who a child feels able to confide in or who understands and is able to give good and sound support to successfully protect them from harm (Cossar, Brandon and Jordan, 2011).

A key point in Working Together to Safeguard Children is a culture of listening to the child and taking their opinions, needs and feelings into account (Gov.uk., 2015a) which is also reflected in the SEND code of practice (DfE, 2015). Professionals must undertake a child-centred/victim-centred approach, always taking the best interests of the vulnerable person into consideration and a child-centred approach is vital to effective safeguarding (Munro, 2011), and that their opinions need to be considered in decision-making around their protection. Furthermore, Baginsky (2008) particularly emphasises the importance of listening to the voice of children with SEND, who are often even more vulnerable to abuse, and empowering them to speak out about the abuse they may be facing.

Unfortunately, however, other aspects can sometimes stand in the way of teachers and other professionals keeping the best interests of the children at heart in order to keep them safe. For example, Cooper (2005) suggests that the emotional trauma and anxiety that can be caused by dealing with difficult cases can lead to professionals 'turning a blind eye' to what is happening and therefore failing to do their duty to safeguard the individual. In addition to this, without an improvement in working conditions (that is, decreasing workload, increasing time, etc.), staff, while they may keep the best interest of the child at heart, will simply not have the capacity to listen carefully to the child's voice and act effectively upon it.

 Pause for reflection

One suggestion has been that due to workload, staff do not have the time to listen to the child (Reder and Duncan, 2004).

■ Can you think of any other reasons as to why a child's story may not be believed, or acted upon?

Safeguarding and Prevent

The Prevent duty came into force as part of the Counter-Terrorism and Security Act in 2015. It places a duty on educational providers and other public bodies to help prevent children, young people and vulnerable adults from being radicalised and drawn into terrorism. This means identifying those at risk and taking the appropriate actions. Those who work with children, young people or vulnerable adults have a legal duty in respect of Safeguarding and Prevent.

 Activity

The Home Office have published an online e-learning package which professionals working within education can access.

This package can be accessed online via the Home Office (2018) website.

Summary

There is a responsibility placed on all staff in schools, regardless of their role, to safeguard and protect children and professionals should have sufficient safeguarding training, specific to their setting (Baginsky, 2008), with those in more senior roles (that is, DSL) having access to more in-depth training.

Furthermore, working successfully with other agencies in safeguarding can impact positively on both staff and pupils, with staff getting the support they need to help children reach their potential (Forbes, 2007; Lindon, 2008). In order to do this successfully, staff must put policies and good intentions into practice (Lindon, 2008). It is vital that staff understand their own responsibility as well as that of other agencies, overcoming professional boundaries and collaborating effectively (Baginsky et al., 2015), with the end result of keeping all children safe from harm.

Finally, staff must always remember to keep the best interests of children at heart (DfE, 2015). They must adopt a whole-school ethos of child-centred care, in which the needs and feelings of individual children are listened to and valued (Baginsky, 2008). The recommendations of Cooper (2005) and Reder and Duncan (2004) should be taken on board by local authorities in order to ensure that teachers and other staff have the capacity to listen to the child's voice and keep their best interests at heart of safeguarding practice. All staff working with children should strive to do their utmost to keep them safe, always keeping the best interests of the individual at heart of their practice in order that they can have a happy and safe childhood.

References

Baginsky, M. (2008). *Safeguarding children and schools*. London: Jessica Kingsley Publishers.

Baginsky, M. (2014). Social work in hiding? The views of other professionals on social workers and working with social workers. *Research, Policy and Planning*, 30(3), pp. 143–154.

Baginsky, M., Driscoll, J. and Manthorpe, J. (2015). Thinking aloud: Decentralisation and safeguarding in English schools. *Journal of Integrated Care*, 23(6), pp. 352–363.

Bandele, F. (2009). The contribution of schools to safeguarding children. In Hughes, L. and Owen, H. (eds.), *Good practice in safeguarding children: Working effectively in child protection*. London: Jessica Kingsley Publishers.

Batty, N. and Metcalfe, J. (2018). Safeguarding. In Cooper, H. and Elton-Chalcraft, S. (eds.), *Professional studies in primary education*, third edition. London: SAGE Publications.

Bergström, H., Eidevald, C. and Westberg-Broström, A. (2016). Child sexual abuse at preschools – a research review of a complex issue for preschool professionals. *Early Child Development and Care*, 186(9), pp. 1520–1528.

Briggs, F. (2006). Safety issues in the lives of children with learning disabilities. *Social Policy Journal of New Zealand*, 29, pp. 43–59

Buckley, H. and McGarry, K. (2011). Child protection in primary schools: A contradiction in terms or a potential opportunity? *Irish Educational Studies*, 30(1), pp. 113–128.

Cleaver, H., Walker, S. and Meadows, P. (2004) *Assessing children's needs and circumstances: The impact of the assessment framework*. London: Jessica Kingsley.

Cooke, P. and Standen, P.J. (2002). Abuse and disabled children: Hidden needs? *Child Abuse Review*, 11, pp. 1–18.

Cooper A. (2005). Surface and depth in the Victoria Climbié inquiry report. *Child and Family Social Work*, 10, pp. 1–9.

Cossar, J., Brandon, M. and Jordan, P. (2011). *Don't make assumptions: Children's and young people's views of the child protection system*. Working paper. London: Office of the Children's Commissioner.

Department for Children, Schools and Families (2005). *Analysing child deaths and serious injury through abuse and neglect: What can we learn?* Available online at: www.dcsf.gov.uk/rsgateway/DB/RRP/u014591/index.shtml (Accessed 05/05/2018).

Department for Education (2011). *Teachers standards; guidance for school leaders, school staff and governing bodies.* Available online at: https://assets.publishing.service.gov.uk/government/uploads/system/uploads/attachment_data/file/665520/Teachers__Standards.pdf (Accessed 19/07/2018).

Department for Education (2016). *Keeping children safe in education: Statutory guidance for schools and colleges.* Available online at: https://assets.publishing.service.gov.uk/government/uploads/system/uploads/attachment_data/file/550511/Keeping_children_safe_in_education.pdf (Accessed 22/04/2018).

Featherstone, B. and Evans, H. (2004). *Children experiencing maltreatment: Who do they turn to?* London: NSPCC.

Ferguson, H. (2009). Performing child protection: Home visiting, movement and the struggle to reach the abused child. *Child and Family Social Work*, 14(4), pp. 471–480.

Forbes, F. (2007). Towards inclusion: an Australian perspective. *Support for Learning*, 22(2), pp. 66–71.

Gov.uk. (2003). *Every child matters.* Available online at: www.gov.uk/government/publications/every-child-matters (Accessed 01/07/2018).

Gov.uk. (2015a). *Working together to safeguard children.* Available online at: https://assets.publishing.service.gov.uk/government/uploads/system/uploads/attachment_data/file/592101/Working_Together_to_Safeguard_Children_20170213.pdf (Accessed 20/04/2018).

Gov.uk. (2015b). *What to do if you're worried a child is being abused.* Available online at: https://assets.publishing.service.gov.uk/government/uploads/system/uploads/attachment_data/file/419604/What_to_do_if_you_re_worried_a_child_is_being_abused.pdf (Accessed 19/04/2018).

Gov.uk. (2018a). *Information sharing. Advice for practitioners providing safeguarding services to children, young people, parents and carers.* Available online at: https://assets.publishing.service.gov.uk/government/uploads/system/uploads/attachment_data/file/721581/Information_sharing_advice_practitioners_safeguarding_services.pdf (Accessed 21/08/2018).

Gov.uk. (2018b). *Keeping children safe in education: Statutory guidance for schools and colleges*, Crown Copyright, [online], Available online at: https://assets.publishing.service.gov.uk/government/uploads/system/uploads/attachment_data/file/550511/Keeping_children_safe_in_education.pdf (Accessed 22/04/2018).

Higgins, D.J. and McCabe, M.P. (2001). Multiple forms of child abuse and neglect: Adult retrospective reports. *Journal of Aggression and Violent Behaviour*, 6, pp. 547–578.

Hobart, C., Frankel, J. and Walker, M. (2009). *A practical guide to child observation and assessment.* 4th ed. Cheltenham: Nelson Thornes.

Home Office (2014). *Multi-agency working and information sharing project.* Available online at: www.gov.uk/government/publications/multi-agency-working-and-information-sharing-project (Accessed 29/04/2018).

Home Office (2018). *Introduction to prevent e-learning package.* Available online at: www.elearning.prevent.homeoffice.gov.uk/screen2 (Accessed 12/07/2018).

Jones, L., Bellis, M.A., Wood, S., Hughes, K., Bates, G., Eckley, L., McCoy, E., Mikton, C., Tom Shakespeare, T. and Alana Officer, A. (2012). Prevalence and risk of violence against children with disabilities: A systematic review and meta-analysis of observational studies. *The Lancet*, 379 (9826), pp. 1621–1629.

Laming (2003). *The Victoria Climbié inquiry*. Norwich (GB): HMSO.Legislation.gov.uk. (2010). *Equality Act 2010*. Available online at: www.legislation.gov.uk/ukpga/2010/15/contents (Accessed 11/03/2018).

Legislation.gov.uk. (1989). *Children Act 1989*. Available online at: www.legislation.gov.uk/ukpga/1989/41/contents (Accessed 29/04/2018).

Legislation.gov.uk. (2004). *Children Act*. Available online at: www.legislation.gov.uk/ukpga/1989/41/contents (Accessed 29/04/2018).

Lindon, J. and Webb, J. (2016). *Safeguarding and child protection*. 5th ed. London: Hodder Education.

McLaughlin, T. (2005). The educative importance of ethos. *British Journal of Educational Studies*, 53(3), pp. 306–325.

Miller, D. and Brown, J. (2014). *'We have the right to be safe': Protecting disabled children from abuse*. NSPCC. Available online at: www.nspcc.org.uk/globalassets/documents/research-reports/right-safe-disabled-children-abuse-summary.pdf (Accessed 29/04/2018).

Munro, E. (2011). *The Munro review of child protection: Final report, a child-centred system*. CM, 8062. London: The Stationery Office.

NSPCC (2018). *Safeguarding and child protection in schools*. Available online at: www.nspcc.org.uk/preventing-abuse/safeguarding/schools-protecting-children-abuse-neglect/ (Accessed 29/04/2018).

Ofsted (2016). *Inspecting safeguarding in early years, education and skills settings*. Available online at: www.gov.uk/government/publications/inspecting-safeguarding-in-early-years-education-and-skills-from-september-2015/inspecting-safeguarding-in-early-years-education-and-skills-settings#safeguarding-and-inspectors-responsibilities (Accessed 24/04/2018).

Parliament of the United Kingdom (2002). *Education Act 2002*. Available online at: www.legislation.gov.uk/ukpga/2002/32/pdfs/ukpga_20020032_en.pdf (Accessed 08/04/2018).

Pettitt, B. (2003). *Effective joint working between child and adolescent mental health services (CAMHS) and schools*. LGA Research Report 412. London: Mental Health Foundation for DfES.

Reder, P. and Duncan, S. (2004). Making the most of the Victoria Climbié report. *Child Abuse Review*, 13, pp. 95–114.

Richards, C. (2018). 'It's a big ask when your job is to teach children to read, write and to count': The experiences of school staff in early help and child protection. *Pastoral Care in Education*, 36(1), pp. 44–56.

Roaf, C. (2002). *Co-ordinating services for included children: Joined up action*. Buckingham: Oxford University Press.

Rogers, M. (2013). *Daniel Pelka serious case review, coventry LSCB*. Avaiable online at: www.lgiu.org.uk/wp-content/uploads/2013/10/Daniel-Pelka-Serious-Case-Review-Coventry-LSCB.pdf (Accessed 22/04/2018).

Sellgren, K. (2011). *Gove: Tougher new teacher standards needed*. Available online at: www.bbc.co.uk/news/education-12717061 (Accessed 27/05/2018).

Stewart-Brown, S. and Edmunds, L. (2003). *Assessing emotional and social competence in primary schools and early years settings.* London: The Stationery Office.

Sullivan, P. and Knutson, J. (2000). Maltreatment and disabilities: A population-based epidemiological study. *Child Abuse & Neglect*, 24(10), pp. 1257–1273.

Walker, G. (2018). *Working together for children – A critical introduction to multi-agency working.* 2nd ed. London: Bloomsbury.

3 The changing role of the SEND practitioner

Introduction

Special Educational Needs and Disability (SEND) Practitioners in the UK have a key role to play in preparing SEND children and young people to take their place in society and in the world of work. There are a number of specialist and support professionals working in this area, including the teaching assistant (TA), the Special Needs Co-ordinator (SENCO), the teacher, the Inclusion Manager, Behaviour Support Manager and Educational Psychologist. A key aspect of the changing role of the SEND practitioner is the role that professionals work within a multi-agency framework. As such multi-agency working is seen to provide improved responses for children and young adults through better communication and information sharing so that a higher quality safeguarding response can be made. There are a range of services involved in the SEND arena, which include:

1. universal services, where everyone can access without a special referral, for example, General Practitioners (GPs), dentists' nurseries, schools and hospitals

2. targeted services, which provide support for certain groups of children and young people and are often accessed from within universal services, for example, children's centres and social services

3. specialist services, which are usually accessed when universal services cannot meet the needs of the individual, for example, family support workers, speech and language therapists, physiotherapists and child and adolescent mental health workers.

This chapter explores how multi-agency practice is at the centre of the changing role of the SEND practitioner and examines the roles that a SENCO and a TA carry out within the SEND context. It aims to:

■ describe how multi-agency working has developed since the start of the century

■ relate this to relevant policy and legislation in the area

- discuss the role of integrated working and the multi-agency team (MAT) in relation to the SEND practitioner

- examine some of the key practitioner roles within practice

- evaluate the benefits and issues surrounding multi-agency working

- use examples to identify three models of multi-agency working

- review the changing roles of the SENCO and the TA in a historical and contemporary context.

The road to multi-agency working

Following the tragic death of Victoria Climbié in 2000, the government set up an independent inquiry to find out how so many professionals had had contact with the family yet failed to provide protection for her from serious harm and, ultimately, death. As a result of the Laming Report (2003) and a series of Chief Inspectors Reports, the government issued a Green Paper called Every Child Matters (ECM) in 2003 (Department for Education and Skills, 2003) to focus on the purpose of early and preventive intervention. This and other inquiries found the failure of professionals to intervene early enough; poor coordination between professionals; a failure to share information; the absence of accountability and poor management and lack of training. In this report, there were clear steers towards addressing the shortcomings of agencies who were not sharing information. These included direction for teams to work better together to determine the child's needs, so that they get the help and support they need, not the needs of organisations. Every Child Matters highlighted the need for agencies to share information about the children they are supporting and their services and to plan for services which were delivered jointly and team up in new ways to better work together, including creating new ways of working across the children's workforce.

In the Children and Young People's Workforce Strategy (2008), the Labour Government's vision was that everyone who worked with children and young people should be ambitious, excellent in practice, committed to integrated working and respected and valued as professions. It was to ensure that professionals had the skills and knowledge to help children and young people develop and succeed through a common core of competencies and knowledge. These were expectations of both paid and unpaid staff whose work brought them into regular contact with children, young people (CYP) and families. These included the effective communication and engagement with CYP and families; safeguarding and promoting the welfare of the child; and supporting transitions and multi-agency working to include the sharing information (Children and Young People's Workforce Development Network, 2008). The Laming Report (2003) put into law the recommendations of Every Child Matters (ECM) agenda (extended into Further Education (FE) to include all young people), which required children's services to plan to work together to improve children and young people's lives, to take all measures to ensure that risks of harm are minimised and to take appropriate action to address concerns about the welfare of children. The Children's Act (2004) (Legislation. gov.uk., 2004) introduced legislation that encouraged multi-agency cooperation (Gillen, 2011) and imposed a duty on Local Authorities (LAs) and partners to improve well-being of children and young people as defined by reference to ECM outcomes.

Under Section 10 of the Children Act 2004 and Section 75 of the National Health Service Act (2006), local authorities and Clinical Commissioning Groups have a statutory duty to consider the extent to which children and young people's needs could be met more effectively through integrating services and aligning or pooling budgets in order to offer greater value for money, improve outcomes and/or better integrate services for children and young people with SEN or disabilities (Legislation.gov.uk., 2006). Under the Care Act (2014), local authorities must ensure the provision of preventative services, the diversity and quality of care and support services for adults, and the provision of information and advice on care and support locally. Partners must agree how they will work together. They should aim to provide personalised, integrated support that delivers positive outcomes for children and young people, bringing together support across education, health and social care from early childhood through to adult life and improve planning for transition points such as between early years, school and college, between children's and adult social care services, or between paediatric and adult health services (Legislation.gov.uk., 2014).

In Working Together to Safeguard Children (2015), there are requirements for local agencies to work together to assess the social care needs of individual children and young people who may benefit from early help and for local authorities and their partners to have a clear line of accountability for the commissioning and/ or provision of services designed to safeguard and promote the welfare of children and young people. The local authority must engage other partners it thinks appropriate to support children and young people with SEN and disabilities. This might include voluntary organisations, child and adolescent mental health services (CAMHS), local therapists, Jobcentre Plus and their employment support advisers, training/apprenticeship/supported employment providers, housing associations, careers advisers, leisure and play services (Gov.uk., 2015).

Contemporary reforms in educational legislation and the revised SEND Code of Practice (DfE, 2015), have put even greater weight on professionals working cohesively in a MAT. It has intensified the multi-agency work between professionals from education, health and social care professions. Fox (2015) highlights that the introduction of Education Health and Care Plans (EHC P) delivered further emphasis on the need for professional to work together in order to put the CYP and their family at the heart of the procedure. This requirement of professionals working together enables them to gather a greater understanding and respect of each other's roles and affirms that education, health and social care services should collaborate to enable children with additional needs to get the best support. Grol and Grimshaw (2003), cited in Kennedy and Stewart (2012), see the exchange between professionals as beneficial, by providing improved interpersonal skills, increasing team work understanding and being clear about achievements.

 Pause for reflection

■ Why do you think there has been so many reforms in this area?

■ What contact have you had with different professionals and organisations, within your practice?

■ What was the experience like for you, the pupils and families concerned?

Multi-agencies, integrated working

Multi-agency working is a generic term and takes different forms locally. It brings together practitioners from different sectors and professions to provide an integrated way of working to support CYP and families. It is a way of working that ensures children and young people who need additional support have exactly the right professionals needed to support them. Multi-agency working could involve anyone whose job or voluntary work puts them in contact with CYP and their families. It is likely to include people from professional backgrounds including social work, health, education, Early Years, youth work, police and youth justice.

Because CYP and family's needs can be very different, the composition of a MAT will differ from case to case. It is important bring with them their own specialist skills, expertise and insight so that the child, young person and family gets the best support possible. Multi-agency working can be described as a single project or initiative where agencies come together to address a specific issue or concern (Atkinson, Doherty and Kinder, 2005). The terms 'multi-agency' and 'multi-professional work' entered the discourse of policy and practice in children's services during the 1990s (Anning et al., 2006).

The idea of multiple professionals working together to ensure the best outcomes for a child has led to the framework of multi-agency working. This initiative first came about as a result of ECM (DfE, 2003), which encouraged various agencies and professionals to come together and work collaboratively around a given plan. This initiative has since been given greater standing in the SEND Code of Practice 0–25 (2015), which states that it is essential for professionals to work together effectively to ensure that all the different needs of the child are being addressed (DfE, 2015). Lloyd, Stead and Kendrick, (2001) defines a MAT, as a collaboration of professionals from different agencies that join together to deliver a cohesive approach to support CYP and families. According to Parr (2016), the notion of multi-agency work has developed and is rooted in the discourses and contemporary legislation directing practice, in addition to policymaking in England. Lucas (2017) states that MATs comprising multiple practitioners demand a lead professional to be appointed, so that services can be directed appropriately to achieve an effective action plan that supports the CYP and their family.

 Activity

There are a number of professionals who work within a MAT including:

1. Head teacher/class teacher

2. Child protection designated teacher

3. Special Educational Needs Co-ordinator (SENCO)

4. Educational psychologist

5. Education welfare officer

6. Paediatric occupational therapist

7. Social worker

8. Specialist teachers from the learning support service

9. Speech and language therapist

10. Home school liaison worker

11. Child and adolescent psychotherapist

- Identify what roles these and other professionals carry out within the area of SEND?

- How are they accessed, who do they report to and how do they work collaboratively?

- By giving a specific example from your practice, describe how these professionals worked together.

Benefits and issues of multi-agency working

Multi-agency working provides benefits for CYP and families because they receive tailor-made support in the most efficient way. The benefits of this include: early identification and intervention; easier or quicker access to services or expertise; better support for parents; CYP and the family's needs addressed more appropriately and groups of professionals working together to meet the complex needs of children and families. Atkinson et al. (2002) outlined outcomes of successful multi-agency working, which include easier access across the range of services and expertise, increasing educational attainment, early identification of special needs and effective support for parents. Abbott Townsley and Watson (2005) further support multi-agency working has led to increased healthcare provision for children with disabilities; however, this had no impact on the social and emotional needs of the child and families.

However, this approach relies on each practitioner contributing their own expertise, specialist skills and perceptions, which could be a barrier to achieving a plan for the CYP and family that is effective and supportive. This view is supported by Lucas (2017) who argues that social relations and forming partnerships may be a limitation to working in a MAT. Similarly, Maddern et al. (2004) claims that, if professionals in MATs do not communicate adequately between themselves, they risk educational settings turning into ideological battlefields, due to professional conflicts from each organisation presenting contending services. It could be argued that the lead professional role should be undertaken by the individual who is in best position to make appropriate judgements on the CYP and family's needs.

 Activity

The Scottish government issued the guide Getting it right for every child (2008) whose principles are to improve outcomes for all children. It does this by creating a single system of service planning and delivery across children's services. It helps to create a positive culture of collaborative working, streamlines systems, achieving valuable savings, in time and resources and develops consistently high standards of practice.

The guide can be obtained from the Government of Scotland's (2018) website.

▓ What are the ten components of this guide?

▓ How would this improve the outcomes for all children, including those with SEND?

Doyle (2008) reviewed barriers and facilitators of multidisciplinary team working and suggested that there were advantages of working collaboratively such as sharing resources, emphasis on team work and interagency training that supports working together. However, issues such as lack of trust or confidence in others, lack of time to meet up and communicate and the duplication of workload were identified. When there is a lack of communication in a MAT, it could lead to issues with sharing information and therefore affect working together in all aspects to meet the needs of the child, which could then lead to child protection and safeguarding issues. Atkinson et al. (2002) suggest that successful multi-agency working is based on effective systems and practices with three positive consequences: improved services, direct outcomes and prevention. These would ensure good communication and adequate resources in terms of staffing and time, alongside a commitment that this actually works in practice. Role release, in which professionals transfer their skills and share expertise and role expansion involving the training of other professionals, were vital.

Parents also play a crucial role in multi-agency working, and Lendrum, Barlow and Humphrey (2015) found that developing positive school-home relationships through structured conversations with parents of learners with special educational needs and disabilities was important. However, there were also problems, including the fact that parents who have children with SEND may have a poor level of education and negative experiences of school themselves; this could mean that they may be reluctant to become involved with their child's school. However, parents who are engaged typically have higher aspirations and expectations of their children, which means that they may expect too much from their child. Also, schools may struggle to communicate with working parents because they are busy at times when school staff are available for meetings.

 Activity

▓ From your practice, what are the benefits of working with other professionals as well as parents in support of their child with SEND?

▓ What are the barriers and facilitators within these relationships?

▓ Describe a situation which had a positive outcome of working with other professionals and identify why this was the case?

Models of multi-agency working

The Department for Children, Schools and Families (DSFC) offers three working models to support educational settings: the multi-agency panel, MAT and integrated services (DSFC, 2007).

Multi-agency panels

Members of a multi-agency panel are each employed by their own agencies, but meet on a regular basis to discuss about children who require additional support from multiple agencies (CWDC, 2007). An example of a multi-agency panel is the Youth Inclusion and Support Panel (YISP), which brings multiple agencies together with the aim of reducing crime and antisocial behaviour (Walker et al., 2007). At the heart of this YISP is the aim to keep the child/young person at the centre and work with them rather than for them, something that follows the requirements set out in the SEND Code of Practice 0–25 (2015) (DfE, 2015).

Multi-agency teams

This is a more formal arrangement where, while professionals maintain contact with their home agency through training, supervision and support, they are actively recruited into the team. Using an integrated approach (Frost, 2014), the team takes on work at a range of levels from an individual level to a whole-school level. Examples of MAT are Behaviour and Education Support Team and the CAMHS that recruit staff from different backgrounds with different expertise, which led to an increase in information from different perspectives and specialisms, resulting in a more holistic and creative approach (Halsey et al., 2005). They consist of a team of people from the education, social care, health and other services to improve the mental and well-being of students by placing emphasis on building resilience, prevention and intervention.

Integrated services model

This consists of various services working together collaboratively in a common location, for example, in a Multi-Agency Safeguarding Hub (MASH), which brings together the Local Authority, the NHS, police force and the probation service under one roof to safeguard CYP and adults (Nottinghamshire.gov.uk., 2018). The aim of a MASH is to bring agencies together and to put the child or young person at the centre of everything they do. They provide a single point of contact for any concerns around the safeguarding of a child, young person or adult. Due to the number of professionals all in one place, referrals can be dealt with efficiently as all professionals can share their intelligence and background knowledge in a timely manner.

Furthermore, the wide range of specialisms provides an array of knowledge from different backgrounds, meaning that MASH can assess these referrals more accurately and be aware of the support that should be provided from all angles. Other benefits include a united vision, which ensures that all professionals understand each other in terms of the professional language and approaches they use, and greater efficiency in terms of ensuring that support is not being duplicated. Nottinghamshire County Council has a dedicated MASH hub and is the single point of contact for all professionals to report safeguarding concerns. It can be accessed online from the Nottinghamshire County Council (2018).

- Thinking about your own practice, can you identify any of these three types of multi-agency models?

- How has the relationship with your context and these professionals changed over the past few years?

- If you are a new member of staff working in the area of SEND, what do you see as the priorities within your role, when working with the range of SEND practitioners?

Multi-agency practice

There are four types of inter-professional practice within multi-agency working, which consist of parallel working, multi-agency casework, project teams and work groups, all of which have different levels of collaboration. Frost (2005) talks about a continuum in partnership:

1. level 1 (cooperation) is recognised as services working together towards consistent goals while maintaining independent management;

2. level 2 (collaboration) consists of services planning together and addressing issues collaboratively;

3. level 3 (coordination) describes how services work together in a planned and systematic manner towards shared and agreed goals;

 Activity

Case study – Thomas

Staff at Ickerby School have become concerned about the progress of Thomas, an 11-year-old boy. His handwriting is extremely poor and many of his letters are incorrectly formed. He is of above-average intelligence but seems lazy and unmotivated in class. Thomas understands the tasks given to him, but is slow to organise himself to start work. He rarely has the correct equipment at school and slouches at his desk. Thomas often looks very scruffy and his clothes are stained with spilt food. Thomas quickly loses concentration during lessons and spends a lot of time gazing out of the window. He finds it difficult to make friends and is often alone at lunchtimes. He lacks confidence and self-esteem and becomes upset easily in class. He has been recently excluded for two days due to an outburst where he had banged his fists on the desk constantly and raced out of the classroom swearing at the teacher.

Staff have noticed that Thomas has a lot of bruises on his knees and elbows and he has told them that he acquired them by falling a lot. Thomas does not seem to cope well in many lessons, but has particular difficulty in those which require large amounts of writing or copying from a book or board. Thomas also hates PE as he is not good at sports and is always last to get changed.

■ What are your initial thoughts about Thomas' difficulties?

■ Which outside (or internal) agencies if any would you refer Thomas to?

■ What steps might the person in your chosen role take to support Thomas?

■ What interventions might they make?

4. level 4 (merger/integration) implies that different services become one organisation in order to enhance service delivery.

The next section of the chapter focusses on two SEND practitioners from the range of professionals who work in the area and assesses how they work collaboratively.

The changing role of the SENCO

Pause for reflection

■ What do you understand as the role of the SENCO?

■ What do you think are the barriers to achieving the role of the SENCO?

■ Do you think the role of the SENCO and responsibility for SEND pupils can be done by just one individual? Can there be a 'whole-school approach' to SEND?

The status of the SENCO was first defined in the Special Educational Needs Code of Practice (DfE, 1994). The descriptive role involved working with, advising and contributing to the training of other teachers; the teaching of, and maintaining records of, children with special educational needs; keeping in touch with the parents of children with SEN and working with other agencies, including the educational psychology service, medical and social services and voluntary bodies. Since 1994, there has been a significant improvement in the status of the SENCO, requiring SENCOs to have qualified teacher status. The SENCO guide (DfE, 1997) offered examples of best practice and the National Standards for Special Educational Needs Co-ordinators (TTE, 1998) (Batod.org.uk., 1998), and also offered structure and reinforcement of the roles of the SENCO.

It also identified the main knowledge, attributes and expertise expected of a SENCO (Hallett and Hallett, 2010). The 2001 SEND Code of Practice 0–25 (2015) (DfE, 2015) further exemplified the position by highlighting the managerial responsibilities of the SENCO, which includes ensuring that there is liaison between parents and carers and that individual educational plans (IEPs) were in place. The role also involved advising and supporting other staff about SEN and having a school policy for dealing with SEN children and putting in place a graduated response system to meet children's needs at the earliest opportunity (Ekins, 2012).

Removing Barriers to Achievement (2004) (Department for Education and Skills, 2004) identified that the SENCO should be a key member of the Senior Leadership Team (SLT), and influenced the development of policy for whole-school improvement, or at least a person to act as champion of SEN and disability issues in the school. The SEND Code of Practice 0–25 (2015) (DfE, 2015) highlights that all newly appointed SENCOs must be qualified teachers to achieve the National Award in SENCO within three years. They still have day-to-day responsibility for SEND policy in school, but need to offer professional guidance to colleagues and works closely with staff, parents and other agencies. Advisory roles include the graduated response, delegation of budget and resources and the key contact for external agencies.

 Activity

The Council for Disabled Children have published the SEN and disability in the early years: A toolkit Section 6: The Role of the Early Years SENCO. It can be accessed online via the Foundationyears (2018) website.

It identifies the role of the SENCO from the SEND Code of Practice 0–25 (2015) 0–25 (2015) as:

■ ensuring all practitioners in the setting understand their responsibilities to children with SEN and the setting's approach to identifying and meeting SEN;

■ advising and supporting colleagues;

■ ensuring parents are closely involved throughout and that their insights inform action, taken by the setting;

■ liaising with professionals or agencies beyond the setting.

It suggests a reflective task for the SENCO working with the manager of the setting to review the SEN and disability policy and practice within the setting and consider:

1. how well children with SEN are learning and developing; what progress they are making and how good outcomes are for them;

2. how well practitioners understand their responsibilities to children with SEN or disabilities;

3. how well practitioners understand the setting's approach to identifying and meeting SEN;

4. how well supported colleagues feel, in terms of information, advice and support in identifying and meeting the needs of individual children, and training in SEN and disability;

5. how closely parents feel they are involved and how well their insights inform action taken by the setting;

6. how well the setting liaises with professionals or agencies beyond the setting and how well this supports the SENCO and other practitioners in the setting.

● Although aimed at SENCOs, do these questions reflect your understanding of the role of the SENCO within your practice?

Activity

The National Award for SEN Co-ordination is a master's level qualification and involves the following competencies:

1. Strategic development of SEN policy and procedures, such as working with senior colleagues and governors, financial planning and budget management.

2. Coordinating provision involving developing, using and monitoring evaluating systems, alongside the collecting, analysing and use of data and deployment of staff.

3. Leading, developing and supporting colleagues with their professional direction, offering leadership and continual professional development (cpd) for staff.

4. Working in partnership with pupils, families and other professionals, drawing on external sources of support/expertise, consulting, engaging and communicating with colleagues, parents /carers and pupils.

Elkins (2012) suggests that there are a number of benefits including increased status, confidence and skills for the role, the development of a SEND-specific discourse in schools and opportunity to catch up with the latest practices. However, issues such as SENCOs still being limited in their opportunity to share knowledge and implement change due to the perception of the role (for example, not on the SLT), balancing the requirements of a Masters degree and full-time work and the Award is only mandatory for teachers new to the post.

■ How does the role of the current SENCO differ from the role in 1994?

■ What are the benefits and issues of ensuring that all newly appointed SENCOs achieve the National Award?

■ What are the thoughts of the SENCO working in your practice?

The changing role of the Teaching Assistant or Support Staff

 Pause for reflection

■ What roles and responsibilities does a TA or Support Staff carry out within your practice?

■ What do you think are the benefits of this role and are there any issues which may prevent staff from carrying out these roles and responsibilities?

TAs have a useful role in supporting teachers in classrooms; in working with teachers to support a wide range of children in their learning; in providing targeted interventions for individuals and small groups of children, under the direction of a teacher, and on programmes and interventions for which they have been trained. Underpinning this is a core principle that the teacher takes responsibility for the outcomes of every child, through planning and monitoring of progress (Lamb, 2009). TA roles in relation to students with SEND include supporting and implementing behaviour management plans for individual and classes; taking part in the assessment process, observing and recording student behaviour; supporting the progress of a pupil's IEP and encouraging positive peer group behaviour/interaction (Groom and Rose, 2005). TAs are often used in two ways allotted to one child, class or teacher for the entire week, or one teacher may work with several different TAs in the course of one day, depending on the needs of their children.

 Activity

It is essential that both teachers and TAs recognise that the teacher is to be responsible for the needs of the whole class (SEND Code of Practice 0–25 (2015), 2015; Lamb, 2009) and that TAs should be deployed in an effective way that leads to the independence and maximum outcomes of the child(ren) in their care, always under the management and supervision of the class teacher (Lamb, 2009). It is essential that teachers and TAs, along with any other relevant staff, work together to ensure the best outcomes for the child (Morewood, 2009).

■ If you were going for an interview for the role of a TA or Higher-Level TA, what key skills and attributes should you possess when working with pupils with SEND?

The National Workforce Agreement (DfES, 2003), sought to restructure the roles and responsibilities of school-based workforce, increase time for planning, reduce classroom teacher responsibilities and management, and recognise the role of school support staff alongside funding for training opportunities including Higher Level Teaching Asssistants (HLTAs). It was clear that the agreement was not about replacing teachers with TAs and other support staff – it makes clear that teachers and TAs are not interchangeable and that each class/group must have an assigned qualified teacher to teach them. It was about looking at the key role currently played by support staff, identifying ways in which that role can be extended in order to raise standards, and seeing the benefits that this can have for pupils, teachers and every aspect of school improvement. In the publication School Support Staff: The Way Forward (2003), the National Joint Council for Local Government Services and Department for Education and Skills offered the first opportunity for support staff to progress in their roles and local authorities began to introduce support staff career structures (Woodward and Peart, 2005).

Activity

The Deployment and Impact of Support Staff project ran from 2003 to 2009 and aimed to examine the impact of TAs on teachers and pupils and the assumptions that support staff help raise pupil standards. It can be accessed online via the maximisingtas (2018) website.

There were a number of findings including the view that TA support leads to pupil separation from the teacher and the curriculum with pupils tending to miss out on everyday teacher-to-pupil interaction. TAs were also given responsibility for pupil tasks and intervention and these supported pupils spend less time in mainstream curriculum coverage. There were differences in how teachers and TA engaged in talk with pupils also, for example, teachers provided more feedback, promoted pupils' thinking and cognitive engagement and linked current lessons to pupils' prior knowledge. On the other hand, TA explanations were sometimes inaccurate or confusing, more likely to prompt pupils, more frequently supplied pupils with answers and have a frontline pedagogical role, but an ineffective one.

▧ If you were a TA at this period of time, how would these findings make you feel?

Overall, it was suggested that TAs are an 'alternative' not 'additional' to the teacher and are given responsibilities for pupil tasks and interventions; however, TA support led to pupil separation between the teacher and the national curriculum and further reported that pupils are missing out on everyday teacher-pupil interactions (Webster et al., 2010).

The report proposed that there was a fundamental rethink required if schools are going to get the best use from their TAs and help their pupils. TAs have become the 'primary educators' of pupils they support (especially those with SEND). It is unreasonable to expect TAs to produce similar learning outcomes to teachers.

▧ Read the report and identify the recommendations suggested. Do you think that much has changed in the roles and responsibilities of TAs currently working with SEND pupils in particular?

The evidence of the impact of these measures is mixed; on the one hand, TAs began to have a more positive role to play to support an inclusive and whole-school approach and pupils reported a positive impact in the assistance they received (Groom and Rose, 2005) and outside the school environment, TAs began to be employed in family centres and child mental health services (Groom, 2006). However, there was a reduction in opportunities for pupils to engage in independent learning, and there was a lack of training of support staff in intervention and child development.

With respect to SEND pupils, many did not develop independent learning strategies and there was a lack of understanding in how to 'question' a pupil with SEND to learn (Ekins, 2012). In their report 'The Special Educational Needs and

Disability Review: A Statement Is Not Enough', Ofsted identified that good lessons were defined by students looking to the teacher for their main learning and to the support staff for support, while less successful lessons were defined by the roles of additional staff not being planned well or additional staff with limited training and the support provided not receiving sufficient monitoring. Students were also found to spend more time with the TA (Ofsted, 2010).

The TA has a crucial role in the education and well-being of a child with SEND. They have a responsibility to promote inclusion in schools and to work in collaboration with other staff such as teachers or SENCOs to ensure the best outcomes for the children in the school (Parker et al., 2012). Furthermore, while TAs are responsible for providing interventions for children with SEND, these interventions should not be in place of mainstream lessons and it is the responsibility of the TA to support children within lessons taught by the teacher as well as supporting the curriculum.

TAs may be designated to a certain child or a small group and children and it is their responsibility to ensure that lessons are broken down in a way that is accessible for the child(ren). The TA should work closely with the teacher and other professionals to plan and review the impact of the interventions that are being put in place to ensure the child are achieving the best possible outcomes (SEND Code of Practice 0–25 2015) (DfE, 2015). Parker et al. (2012) state that, as well as supporting the academic side of the curriculum, TAs should also take some responsibility for supporting the emotional well-being of the individuals in their care.

The relationship between teachers and TAs is one that has been studied at length. Policies and procedures have been put in place to ensure that the two professionals work together to ensure positive outcomes for pupils. However, this aim has not always been achieved. The National Agreement (2003) aimed to reduce the workload of teachers and therefore gave TAs a more prominent role. Teachers saw this as beneficial as it succeeded in its aim and enabled them to focus on the more important and demanding parts of their job; however, it leads to unforeseen negative results on the education and engagement of vulnerable students such as those with SEND. The Lamb Inquiry (2009) discovered that these vulnerable students who needed the most support were, in reality, being taught by under-qualified staff such as TAs, often in place of being taught by the teacher. This led to a range of negative impacts such as a lack of independence in learning for students with TA access, lower attainment and slower progress rates (Lamb, 2009).

 Activity

Think about the models of disability, described throughout this book.

- How would the social and medical/charity models in particular view the role of the TA and how might these discourses impact how pupils with SEND are supported?

Cajkler et al. (2006) state that TAs had begun to view themselves as co-educators with the teachers. Furthermore, studies have shown that many TAs were given the responsibilities of whole-class teaching and learning, whether for specified short periods of time or covering teacher absences (Hammersley-Fletcher and Lowe, 2011). Many TAs were taking on responsibilities that were not in their remit, thus blurring the professional boundaries. Not only did this lead to poorer outcomes for students, but it also led to conflict between teachers and TAs as some teachers saw the ambiguity of roles as threatening their professional identity.

Radford et al. (2014) state that the lack of training and preparation for undertaking a pedagogical role that TAs receive leads to lower quality interactions and a lack of independence for the pupils due to the TA being task-focussed rather than process-focussed (Lamb, 2009). It has been suggested that TAs should be given more training before undertaking their role to ensure best practice and maximum outcomes from the children they work with (Radford et al., 2014). When trained and used effectively, TAs can be a valuable asset to the primary school environment and a greater correlation between the demands of the role of the TA and the training they receive would result in professionals who are well equipped for their role (Symes and Humphrey, 2011).

 Activity

The Open University has an online free course entitled 'Teaching Assistants: support in action'. It looks at how the role has developed across the UK over time and explores the skills and attributes that TAs use to provide effective support and contribute to productive teamwork.

It can be accessed online via the Open University website (Open University, 2018).

Summary

Within multi-agency working, professionals act as a 'team around the child' to work closely with both the child and family (Limbrick, 2004). The team provide practical inputs, work towards a shared goal, meet regularly to agree on a service plan for the child and then further review their progress. Whether the professional works within the context of education, social services or health, the SEND Code of Practice 0–25 (2015) (Dfe, 2015) advocates the importance of the 'joined up' approach to supporting CYP and adults and the need to work with families and the person themselves. Differences in roles and training should be celebrated and used to the advantage of the individual with SEND and their family in order to ensure the best outcomes for these individuals. There may be issues with professional boundaries, specialist knowledge and communication channels, but SEND practitioners work together to share knowledge and specialist understanding, while respecting professional boundaries.

References

Abbott, D., Townsley, R. and Watson, D. (2005). Multi-agency working in services for disabled children: What impact does it have on professionals? *Health & Social Care in the Community*, 13(2), pp. 155–163.

Anning, A., Cottrell, D., Frost, N., Green, J. and Robinson, M. (2006). *Developing multi-professional teamwork for integrated children's services*. Maidenhead: Open University Press.

Atkinson, M., Doherty, P. and Kinder, K. (2005). Multi-agency working: Models, challenges and key factors for success. *Journal of Early Childhood Research*, 3, pp. 7–17.Atkinson, M., Wilkin, A., Stott, A., Doherty, P. and Kinder, K. (2002). *Multi-agency working: A detailed study (LGA Research Report 26)*. Slough: NFER.

Batod.org.uk. (1998). *National standards for specialist teachers*. Available online at: www.batod.org.uk/index.php?id=/batod/workbatod/workbatodarchive/standards/senstandards.htm (Accessed 12/04/2018).

Cajkler, W., Tennant, G., Cooper, P.W., Sage, R., Tansey, R., Taylor, C., Tucker, S.A. and Tiknaz, Y. (2006). *A systematic literature review on the perceptions of ways in which support staff work to support pupils' social and academic engagement in primary classrooms (1988–2003)*. Research Evidence in Education Library. London: EPPI-Centre, Social Science Research Unit, Institute of Education, University of London.

Children and Young People's Workforce Development Network (2008). *Consultation on the children and young people's workforce strategy and the common core of skills knowledge and understanding for the children and young people's workforce in wales*. Care Council.

Department for Children, Schools and Families (DCSF) (2007). *Effective integrated working: findings of concept of operations study. Integrated working to improve outcomes for children and young people*. London: DCSF.Department for Education (1994). *Code of practice on the identification and assessment of special educational needs*. London: DfE.

Department for Education and Skills (2003). *Every child matters*. London: DfE.

Department for Education (2015). *Special educational needs and disability code of practice: 0 to 25 years*. Department for Education.

Department for Education and Skills (2004). *Removing barriers to achievement; the Government's Strategy for SEN*. Available online at: http://webarchive.nationalarchives.gov.uk/20130401151715/http://education.gov.uk/publications/eorderingdownload/dfes%200117%20200mig1994.pdf (Accessed 10/12/2017).

DFES (2003). *Time for standards-raising standards and tackling workload: A national agreement*. London: DfES.

Doyle, J. (2008). Barriers and facilitators of multidisciplinary team working: A review. *Paediatric Care*, 20(2), pp. 26–29.

Ekins, A. (2012). *The changing face of special educational needs: Impact and implications for SENCOs and their schools*. London: Routledge.

Foundationyears (2018). *Section 6: The role of the early years SENCO*. Available online at: www.foundationyears.org.uk/files/2015/06/Section-6-Role-of-SENCO.pdf (Accessed 16/03/2018).

Fox, M. (2015). 'What sort of person ought I to be?' – repositioning EPs in light of the children and families bill (2013). *Educational Psychology in Practice*, 31(4), pp. 382–396.

Frost, N. (2005). *Professionalism, partnership and joined-up thinking: A research review of frontline working with children and families*. Sheffield: Children and Families Research Group.

Gillen, A. (2011). *Multi-agency working with children and families: A focus on facilitators and using activity theory principles to explore this topic area.* PhD. Newcastle: Newcastle University.

Gov.scot. (2018). *A guide to implementing getting it right for every child: Messages from pathfinders and learning partners.* Available online at: www.gov.scot/Publications/2010/07/19145422/2 (Accessed 12/03/2018).

Gov.uk (2015). *Working together to safeguard children.* Available online at: www.gov.uk/government/publications/working-together-to-safeguard-children--2 (Accessed 13/01/2018).

Groom, B. (2006). Building relationships for learning: The developing role of the teaching assistant. *Support for Learning*, 21(4), pp. 199–203.

Groom, B. and Rose, R. (2005). Supporting the inclusion of pupils with social, emotional and behavioural difficulties in the primary school: The role of teaching assistants. *Journal of Research in Special Educational Needs*, 5, pp. 20–30.

Hallett, F. and Hallett, G. (2010). *Transforming the role of the SENCo: Achieving the national award for SEN coordination.* 1st ed. Maidenhead: Open University Press, McGraw-Hill.

Halsey, K., Gulliver, C., Jonson, A., Martin, K. and Kinder K. (2005). *Evaluation of behaviour and education support teams.* Nottingham: NFER trading ltd.

Hammersley-Fletcher, L. and Lowe, M. (2011). From general dogsbody to whole-class delivery - the role of the primary school teaching assistant within a moral maze. *Management in Education*, 25(2), pp. 78–81.

Kennedy, S. and Stewart, H. (2012). Collaboration with teachers: A survey of South Australian occupational therapists' perceptions and experiences. *Australian Occupational Therapy Journal*, 59(2). pp. 147–155.

Lamb, B. (2009). *SEN and parental confidence.* London: Crown Copyright.

Laming, H. (2003). *The Victoria Climbie inquiry.* Norwich: HMSO.

Legislation.gov.uk. (2004). *Children Act 2004.* London: Her Majesty's stationery office. Available online at: www.legislation.gov.uk/ukpga/2004/31 (Accessed 12/12/2017).

Legislation.gov.uk. (2006). *National Health Service Act 2006.* Available online at: www.legislation.gov.uk/ukpga/2006/41/section/6 (Accessed 11/12/2017).

Lendrum, A., Barlow, A. and Humphrey, N. (2015). Developing positive school-home relationships through structured conversations with parents of learners with special educational needs and disabilities (SEND). *Journal of Research in Special Educational Needs*, 15(2), pp. 87–96.

Limbrick, P. (2004). *Early support for children with complex needs: Team around the child and the multi-agency keyworker.* Worcestershire: Interconnections.

Lloyd, G., Stead, J. and Kendrick, A. (2001). *Inter-agency working to prevent school exclusion.* Available online at: www.jrf.org.uk/report/inter-agency-working-prevent-school-exclusion (Accessed 14/01/2018).

Lucas, S. (2017). A children's space? Participation in multi-agency early intervention. *Child & Family Social Work*, 22(4), pp. 1383–1390.

Maddern, L., Franey, J., McLaughlin, V. and Cox, S. (2004). An evaluation of the impact of an inter-agency intervention programme to promote social skills in primary school children. *Educational Psychology in Practice*, 20(2), pp. 135–155.

Maximisingtas (2009). *Deployment and impact of support staff project.* Available online at: http://maximisingtas.co.uk/assets/content/dissressum.pdf (Accessed 26/01/2018).

Morewood, G.D. (2009). Making optimum use of SENCo time. Optimus publishing. *Curriculum Management Update*, 95, pp. 7–10.

Nottinghamshire.gov.uk. (2018). *Multi-agency safeguarding hub (MASH)*. Available online at: www.nottinghamshire.gov.uk/care/childrens-social-care/nottinghamshire-childrens-trust/pathway-to-provision/multi-agency-safeguarding-hub-mash (Accessed 12/05/2018).

Open University (2018). *Teaching assistants: Support in action*. Available online at: www.open.edu/openlearn/education-development/education/teaching-assistants-support-action/content-section-0?active-tab=description-tab (Accessed 07/05/2018).

Ofsted (2010). *The special educational needs and disability review a statement is not enough*. London: Ofsted.

Parker, P.D., Martin, A.J., Colmar, S. and Liem, G.A. (2012). Teachers' workplace well-being: Exploring a process model of goal orientation, coping behavior, engagement, and burnout. *Teaching and Teacher Education*, 28(4), pp. 503–513.

Parr, J. (2016). *How can i use my position as a local system leader to encourage more effective multi-agency working to 'turn the curve' thus ensuring that outcomes are improved for vulnerable children?* MA Integrated System Leadership. Birmingham City University. Available online at: www.crec.co.uk/research-paper- archive/ (Accessed 14/04/2018).

Radford, J., Bosanquet, P., Webster, R., Blatchford, P. and Rubie-Davies, C. (2014). Fostering learner independence through heuristic scaffolding: A valuable role for teaching assistants. *International Journal of Educational Research*, 63, pp. 116–126.

Symes, W. and Humphrey, N. (2011). School factors that facilitate or hinder the ability of teaching assistants to effectively support pupils with autism spectrum disorders (ASDs) in mainstream secondary schools. *Journal of Research in Special Educational Needs*, 11(3), pp. 153–161.

Walker, S., Wachs, T., Meeks Gardner, J., Lozoff, B., Wasserman, G., Pollitt, E. and Carter, J. (2007). Child development: Risk factors for adverse outcomes in developing countries. *The Lancet*, 369(9556), pp. 145–157.

Webster, R., Blatchford, P., Bassett, P., Brown, P., Martin, C. and Russell, A. (2010). Double standards and first principles: Framing teaching assistant support for pupils with special educational needs. *European Journal of Special Needs Education*, 25(4), pp. 319–336.

Woodward, M. and Peart, A. (2005). *Supporting education: The role of higher-level teaching assistants*. London: ATL.

4 Working with families in the SEND context

Introduction

For children to receive the best education possible, it is important for schools to understand and respect that parents must become advocates for their child. Schools should be thoroughly educated on placing students into more inclusive environments successfully and understand that disability is only one component of a child's unique identity (Bacon and Causton-Theoharis, 2013). Opportunities need to be provided to parents by educators to describe their children and their aspirations for their child. Parents feel respected and valued when educators develop strong, productive relationships with them and conflicts can be easily addressed (Lake and Billingsley, 2000). The role of the practitioner is to liaise with parents, carers and families and here is no doubt that it is beneficial to work closely with families including parents, carers and caregivers, but it is not always easy to do so and how to engage with these advocates can be a daunting task.

This chapter aims to develop your understanding of the complexity of working with families in the SEND context and how policies and legislation have supported the move towards families' having of voice in how their child is supported. It both focusses on the theoretical underpinning of the professional/family relationship and outlines some of the practical applications arising from this. It aims to:

- emphasise the critical role that families play in the education of their children living with SEND

- examine key reforms which have underpinned the change in the relationship between families and the professionals they come in contact with

- reflect on how to engage hard-to-reach parents

- use the example of critical incidences to reflect on practice

▨ analyse the importance of communicating with families

▨ examine the use of a personal toolkit to help support your practice

▨ explore the use of models and power in engaging families in the relationship.

The policy context: SEND reform

With the Children and Families Act (2014) (Legislation.gov.uk., 2014), advocating giving more power to parents and others, it is vital that practitioners are all involved in working with families. Parents have a critical role to play and hold key information in their child's education and have unique experience, knowledge and strengths to contribute to the shared view of a child's needs. Therefore, it is essential that all professionals value the contribution parents make and actively seek to work with them.

The 1967 Plowden Report (Central Advisory Council for Education, 1967) evaluated all aspects of primary education in England including the link between home and school and advocated that a closer relationship between schools and parents was necessary for 'educational advance' (Allen and Gordon 2011, 61). The report stated, 'that one of the essentials for educational advance is a close partnership between the two parties to every child's education' (Gillard, 2018). Before the report, the widely held view of the association between school and a child's home life was how school should as much as possible recompense for any disadvantages that a child may experience within their family life. The parent's key role in the home-school relationship was merely to make certain their child was prepared and able to engage in school life. It was now argued that the way to achieve this was by setting outcomes of frequent contact between home and school and that child's achievement at school was influenced as much by family life as their level of intelligence and readiness to perform well at academic tasks (Alexander, 2010).

There was focussed attention on the child being at the core of the educational system, and the fundamental role that parents should play in reinforcing their child's education was prioritised, with the responsibility of the school to embrace a flexible and determined perspective to enlist parental support (Feiler, 2010). For the relationship between the setting and parent to be successful, engagement and enthusiasm from parents are required with parental participation being reciprocal, constructive and empowering (Grady, Ale and Morris, 2012). Moving forward a decade, the 1978 Warnock Report analysed the educational provision of children and young people with SEND in England. An entire chapter of the report was assigned to the need for a partnership to be forged between professional and parent arguing that efficient education of children with SEND was subject to comprehensive involvement of their parents (Feiler, 2010).

The Lamb Inquiry (Lamb, 2009) reported that parents felt their child's school did little to enquire about their aspirations or to encourage high expectations. More than a third of parents (39 per cent said that the school had not discussed outcomes with them at all. Instead the focus was on provision. The report concluded that a 'radical recasting' of the partnership between schools, parents and the local authority needed to take place. It highlighted that an integral element of a successful partnership from a parent's perspective was to be treated as an 'equal partner' with mutual respect. Professionals needed to acknowledge parents as experts of their child's needs and the need for clear communication and information sharing from professionals. It sought to improve parental confidence in the special educational needs (SEN) system and concluded that the system needed to refocus its efforts in securing better outcomes for children and delivering the support they need to make progress and achieve. There were concerns raised that there was not enough focus on the outcomes for children and it also highlighted that engagement with parents through honest, open communication is crucial to a child's progress (Holland and Pell, 2017).

Lamb (2009) summed up key areas where change was needed, which included giving parents a stronger voice and putting outcome for children at the heart of the system (Tutt and Williams, 2015):

1. placing outcomes for children and young people at the heart of the system

2. a stronger voice for parents in decisions about their children

3. a greater focus on the needs of children and young people

4. a more accountable system that delivers better services.

Pause for reflection

■ Do you think the Lamb Inquiry was a turning point for how practitioners work with families?

In 2012, the government's Green Paper, *Support and Aspiration: A New Approach to SEN and Disability* (Association of Teachers and Lecturers, 2016) recognised that better communication and greater engagement with parents and carers are the keys to putting the child or young person at the centre of provision to meet their needs, and it set the direction of travel for the relationship between parents and services.

Perhaps the most fundamental legislation emerging from the Lamb Inquiry (2009) was the introduction of Part 3 of the Children and Families Act (2014) (Legislation.gov.uk., 2014), placing legal duties on stakeholders in the recognition of the importance of their views and wishes of parents, the promotion of their full involvement in decision-making and the need for parents to be supported in achieving the best possible outcomes for their children. The act built upon and extended parent partnership services to provide information and advice to children and young people as well as their parents and carers and impartial information, advice and support (IAS) service became important source of support for parents to enable them to participate more effectively in decisions affecting their children.

The accompanying Special Educational Needs and Disability Code of Practice 0–25 (2015) (DfE, 2015) reinforced these legal requirements in the form of statutory guidance, highlighting the responsibilities of stakeholders in providing more choice and control for parents and increasing their participation in decision-making and planning outcomes for children and young people. Similarly, inclusivity and collaboration with parents was echoed in the Statutory Framework for the Early Years (2014) (DfE, 2014), advocating that the future educational development of children should be promoted through a strong relationship/partnership between the practitioner and families. The common theme that has emerged from the aforementioned is undoubtedly the 'voice of the parent'. One criticism of much of this literature has been that it appears to assume that parents lie within a homogenous group with little regard to individuality.

Activity

■ Produce a timeline which identifies how the models and discourses, such as the medical and social models have impacted the nature of working with families

■ How could these models be mapped to legislation and policy from the Warnock Report to the SEND Code of Practice 0–25 (2015) (DfE, 2015)?

Partnership working in a SEND context

Parents are seen as key partners in supporting children's learning and development and partnerships can range from attending parents' evenings, Parent and Teachers' Associations, to being a parent-school governor, etc. Draper and Duffy (2010) suggest that such partnerships can be interpreted as parents and staff working together, running toy libraries, teachers visiting families, or parents attending workshops. Whalley (2001) suggests that true partnerships work on an equal basis with the sharing of practice, including recognising parents' skills, competencies and commitment to their child's learning, not simply in sharing information.

The role of parents in Early Years settings, for example, has significantly evolved and increasing knowledge about the role that parents' play in the lives of their children has led to an emphasis of involving them as much as possible to enhance outcomes for children's development. Even the smallest amount of involvement can be helpful (Abbot and Langston, 2006). The Early Years Foundation Stage (EYFS) Framework (DfE, 2014), sets the standards that all Early Year providers must ensure that children develop and learn well and are kept safe and happy. Good parenting and high-quality learning provide the foundation needed for children to grow and make the most of their abilities. The framework also states the importance of assessment, by helping practitioners and parents to recognise a child's progress, understand and support their needs and to plan activities.

Parents must be kept up-to-date with their child's development needs and progress and the significance of creating positive relationships with parents and carers is also emphasised in the Statutory Framework for the Early Years Foundation Stage (2014). It outlines the importance of working with parents and carers, and the need for ensuring inclusivity and creating partnership between practitioners (DfE, 2014). This should include providing information to parents and carers about how their child will be supported, helping create a person-centred approach in line with current legislation. Practitioners need to be respectful of parents' views. However, it fails to suggest how practitioners ought to create the relationships with parents and carers. It is considered that the responsibility of creating relationships should not exclusively be the settings, but for parents to be responsible for it too.

Communication with families

Communication is at the heart of effective parental participation, and the Lamb Enquiry highlighted the importance of good communication as the basis for the development of trust:

> Good, honest and open communication is the key to the development of positive working relationships and requires practitioners who listen to parents and are trusted by them. The quality of communication both reflects and reflects the working relationships between professionals and parents. The worst communication generates significant levels of hostility whilst the best communication engenders impressive levels of confidence and a sense of partnership.
>
> (Lamb, 2009)

Fundamental to a continuing relationship with parent is the understanding of their point of view, empathetic listening and the valuing of their expertise. If a parent feels listened to, then the relationship will flourish. The leading predictor of a child's academic success while at school is the extent of their parent's participation (Henderson and Berla 1994, cited in Olender, Elias and Mastroleo, 2015). The partnership should be built on recognition and mutual trust of both practitioner and parent and it is crucial for practitioners to realise that parents will have individual values and attitudes, which they will bring to the setting. Constructive relationships will be born out of appreciation of them. In addition, an outstanding feature of a successful partnership is communication.

Positive communication should amount to a positive relationship (Olender, Elias and Mastroleo, 2015) and the use of words, tone, body language, facial expressions and the space between people are all means of communication, which are indivisibly linked to alliances. In a setting, when involved with face-to-face contact with a parent or carer, communicating positively involves the practitioner developing techniques such as empathy to aid insight into a parent's feelings on a particular issue, active listening skills to fully engage with what is being said and importantly how it is being said to steer away from misinterpretation and reflective speaking to summarise key issues as they are discussed to ensure clear understanding throughout dialogue.

Where face-to-face contact is not possible, there are numerous ways in which the practitioner can communicate with parents. Routine contact over the telephone, email or written information in a daily school-to-home diary, which details events of the day or forthcoming planned activities or change to routinely ensure regular information sharing. This communication is of relevance to parents and carers of children with SEND as the child may not have the ability to convey any information about their time away from home themselves. This communication works both ways, allowing parents the opportunity to discuss and document progress or difficulties at home to inform the school (Dukes and Smith, 2007).

There are a number of communication skills that professionals need when working with parents, for example, during an Education, Health and Care plan meeting, including empathy, active and reflective listening, positive body language, reflection and clarification (Sabanci et al., 2016). Sen (2008) states that empathy is a core element to interpersonal skills which contribute to effective communication, it involves sensing other's feelings and taking 'active interest' in their feelings and concerns. Professionals must also have understanding and patience as parents may have feelings of anxiety when speaking to professionals. When speaking to a parent, the practitioner must allow time to consider their responses and may need to seek advice from others. The professional must acknowledge the parent at the time of speaking, but make them aware that they would have to discuss their concerns at a later date when they can be provided with the information they require. Good active listening ensures that there are no misunderstandings, it is important to reflect back to ensure that there are no miscommunications (Dukes and Smith, 2007).

Developing a personal toolkit

 Activity

The **Foundation Years** website (Foundationyears.org.uk., 2018) is a good place to find information and support if you work in the Early Years and childcare-delivering service.

A Guide for working with parents of children with Special Educational Needs or Disabilities can be found online. Section 5 is entitled 'Developing a Personal Toolkit'.

■ Read this section and reflect on how you would evidence the seven personal skills.

■ What support would you need to develop these skills further?

Critical incidences

A critical incident need not be a dramatic event: usually it is an incident which has significance for you. It is often an event which made you stop and think, or one that raised questions for you. It may have made you question an aspect of your beliefs, values, attitude or behaviour. It is an incident which in some way has had a significant impact on your personal and professional learning and/or on your teaching. In an educational setting, a critical incident might include:

- an aspect of your work that went particularly well;
- an aspect of your work that proved difficult;
- a piece of work or a group that you found particularly demanding;
- a piece of work or a group that increased your awareness, or challenged your understanding, of say inclusion;
- an incident involving conflict, hostility, aggression or criticism. This may concern a colleague or a learner.

 Activity

Taking a critical incident where you have worked with a parent or family in relation to supporting a child with SEND, use the key points below from Johns' (2013) model of reflection, to examine your response to the incident.

1. Bring the mind home.
2. Focus on a description of an experience that seems significant in some way.
3. What particular issues seem significant to pay attention to?
4. How were others feeling and why did they feel that way?
5. How was I feeling and why did I feel that way?
6. What was I trying to achieve, and did I respond effectively?
7. What were the consequences of my actions on the family and myself?
8. What factors influence the way I was/am feeling, thinking and responding to this situation?
9. What knowledge did or might have informed me?
10. To what extent did I act for the best and in tune with my values?
11. How does this situation connect with previous experiences?
12. Given the situation again, how might I respond differently?
13. What would be the consequences of responding in new ways for the family, others and me?
14. What factors might constrain me from responding in new ways?
15. How do I NOW feel about this experience?
16. Am I able to support myself and other families as a consequence?
17. What insights have I gained?
18. Am I more able to realise desirable practice?

Power relationships

Schools should enable parents to share knowledge about their child and give them confidence, and a fundamental factor to the succession of this statement in practice is much reliant on the balance of power within parent/practitioner relationships. French and Raven (1959) denote several sources of power in relationships:

1. Legitimate – this comes from the belief that a person has the formal right to make demands, and to expect others to be compliant and obedient. Legitimate power often applies to those of professional status giving an immediate power imbalance between practitioners and parents, placing the practitioner as the driving force in relationships.

2. Reward – this is a result of one person's ability to compensate another for compliance. This could be beneficial to either the parent, child, or both.

3. Expert – this is based on a person's high levels of skill and knowledge. This could relate to a range of professionals in the SEND context.

4. Referent – this is the result of a person's perceived attractiveness, worthiness and right to others' respect. The belief that the status of professionals within the field should be respected with loyalty is a friendlier approach, where the individual is enticed into a process.

5. Coercive – this comes from the belief that a person can punish others for noncompliance.

Six years later, Raven added an extra power base:

6. Informational – which results from a person's ability to control the information that others need to accomplish something.

 Activity

- Identify specific scenarios when one or more of these power bases have or could be used.

- How would the parent or family know how a specific source of power is being used within their relationship with professionals?

Engaging families in the relationship

Constructing an effective relationship between the practitioner and the parent is complex, which may be due to a lack of respect between both parties. A common assumption within educational establishments is that many parents refer to their own experiences of school. If it was an unpleasant one, parents and carers are then impassive and belligerent to educational intention for their children (Alexander, 2010). Some parents may lack confidence to engage and converse with the practitioner and therefore find it difficult to forge a relationship from the start. Having a child with SEND can affect how parents look at themselves, harbouring the feeling that they are judged by others who consider they are to blame for their child's additional needs.

From the very beginning of their child's life, many parents begin an often-exhausting journey of hospital appointment attendance and meetings with various professionals in addition to dealing with the complexities of raising a child with SEND. For this reason, some parents may appear forceful and present as 'coming out fighting' to practitioners as they grapple to do what they feel is best for their child. Essential components of successful parental partnership are: first, attentiveness to the views and wishes of the parent; second, recognition from the practitioner of the advantages of partnership and third, the parents need to feel empowered. These points are of distinct importance to parents of children with SEND as many will have experienced discord with support agencies and have an acute sense of mistrust. Establishing trust is therefore crucial from the start, as it will determine the quality of the relationship and equality within it. Furthermore, practitioners should ensure they embrace a varied approach to working with parents. A family of a child with SEND bring with them 'unique demands and stressors' and should be allowed choice of when, how and what level of participation they want in discussions regarding their child. In addition, if they choose to have little or no involvement, the practitioner should show regard for their decision (Abbott and Langston, 2007, 118).

Often parents of a child with SEND require support and advice in addition to what can be offered by the practitioner. In the setting, the role of the family support worker is to work directly with parents and contact and liaise with additional outside agencies to support the needs of the child and family. The operation of defining and meeting the needs of a child with SEND can be complex and usually involves several assessments and appointments, which the family support worker can assist the family with (Digman and Soan, 2008). Many parents are faced with further challenges that force time constraints such as job demands, health issues and relational complications. This can often cause difficulty to remain involved and positively engaged with the practitioner. However, the setting can provide a rich source of information that parents can have direct access to when they need it. One example is that of Staffordshire SEND Family Partnership Service which aims to ensure the parents of children with SEND can obtain guidance, advice and information regarding their child's educational needs, for them to make well-judged decisions (SENDIASS – Staffordshire Family Partnership, 2018).

Hard-to-reach parents

There is significant research, nationally and internationally, to suggest that parental involvement in children's learning is positively related to achievement. Cotton and Wikelund (1989) in their study on parental involvement in education propose that the more intensely parents are involved in their children's learning, the more beneficial are the effects on achievement. Moreover, they state that this holds true for all types of parental involvement in children's learning and for all types and ages of pupils. Research also suggests that there is significantly more evidence of parental engagement in the early stages of primary school than in secondary schools, although parental support of learning in the home has been seen to have a significant effect on children of all ages from preschool to 16 (Sammons et al., 2007).

An effective home-school partnership is a process that demands time and commitment from both partners (Pirchio et al., 2013). Difficulties arise, however, as some parents can have problems engaging with schools or seem disinterested. These hard-to-reach parents are undoubtedly one of the most demanding issues facing teachers in today's schools (Feiler, 2010). Practitioners who have difficulty forming professional relationships with parents have used the term 'hard-to-reach' widely. Such parents can be identified as having little involvement or engagement with school, often not attending parent's evenings or replying to school communications. However, 'hard-to-reach' is considered a convenient phrase, which simply indicates problems faced by practitioners when creating relationships with parents. Parental engagement is strongly influenced by social background factors and there is increasing concern that this terminology promotes deficit views of families.

 Activity

Below are some examples of how schools could try to engage with families:

1. Implementing training programmes for parents, where they learn to communicate and work directly with their child.

2. Enabling parents to recognise that they are partners and consumers in the educational process and providing them with suitable arenas to critique and formulate agendas.

3. Making it easier for parents to participate by giving them meaningful roles in school decision-making.

4. Emphasising to parents how needed and valued their involvement is.

   ● How would you go about formulating a policy for your school which incorporates these suggestions on how to engage with hard-to-reach families?

How can parents support professionals?

There are a number of ways in which parents can support their child's education. For example, the SEND Code of Practice 0–25 (2015) (DfE, 2015) states that parents should be provided with IAS to enable them to make decisions. Dukes and Smith (2007) suggest that information leaflets and booklets are a great way to let parents know about what is taking place in the school and can also give ideas on how parents can support their child in their home environment. This links in with the idea of 'the transplant relationship', in which the professional shares their skills or ideas with the parent to enable them to assist at home, and even become a 'co-educator' (Jeffree cited in Dale, 1996). Within the setting, a particular child may have difficulty in learning to read new words and difficulties with working memory (Ehlis, 2008). In order to try and help children to develop their reading will require a great deal of practice and reminders, sending a folder home with some tasks and activities to help develop the child's reading skills, alongside an information sheet to explain how the parent could help their child to complete the tasks and practice their reading skills at home.

Key workers who support children with SEND often communicate with parents at the beginning and end of each day, thus providing a vital home school link. This informal information sharing helps create a trusting relationship between parent and practitioner. An informal way of communicating with parents about their child's day is through the home/school diary. One advantage of this system is the ease at which parents can use them to communicate with practitioners, especially if their child has a communication difficulty (Runswick-Cole, 2016). Conversely, home school diaries, if not used correctly, can cause difficulties. Schools need to ensure that parents are aware of the other communication channels available to them, such as emails, parents' evenings, etc., so they do not become reliant on home school diaries. Confidentiality can be a concern especially if the diary gets lost, as well as the system failing to consider the parents' own literacy skills.

Some parents may also need guidance from the practitioner in dealing with behavioural issues at home. Practitioners may use star charts or other methods for behaviour management dependent on the individual child, if the method is effective in the setting, but there are still reports of negative behaviour at home, the practitioner could provide the parent with the same chart to try to promote the consistency of behaviour management. It is important that the practitioner encourages the parent to feel that they are helping by doing and that behavioural support is a dual responsibility.

 Activity

Parents are also often invited into school to take an active role in the classroom, by either supporting their child or even learning themselves.

- From your own practice or placement, can you think of any examples where you have witnessed parents to support their child in the classroom?

- What are the benefits to both the parents and their child in such an activity?

- Can you give any other examples where parental involvement has supported the academic or social development of a child?

Models of working with families

The Warnock Report stated that parents can be effective partners if professionals take notice of how they feel and what they say in relation of needs and treat their contribution as intrinsically important (Wolfendale, 2002). However, according to Dale (1996), the role of a parent occupies a lower social status than professionals. Where the professional and the parent stand in relation to each other, in the terms of authority and power, it can affect the type of relationship they can sustain. Parents lack expert power, and in the event of a challenge from the parent, a professional can draw on backup forms of power to maintain their position of authority. Even with the positive benefits of parental involvement, the one-way delivery of professional expertise can still dominate the interactions of some professionals with parents.

Teacher resistance has been the most persistent barrier to family engagement in their child's education. Educators will often justify their opposition based on being a professional, and there are considerable strengths as well as limitations in what professionals and parents can offer. Decision-making proceeds through a two-way dialogue, whereby each partner brings in their own perspective to assist in deciding. Through negotiation, two different outcomes can be met, one being a shared understanding and consensus or dissent and lack of shared understanding. Due to differences between perspectives and roles, working together may not be straightforward; it might not even be possible to gain openness and mutual trust.

There are various models of working with families ranging from the traditional approach of 'the professional as expert' to 'the negotiating model' (Dale, 1996). Prior to the 1970s, the professional as expert model was the common way of working with parents of children with SEND. The role of the parent was to provide basic information to the professional when required, but viewpoints and feelings were not sought with parents not becoming involved in the process of supporting their child.

The transplant relationship model sees the parent's knowledge as an untapped resource to share skills and expertise, empowering them to become more confident, competent and skilled. The downside of this approach is that parents may have unrealistic ideals or goals, making the process more difficult. However, in EHC plan Statement Reviews, personal plan meetings, pupil support plans, mean parents are regularly involved in every aspect of their child's learning.

With the parent as a consumer model, the parent has the expertise; a relationship is built between the parent and setting by listening and understanding views, aims and expectations. This may be limited if parents are over demanding with unrealistic expectations but can be an effective way to build relationships between parents and the setting relationship, and be effective when parent and setting.

The empowerment model is a mix of the parent as consumer and the social network or systems model, offering empowerment combined with the view of the parent as consumer. The limitations of the model are that the setting would need to guide the parent to start to ensure effective use; this could be like the professional as expert model, but it is an excellent model if the parent is open minded and feels comfortable working with the setting, being supportive and building a positive relationship. Parents are active and supportive in decisions relating to their child.

In the negotiating model, negotiation is the key transaction; working relationships use negotiation and joint decision-making to resolve conflict reaching a shared mutually agreeable decision. It focusses on cooperation as the key transaction for partnership work. Its principle in the model is that professionals and parents have separate and highly potential contributions to offer to children and it can lead to multiple and varying perspectives of the same situation. This model can be used to promote joint decision-making, resolve conflict and reach mutual satisfaction.

Until the 1960s, parental involvement was often in the form of supporting children with low achievement, but Draper and Duffy (2010) suggest that there has been a movement from the compensatory to a participatory model, with Whalley (2007) identifying that parents are experts in their own children and are a resource in themselves. Positiveness, sensitivity, responsiveness and friendliness can all be demonstrated through effective communication and effective partnership with parents and families can become possible (Fitzgerald, 2012). Parental involvement can also be seen as the action of participating in activities, such as parents' evenings and open days; while parental engagement is considered to encompass more than just activity, there is some feeling of ownership of that activity (Goodall and Montgomery, 2013).

 Activity

- Think about your own practice and identify situations where each of the aforementioned models has been used in working with families of a child you have worked with.

- What were the outcomes of such situations?

Summary

Historically, parents viewed education of their children as the responsibility of the school (Feiler, 2010). This, in part could be a result of 'the no parents beyond this point' signs seen at schools in the decades after the Second World War. Alternatively, some parents' own negative experiences of school results in them being 'apathetic' or 'openly hostile' towards educational objectives believing responsibility for their children's education ends at the school gates. Recent policies and legislation such as the Lamb Inquiry (2009) along with the SEND Code of Practice 0–25 (2015) (DfE, 2015), have done much to give families a greater say in how their child is supported in their education and highlights the importance of putting children and their families 'at the heart of the process' (Tutt and Williams, 2015).

In addition to outlining the duty of the local authority to tell parents what they need to know about SEND, the underlying principles of the act and the code were devised to support parental and carer involvement in decision-making, and provide access to information to aid the process of decision-making, monitoring the type of help they can receive from social care services, health services and education and also the opportunity to participate in and review the help that is available to them in their local area by contributing to the 'local offer'. For all settings, engaging parents and carers of children and young people with SEND means putting them at the heart of the SEND process, including working with them and encouraging their active participation in assessment, planning and service delivery for their own child and ensuring that they have a voice in policy, strategic planning, decision-making and commissioning and evaluating services.

References

Abbott, L. and Langston, A. (2006). *Parents matter.* Berkshire: Open University Press.

Allen, S. and Gordon, P. (2011). *How children learn 4: Thinking on special educational needs and inclusion.* London: Practical Pre-School Books.

Alexander, R. (2010). *Children, their world, their education: Final report and recommendations of the Cambridge Primary Review.* Oxon: Routledge.

Association of Teachers and Lecturers (2016). *Green Paper "Support and Aspiration: A new approach to special educational needs and disability" Response from the Association of Teachers and Lecturers,* June 2011. London: ATL.

Bacon, J.K. and Causton-Theoharis, J. (2013). 'It should be teamwork': A critical investigation of school practices and parent advocacy in special education. *International Journal of Inclusive Education,* 17(7), pp. 682–699.

Barnes, P. (2008). Multi-agency working: What are the perspectives of SENCos and parents regarding its development and implementation? *British Journal of Special Education,* 35(4), pp. 230–240.

Central Advisory Council for Education (1967). *The Plowden Report, children and their primary schools.* London: HMSO.

Cotton, K. and Wikelund, K.R. (1989). *Parent involvement in education.* School Improvement Research Series, Close-Up No. 6, Northwest Regional Educational Laboratory.

Dale, N. (1996). *Working with families of children with special needs. Partnership and practice.* London: Routledge.

Department for Education (2014). *Early years foundation stage statutory framework (EYFS).* Available online at: www.gov.uk/government/publications/early-years-foundation-stage-framework--2 (Accessed 12/07/2018).

Department for Education (2015). *Special educational needs and disability code of practice: 0 to 25 years.* Department for Education.

Digman, C. and Soan, S. (2008). *Working with parents: A guide for education professionals.* London: Sage Publication Ltd.

Draper, L. and Duffy, B. (2006). Working with parents. In Pugh, G. (ed.), *Contemporary issues in the early years.* 4th ed. London: Sage Publications.

Draper, L. and Duffy, B. (2010). Working with Parents In Cable, C.; Miller, L. and Goodliff, G. (ed). *Working with Children in the Early Years,* Oxon: Routledge.

Dukes, C. and Smith, M. (2007). *Working with parents of children with special educational needs.* London: Paul Chapman Publishing.

Ehlis, C. (2008). Reduced lateral prefrontal activation in adult patients with attention-deficit/hyperactivity disorder (ADHD) during a working memory task: A functional near-infrared spectroscopy (fNIRS) study. *Journal of Psychiatric Research,* 42(13), pp. 1060–1067.

Feiler, A. (2010). *Engaging 'hard to reach' parents.* 1st ed. Chichester: John Wiley & Sons.

Fitzgerald, D. (2012). Working in partnership with parents. In Kay J. (ed.), *Good practice in the early years.* London: Continuum.

Foundationyears.org.uk. (2018). *A guide for working with parents of children with special educational needs or disabilities (SEND).* Available online at: www.foundationyears.org.uk/files/2015/05/Guide-for-working-with-parents-of-children-with-SEND.pdf (Accessed 12/07/2018).

French, J. and Raven, B. (1959). The bases of social power. *In studies in social power.* Ann Arbor: University of Michigan, Institute for Social Research, pp. 150–167.

Gillard, D. (2018). *Education in England.* Available online at: www.educationengland.org.uk/history/chapter02.html (Accessed 12/03/2018).

Goodall, J. and Montgomery, C. (2014). Parental involvement to parental engagement: A continuum. *Educational Review,* 66(4), pp. 399–410.

Grady, J., Ale, C. and Morris, T. (2012). A naturalistic observation of social behaviours during preschool drop-off. *Early Child Development and Care,* 182(12), pp. 1683–1694.

Holland, J. and Pell. G. (2017). Parental participations of the 2014 SEND legislation. *International Journal of Personal, Social and Emotional Development,* 35(4), pp. 293–311.

Johns, C. (2013). *Becoming a reflective practitioner.* 4th ed. Chichester: Wiley-Blackwell.

Lake, F. and Billingsley, B. (2000). An analysis of factors that contribute to parent school conflict in special education. *Remedial and Special Education,* 21, pp. 240–251.

Lamb, B. (2009). *Lamb inquiry special educational needs and parental confidence.* Annesley: DCSF Publications.

Legislation.gov.uk. (2014). *Children and Families Act 2014.* Available online at: www.legislation.gov.uk/ukpga/2014/6/contents/enacted (Accessed 10/07/2018).

Olender, R.A., Elias, J. and Mastroleo, R.D. (2015). *The school-home connection: Forging positive relationships with parents.* New York: Skyhorse Publishing.

Pirchio, S., Tritrini, C., Passiatore, Y. and Taeschner, T. (2013). The role of the relationship between parents and educators for child behaviour and wellbeing. *International Journal about Parents in Education,* 7(2), pp. 145–155.

Runswick-Cole, K. (2016). End of normal: Identity in a biocultural era. *Disability & Society.* DOI: 10.1080/09687599.2016.1221667.

Sabanci, A., Sahin, A. Sonmez, M. and Yilmaz, O. (2016). School managers' interpersonal communication skills in Turkey. *International Journal of Academic Research in Business and Social Services,* 6(8), pp. 13–30.

Sammons, P., Sylva, K., Melhuish, E.C., Siraj-Blatchford, I., Taggart, B. and Grabbe, Y. (2007). *Effective pre-school and primary education 3–11 project (EPPE 3–11): Influences on children's attainment and progress in key stage 2: Cognitive outcomes in year 5.* Full Report. London: Institute of Education, University of London.

Sen, S. (2008). Interpersonal skills through emotional intelligence: A psychological perspective. *The Icfai University Journal of Soft Skills*, 2(4), pp. 25–30.

SENDIASS – Staffordshire Family Partnership (2018). Available online at: www.staffs-iass. org/home.aspx (Accessed 08/06/2018).

Tutt, R. and Williams, P. (2015). *The SEND code of practice 0–25 years*. 1st ed. London: SAGE Publications Ltd.

Whalley, M. and the Pen Green Team. (2001). *Involving parents in their children's learning*. London: Paul Chapman Publishing.

Wolfendale, S. (2002). *Parent partnership services for special educational needs: Celebrations and challenges*. London: David Fulton Publishers.

5 Inclusivity, models and discourses

Introduction

Nothing is debated more in education, than the issue on where pupils with additional needs should be educated. The complex nature of SEND with its categories of need, language used and competing models identifying the causes of disability and how these impact children and young people, their families and practitioners add to the debate. Where should pupils with SEND be educated, in mainstream classrooms, specialist provision or in a unit located within a mainstream school? What are the advantages of each of these types of provision and what support is available once a decision has been made? This chapter examines some of these theoretical and practical issues and aims to:

- define the terms Inclusion, Integration and Segregation

- identify some of the key issues within the area of inclusivity

- outline how the Index for Inclusion might relate to a school

- review what characteristics an inclusive teacher might possess

- discuss the role of the Waves Model within the Quality First Teaching approach to SEND

- evaluate how the medical, social and biopsychosocial models of disability relate to SEND

- examine how the notion of the "Dilemma of Difference" relates to labelling

- outline some examples of the language and discourses surrounding SEND

- identify dyslexia as an example of competing discourses.

Inclusion, integration or segregation?

Pause for reflection

What is your understanding of the terms segregation, integration and inclusion?

There is no set definition of inclusion, it is an elusive term the complexities of which are argued by Rose (2010) to be an indication as to why it has remained the centre of attention for a prolonged period. As an approach, it has no agreed definition (Armstrong, Armstrong and Spandagou, 2010), and is reportedly criticised by some as inconsistent in places, comprising of ideological rhetoric and unrealistic utopianism (Thomas and Loxley, 2007). In the face of much debate about its meaning, Florian (2007) suggests that the concept is destined to persist rather than represent the latest educational fad or bandwagon.

Integration is usually taken to assume that a pupil with Special Educational Needs (SEN) attends a mainstream school whose systems remain unchanged and in which extra arrangement are made to provide for the pupil's education. Mittler (2000) states that integration suggests that the pupil must adapt to the school and there is no necessary assumption that the school will change to accommodate a greater diversity of pupils. Inclusion, on the other hand, implies a radical reform of the school in terms of ethos, curriculum, assessment, pedagogy and grouping of pupils. Inclusion is related to mainstream schools and encourages the school to review its structures, approaches to teaching, pupil grouping and use of support to enable the school to meet the diverse learning needs of all its pupils. There are a number of differing understandings of inclusion including a human rights issue where diversity is considered the norm; social Inclusion with issues relating to who is at risk of exclusion and marginalisation and pertaining to mainstream education – developing a whole school culture of inclusion (Liasidou, 2012). Thus, with integration, the pupil is placed in the school and the school does not adapt its attitudes, policies or practices before, during or after their arrival. The child has to change to fit into the school or simply tolerate exclusion. It responds to the diversity of its learner population by removing barriers to learning (continually and flexibly). The school changes around the child (and the diversity of its learners).

Segregated education is a potential violation of the UN Convention on the Rights of the Child (1989), which also protects the child's right to inclusive education in their community. If the right to an inclusive education is a human right, then the need for evidence in support of whether inclusive education is appropriate becomes redundant. On this basis, therefore, could it be established that segregated education may not only be morally objectionable, but also contrary to International Law? However, the case for inclusive education is marginally positive with

Lindsay (2003) arguing that there is a need for a dual approach focussing on both the rights of children and the effectiveness of their education.

The Centre for Studies on Inclusive Education (CSIE) (2004) makes the case against segregation, claiming that research findings do not meet the case for segregated SEND education provision and that no compelling body of evidence that segregated 'special' education programmes significantly improve learner outcomes. On the other hand, research seems to suggest that the inclusion of SEND pupils is not always advantageous and that there is no demonstrable advantage for mainstream education. However, Farrell (2000) argues that poor teaching practices in mainstream schools may explain negative and inconclusive findings about the benefits of mainstreaming. Children in special units attached to mainstream schools or those who are withdrawn for individual support may not be viewed as truly included and that these processes can isolate children and perpetuate segregation. Wilson (2000) is critical of the purist model of full inclusion and advocates a more responsible or cautious form of inclusion. Proponents of this paradigm argue that individuals have a paramount entitlement to appropriate education and a 'one size fits all' model has been tried and found to fail.

 Activity

Think about the continuum of SEND from Profound and Multiple Learning Difficulties (PMLD), through Severe Learning Difficulties (SLD) and Moderate Learning Difficulties (MLD) to Specific Learning Difficulties (SpLD).

■ Take each of these categories and suggest an inclusive approach which may allow these pupils access to a specific aspect of the curriculum.

■ What are the arguments for and against the view that pupils with greater needs, such as those with Education Heath and Care Plans (EHC plans), should be educated in specialist provision?

What are the key issues?

There are tensions between two agendas within inclusive practice, that of standards and needs (MacBeath et al., 2006). Their study, commissioned by the National Union of Teachers, identified that schools, parents, teaching staff and children commonly held the view that the presence of diverse learners improved teaching and learning for all. However, they also identified some challenges including isolation of SEND pupils who were often segregated due to behavioural problems along with professional inexperience in working with this group of pupils. Stress and overload were also identified with the necessity to balance the needs of individuals with those of wider group, with the result that teachers and support staff often did far more than their normal work load.

Round, Subban and Sharma's (2016) research in secondary school teachers in Australia revealed mild concern about inclusion; however, these were not linked to anxiety about the impact of inclusion on their personal performance as teachers, nor was the disquiet linked to the impact that inclusion would have on overall academic performance. Teachers remained concerned about the provision of appropriate resources to assist with effective inclusion, including teaching materials appropriate to inclusion and access to specialised support staff that would assist with the process of inclusion.

 Activity

In an apt named report 'Inclusion: does it matter where pupils are taught?', Ofsted (2006) identified the following key findings:

1. There was little difference in the quality of provision and outcomes for pupils across primary and secondary mainstream schools and special schools. However, mainstream schools with additionally resourced provision were particularly successful in achieving high outcomes for pupils academically, socially and personally.

2. Pupils with even the most severe and complex needs were able to make outstanding progress in all types of settings. High-quality, specialist teachers and a commitment by leaders to create opportunities to include all pupils were the keys to success.

3. Pupils in mainstream schools where support from teaching assistants was the main type of provision were less likely to make good academic progress than those who had access to specialist teaching in those schools.

4. Fewer pupils with PMLD or those with SLD and challenging behaviour were placed in mainstream schools than other groups, even when specialist facilities were available. Those included in such provision were as likely to do well as those taught in special schools, when they had access to teaching from experienced and qualified specialists.

● You are talking to a parent of a child with SEND who asks you which the better choice for his child is, a mainstream school with support, or a special school with additional facilities and trained SEND staff? What suggestions might you make in order for him to make an informed decision?

Index for Inclusion

The Index for Inclusion (Booth and Ainscow, 2011) summarises some of the ideas which make up a view of inclusion including supporting everyone to feel that they belong; increasing participation for children and adults in learning and teaching activities, relationships and communities of local schools; viewing differences between children and between adults as resources for learning and recognising that inclusion in education is one aspect of inclusion in society.

Activity

The Index for Inclusion is organised in three dimensions:

1. creating inclusive cultures

2. producing inclusive policies

3. evolving inclusive practices

Each section contains up to 11 indicators and the meaning of each indicator is clarified by a series of questions. It can be accessed online via the CSIE website (CSIE, 2018):

■ Identify one of the dimensions which is relevant to your practice. Using the indicators which are mapped to this, and the sample questions, or ones you devise, identify how your organisation and your own practice maps onto the index.

What characteristics does an inclusive teacher possess?

In a longitudinal study in Canada, Jordan, Schwartz and McGie-Richmond (2009) found that inclusive/exclusive teaching practices are the result of: school attitudes; feelings of responsibility for students with SEND; and feelings of self-efficacy for working with pupils identified with SEND and fixed/fluid views of ability. Teachers have beliefs about the causes of learning difficulties and adopted perspectives or models, which embodied their beliefs about inclusion and SEND both of which had the potential to impact SEND and inclusion in schools.

The Pathognomonic Perspective is one in which teachers focus on the pathology of the learner. Therefore, difference is attributed to internal and innate factors which the teacher cannot change and teachers who adopt this approach to understanding SEND:

1. frequently refer students to support services

2. expect parents to undertake remedial work outside of school hours to enable students to catch-up

3. are less likely to cooperate with others

4. do not see themselves as responsible for students' progress

5. relied on transmission teaching, testing of memory, etc., so students have less ownership of the process.

The Interventionist Perspective saw learning and ability as incremental and malleable and they focussed on interventions which help the student learn. Key features of this approach:

1. teachers believe that they were responsible for progress of all students

2. widespread use of flexible, adaptable and responsive pedagogy

3. collaboration with others

4. systematic tracking of progress

5. better classroom management

6. engaging teaching methods

7. extended interactions with students with SEND

8. use of social constructivist approaches.

They concluded that the extent to which a teacher is inclusive is dependent on a number of factors, including:

■ dominant attitudes in the school towards inclusion

■ beliefs of individual teachers about their responsibility for learners with SEND

■ the belief of individual to teach those with SEND (that is, self-efficacy)

■ the belief of individuals about the cause of difficulty

■ the belief of individuals about whether ability is fixed or fluid.

 Activity

Susan is a 9 year old pupil who attends a local primary school (Year 5), who has been identified as living with both high-functioning autism and Attention Deficit Hyperactivity Disorder (ADHD).

■ Taking the different perspectives identified above, how would these suggest that teachers should plan lessons and support for Susan to be able to access the curriculum?

Quality First Teaching

According to the SEND Code of Practice 0–25 (2015) (DfE, 2015), this is high-quality, inclusive teaching which ensures that planning and implementation meets the needs of all pupils, and builds in high expectations for all pupils, including those with SEN. It is about the day-to-day interactions that take place in the classroom and the different pedagogical approaches teachers use to engage and motivate learners, which ensure good pupil progress. Teachers are responsible and accountable for the progress and development of the pupils in their class, including where pupils access support from teaching assistants or specialist staff.

Inclusive teachers plan lessons carefully so that all pupils are able to participate and can access the key learning at their own level; take some new learning away with them. In successful lessons, pupils are made aware of what is to be learned and how it matches with what they already know, what the next steps in their learning will be and where the learning is going over time. During lessons, inclusive teachers secure access to the key points of the learning for all; scaffold the involvement of pupils and model good practice.

The three waves model of intervention is a useful approach to inclusive practice and can be outlined as follows (Figure 5.1):

The Waves Model of Intervention

Wave 1: Quality First Teaching is structured and managed according to the needs of the pupils and the learning objective with a very strong focus on learning rather than on engagement and being busy. There are challenging and motivating activities – making effective use of knowledge about pupils' attainments and interests at which pupils are working and the level of challenge then offered by

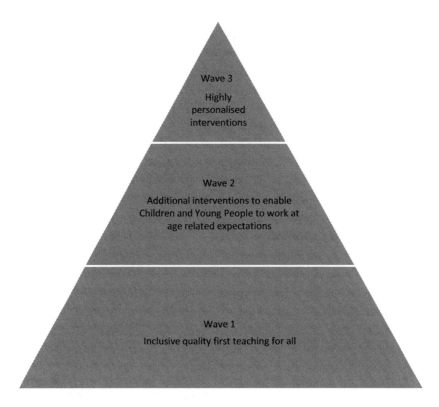

Figure 5.1 The Waves model of Intervention

staff. There is a need to have knowledge of the pupils and the implications of their special needs with the need for effective feedback with the development of advocacy, choice and decision-making.

Wave 2: Wave 1 plus additional, time-limited, tailored intervention support programmes. These might include small group activities for a specified period of time, designed for pupils with the potential to 'catch up' and reach age-related norms by the end of the programme delivery. The class teacher has a full understanding of the intervention and how to integrate learning into the classroom, but it is not a stepping stone to Wave 3.

Wave 3: Wave 1 plus increasingly individualised programmes, for a small percentage of children and young people even with high-quality Wave 1 teaching and support do not make progress and have significant needs. Wave 3 involves a structured and intensive programme that is tailored to individual's specific difficulties. It is delivered as a one-to-one programme by a teacher/teaching assistant who has undertaken some additional training, with the aim to narrow the gap between an individual and their peers.

 Activity

■ What interventions are used in your school in each of the three waves?

■ Are they successful?

■ What evidence would you use to validate your response?

 Activity

Sam has difficult sitting still and concentrating. He is easily distracted, and he is becoming disruptive to the rest of the class. Joshua has great difficulty in remembering, retaining and recalling information. He can focus on the lesson, if it is presented in a visual way. Samira has impaired hearing.

■ Identify what could be done at each of the three waves to support these pupils.

Models of disability

Understanding the different models of disability is important not just for people directly involved with a child or adult with a disability, but also for everyone in society in order to build positive attitudes and a better understanding. The two most prominent models of disability discourse over the past 50 years have been the Social and Medical Models.

The Medical Model

In the Medical Model, disability is the result of impairment of the mind or body and is viewed similarly to ill health and the problem can be medically cured to function in society and gain independence (Haegele and Hodge, 2016). Within this model, medical professionals are employed to judge the limitations of a child with special needs or a disability against functional and developmental norms. The child's performance is compared to the functions carried out by others of the same age to determine the severity of the child's SEN. The child's limitations are labelled through screening and assessment and are described using clinical terminology including 'the pathology of impairment' or 'aetiology of the syndrome'. In attempt to cure the condition, the symptoms displayed by the child are treated using therapeutic or educational interventions and drug therapy (Hodkinson, 2016).

People who adhere to the Medical Model might hold the assumptions that the 'problem' lies within the individual. Also, a person with disability occupies a new role, that of needing care; a wish to be rehabilitated and to return to 'normal'. Often the focus is on rehabilitation and cure with a return to 'normalisation', with a person with a disability being disempowered. Thus, the discourse which follows is identified by terminology such as syndrome, symptoms, disorder, treatment, assessment and therapy, leading to the creation of special pedagogy and support. However, this kind of approach is no more effective than a teacher's own gut assessment of the difficulty and his/her own solution to it (Thomas and Loxley, 2007) and the view that the majority of teachers are not skilled enough to teach 'special' children.

A major critique of the Medical Model is the influence that medical professionals have over the treatment of individuals with disabilities in society. They act as important gatekeepers in society and use diagnoses and labelling to determine which individuals receive services (for example, educational services), types of services and benefits (Humpage, 2007). This process defines an individual's needs and how they receive those needs based on their impairment and may not take into consideration what individuals with disabilities value or want. Rather they create labels and categorisations based largely on the individual's bodily function. Labels and categories can then lead individuals with disabilities to feel as though they have limited options. It also conflates individuals with disabilities with the sick role and discusses disability in a deficit model orientation (Mitra, 2006), but Frederickson and Cline (2015) also highlight that the Medical Model continues to have an extensive influence on the way people think about SEND.

The Social Model

The Social Model of disability, developed over the last 40 years by disabled people, is a radically different model to the medical and charitable approach to disability. It states that people have impairments but that the oppression, exclusion and discrimination people with impairments face are not an inevitable consequence of having an impairment, but are caused instead by the way society is run and organised. The Social Model holds that people with impairments are 'disabled' by the barriers operating in society that exclude and discriminate against them in that impairments did not create disability, but barriers created by society did (Hodkinson, 2016). The approach was founded on the understanding that disabled people who experienced disadvantage, poverty and social exclusion stemmed from environmental barriers and was not a predictable result of their impairment. Many disabled people found the Social Model revolutionary after experiencing years of segregation and medicalisation. The focus shifted away from disabled individuals who were seen as the problem to external factors created by society that restricted access. An example would be a wheelchair user who will only be 'disabled' if the building is not designed with accessibility in mind. That individual may not be able to function independently without the use of lifts, ramps, wide doors and accessible toilets (Hodkinson, 2016).

Thus, the Social Model not only identifies society as the cause of disability, but, equally importantly, it provides a way of explaining how society goes about disabling people with impairments. Sometimes referred to as a 'barriers-approach', it provides a 'route map' that identifies both the barriers that disabled people may face and how these barriers can be removed, minimised or countered by other forms of support. This model views SEND to be a socially constructed phenomenon, relative and context specific, with the rejection of disorders and syndromes. From a Social Model perspective, there is a radical difference between impairment and disability:

- Impairment is an individual's physical, sensory or cognitive difference (for example, being blind, experiencing bipolar disorder or a learning difficulty).

- Disability is the name for the social consequences of having an impairment. People with impairments are disabled by society, so disability is therefore a social construct that can be changed and removed.

The Social Model has been subjected to criticism in that it separates disability from impairment and has not accounted for lived experiences of disabled individuals (Haegele and Hodge, 2016). Another critique of this model is that it distinguishes disabled people as one similar group rather than a complex group of people who vary in terms of age, gender, race, sexuality and impairment (Hodkinson, 2016) with the disability community not being homogenous. The Social Model ends up misplacing responsibility and over-socialising causes for disablement and impairment (Frederickson and Cline, 2015) and there is a lack of consideration of the differences of impairment – effectively 'writing' the body out of consideration (Bury, 2000) with specific impairments continuing to exclude some from society (Shakespeare, 2006), ignoring biological factors and it is unclear who has a disability, society or the individual?

Activity

There are a number of both positive and negative consequences of adopting a social or medical approach to practice.

- Examine the following statements and identify which relate to the medical and Social Models and the positive and negative consequences arising from the use of these models in education:

1. Identification or diagnosis may trigger additional resources and the support of professionals who have expert knowledge that can inform teachers' practice.

2. Pupils' deficits may be the focus of assessment rather than their capabilities or potentialities.

3. Responsibility given that the cause of the difficulty is located within the learner and not in their practice.

4. There may be a reduced tendency to stigmatise pupils with the label of SEND.

5. Pupils may feel some absolution of responsibility for their own progress and learning due to the recognition of the difficulty.

6. Knowledge and understanding of a 'condition' may inform practice in positive ways, including forms of differentiation that are closely tuned to individual needs.

7. Teachers will feel a stronger sense of self-efficacy and they do possess the skills to support all pupils.

8. High expectations of pupils may prevail.

9. Pupils may feel isolated from their 'normal' peers in that they are given a 'different work' to carry out.

The Biopsychosocial Model

The Biopsychosocial Model of disability sees disability as an interaction between a person's health condition and the environment they live in. It advocates that both the Medical and Social Models are appropriate, but neither is sufficient on its own to explain the complex nature of one's health. The Biopsychosocial Model shows the complex and dynamic relationship between a number of interrelated factors. In this model, a person's ability to function is viewed as the outcome of the interactions between a medical factor and contextual factors. The contextual factors include external environmental factors such as social attitude and buildings, and internal personal factors, which include coping styles, social background, education and other factors that influence how disability is experienced by the individual.

It attempts to comprehend a disability as a multitude of experiences and suggests creative approaches or coping mechanisms. This approach or model takes the focus beyond the individual and addresses issues that interact to affect the ability of the individual to maintain as high a level of health and well-being as possible and to function within society. It recognises that disabilities are often due to illness or injury and do not dismiss the importance of the impact of biological, emotional and environmental issues on health, well-being and function in society (Smeltzer, 2007).

 Activity

There are other models of disability, including:

1. Professional – Defined by the professional's process of identifying an impairment and deciding about what is the correct course of action.

2. Customer – In a consumer society, it is becoming more widely recognised that disabled people are large consumers, and businesses are moving towards providing accessibility to suit their business development models.

3. Economic – Based upon an individual's ability to contribute to society and support himself. This ties in with the Social Model, as ability to work is largely dependent upon access provided, and facilities to support disabilities.

4. Transhumanist model of disability – does not see the 'disabled person's body' as abnormal. It rather sees the human body in general as deficient as something in need of improvement. Therefore, it believes in improving any human body if possible whether it's he one of disabled people or that of the so-called non-disabled. In this model in essence everyone is disabled, everyone has defects in need of fixing. At the societal/political level, the principal response is the support for the development of any new technology offering the improvement of the human body and the norm.

5. The Affirmation Model attempts to extend the Social Model to include disability culture and community, personal identity as shaped by disability and impairment, and personal acceptance of impairment. Some barriers exist that we need removed in order to have full civil rights, but impairments are an important part of ourselves and our lives.

(Open University, 2008)

■ How do these models of disability impact a pupil with SEND and their family?

■ How might they impact on professionals working in a school?

The dilemma of difference

Norwich (2009) describes the dilemma of difference in the following way. On the one hand, if we identify difference (through diagnosis, for example) we run the risk of stigmatizing and marginalizing learners in ways that may limit their opportunities. On the other hand, if we do not identify difference and respond in the form of positive action, we run the risk of neglecting learners in ways that may limit their opportunities. If children experiencing difficulties in learning are identified and labelled as having 'SEND', then they are likely to be treated as different and even stigmatised and devalued. If children experiencing difficulties in learning are not identified as having 'SEND', then it is less likely that additional educational resources will be identified and ensured for them.

However, inaccurate labels may lead to inappropriate interventions or assumptions about what a learner can and cannot do and what they do and do not need. There may be a focus on the 'label' rather than on the capabilities and complexities of an individual learner. Some labels are less acceptable and may trigger judgemental and dismissive actions by others and hence further stigmatisation. Labels may place the deficits within the learner rather than in the teaching or curriculum which will remain unchanged and continue to be a barrier.

According to Ofsted (2010) cited in Riddick (2012), there is a growing concern that too many children are being labelled as having SEND when all that is needed is a style of teaching that caters for a wide range of abilities therefore avoiding the need for a label. There are advantages of labelling in the area of SEND in that a label can give us an accurate understanding of a child's learning differences and hence be a starting point for addressing their needs appropriately. It may enable access to 'gatekeepers' of resources such as medical practitioners. Also, those with a similar type of difference can develop their own identity, culture and advocacy groups. Labels can lead to a greater self-understanding and empowerment, and used as mediators in explaining behaviour that might seem unacceptable to the wider public, perhaps leading to greater understanding.

A key issue is that labels could perpetuate a stereotype and, as a result of this, each child is viewed as their disability rather than individual needs that may differ between each child with the same label. This could lead to stigmatisation and the view that labels are 'sticky' and are attached for life. However, Riddick (2012) said that this can be felt by those who have not received a label as it already exists in society due to the way a person behaves, but the label emphasises the existing negative attitudes. Assigning categories to certain learners predisposes educators to believe that they cannot effectively teach all learners together, or that they lack the knowledge to work with pupils who belong to that particular category.

 Activity

You are introduced to a new member of your class named John. He is referred to as 'This is John, he has autism', by another member of staff.

■ What are the differing perspectives you could hold about John and his autism?

■ What would be the differing approaches in working with John, if a member of staff sees the autism as the issue, compared with another who sees the need to identify what works for John rather than the focus on the autism?

The language and discourses surrounding special educational needs

The Union of the Physically Impaired Against Segregation as long ago as 1976 rejected the whole idea of 'experts' and professionals holding forth on how we should accept disabilities with the view that descriptions of how awful it is to be disabled. The key is the changing of the conditions of life, and thus overcoming the disabilities which are imposed on top of any physical impairment by the way society is organised to exclude us.

The label of special educational needs causes much debate. For example:

■ special – euphemism for 'problem'

■ needs – implying 'neediness' (not about a learning requirement), a within-child model

■ Scotland uses the term additional support needs and the Netherlands takes the view of educational needs.

Mallet and Slater (2014) identify the difference between the terms disabled people (Social Model) and people with a disability (Medical Model). Why the distinction? In the Social Model, impairment is seen as injury, illness or congenital condition that causes or is likely to cause a loss or difference of physiological or psychological function, whereas disability is the loss or limitation of opportunities to take part in society on an equal level with others, due to social and environmental barriers. Many authors on the topic of inclusion argue that labels affect the views, responses and actions of teachers (Ainscow, 2007; Frederickson and Cline, 2015; Trussler and Robinson, 2015).

Activity

Consider these statements:

'I feel so sorry for…', 'I pity the family…', 'We need to fund raise to support…'.

'Stephen has a poor working memory and impaired social communication'.

'Farah is struggling with…' 'Jane is suffering from…'.

'These children are normal, but your children…'.

Which of these relate to the following discourses:

- Tragedy/charity

- Deficit language

- The language of problems

- Colloquial language

Language reflects the cultural assumptions and thinking of the society around us. It follows then that for much of history, the language and words used to describe Disabled people have reflected a negative, charitable or medical view of disability. Words that reflect these views of disability include: 'handicapped', 'cripple', 'wheelchair-bound', 'retarded', 'suffering from' and 'special needs'. Social Model language rejects this negative or medical language and replaces it with language that describes more accurately our experience. For example, 'Disabled person' (not 'handicapped' or 'cripple'), 'wheelchair user' (not 'wheelchair-bound'), 'person with learning difficulties' (not 'retarded'), 'person with an impairment' (not 'suffering from') and 'access needs' (not 'special needs').

According to the SEND Code of Practice 0–25 (2015) (DfE, 2015), a child or young person has SEN if he or she has a learning difficulty or disability, which calls for special educational provision to be made for him or her, which is 'additional' to or 'different' from that made generally for other children or young people of the same age. In the normative model of difference, provision is additional to or different from that made generally for other children or young people of the same age by mainstream education (Florian, 2014). SEND children may become labelled as 'abnormal or deviant', separated, marginalised and perceived as different (Trussler and Robinson, 2015). This discourse and practice may promote a sense that ability is fixed and that both teachers and support staff may view that it is difficult to progress children at both ends of the normal distribution curve, who may be limited in their progress (Hart et al., 2004). Thus, this nomothetic approach may fail to consider the uniqueness of individuals which may lead to view that testing, league tables and teaching to the middle, are important (Trussler and Robinson, 2015) and related specialised curricula and associated pedagogy.

Dyslexia: an example of competing discourses

Pause for reflection

Dyslexia can be viewed as:

1. a label

2. a condition

3. an experience

4. a disability

5. a difference

6. a problem

- As a professional what does dyslexia mean to you?
- Which models do these views support?

The term dyslexia could have both negative and positive connotations depending on an individual's world view of what it means to have a difficulty/disability. Whereas the Social Model of dyslexia advocates the need for society or educational settings to make reasonable adjustments to ensure full participation of individuals with learning difficulty, the Medical Model emphasises the problem with the individual. Here dyslexia is a neurological problem of genetic origin, which makes the acquisition of language skills extremely difficult with the problem being located within the individual. Look at these examples of defining the experience of an individual living with dyslexia: people suffering from dyslexia; people who have dyslexia; people who experience dyslexia and people who are dyslexic. The word 'suffering' has negative connotations and dyslexia is not a disease but a difference in neurological function.

The Social Model advocates difference and neurodiversity and that dyslexia is an experience that arises out of natural human diversity, on the one hand, and a world, on the other, where the early learning of literacy, and good personal organisation and working memory are mistakenly used as a marker of 'intelligence', thus the difference is mislabelled as a deficit (Cooper, 2006). Dyslexia could also be seen as a difference in the way people experience information processing and learning. Thus, dyslexia is not a neurological dysfunction, as it is presented by the Medical Model rather a diversification of neurological function which is now one of the cornerstone ideologies on which the Social Model and the neurodiversity movement is built.

Summary

Writing in the Telegraph (2005), Graham Barton, the spokesman for the Special Schools' Protection League, stated that inclusion has been used as a politically correct panacea by politicians, but thousands of parents know they have been sold an illusion and that their children, the ones who most need help, have suffered in mainstream schools. This sentiment was echoed when Baroness Warnock suggested that vulnerable children with severe problems can become isolated in mainstream schools. The concept is still hotly contested today, but we have come a long way since the Warnock Report in 1975. There has been a fundamental shift in discourse on special needs and disability, and accelerated progress towards inclusive approaches to education. The SEND Code of Practice 0–25 (2015) (DfE, 2015), alongside attitudinal change in thinking about the rights of individuals with disabilities, gives us the opportunity to decide what inclusion might look like in 40 years of time.

References

Ainscow, M. (2007). Taking an inclusive turn. *Journal of Research in Special Educational Needs*, 7(1), pp. 3–7.

Armstrong, A., Armstrong, D. and Spandagou, I. (2010). *Inclusive education*. Los Angeles: SAGE.

Booth, T. and Ainscow, M. (2011). *Index for inclusion: Developing learning and participation in schools*. Bristol: CSIE.

Bury, M. (2000). On chronic illness and disability. In Bird, C.E., Conrad, P. and Freemont, A.M. (eds.), *Handbook of medical dociology*, 5th ed. Upper Saddle River: Prentice Hall International.

Centre for Studies on Inclusive Education (CSIE) (2004). *What is inclusion?* Available online at: http://inclusion.uwe.ac.uk/csie/csiefaqs.htm (Accessed 17/9/2004).

Cooper, R. (2006). The point is to make a difference. *PATOSS Bulletin*, Nov 20(1), pp. 50–55.

CSIE. (2018). *Index for inclusion: Developing learning and participation in schools*. Available online at: www.csie.org.uk/resources/inclusion-index-explained.shtml#definitions (Accesssed 04/05/2018).

Department for Education (2015). *Special educational needs and disability code of practice: 0 to 25 years*. Department for Education.

Farrell, P. (2000). The impact of research on developments in inclusive education. *International Journal of Inclusive Education*, 4(2), pp. 153–162.

Florian, L. (2007) Reimagining special education. In Florian L. (ed.) *The sage handbook of special education*. London: Sage Publications.

Frederickson, N. and Cline, T. (2015). *Special educational needs, inclusion and diversity*. Maidenhead: McGraw Hill/Open University Press.

Haegele, J.A. and Hodge, S. (2016) Disability discourse: Overview and critiques of the medical and social models. *Quest*, 68, pp. 193–206.

Hart, S., Dixon, A., Drummond, M.J. and McIntyre, D. (2004). *Learning without Limits*. Maidenhead: Open University Press.

Hodkinson, A. (2016). *Key issues in special educational needs and inclusion*, 2nd ed. London: SAGE.

Humpage, L. (2007). Models of disability, work and welfare in Australia. *Social Policy & Administration*, 41(3), pp. 215–231.

Jordan, A., Schwartz, E. and McGhie-Richmond, D. (2009). Preparing teachers for inclusive classrooms. *Teaching and Teacher Education*, 25, pp. 535–542.

Liasidou, A. (2012). Inclusive education and critical pedagogy at the intersections of disability, race, gender and class. *Journal for Critical Education Policy Studies*, 10(1), pp. 168–184.

Lindsay, G. (2003). Inclusive education: A critical perspective. *British Journal of Special Education*, 30, pp. 3–12.

Macbeath, J., Galton, M., Steward, S., Macbeath, A. and Page, C. (2006). *The costs of inclusion*. Report prepared for the National Union of Teachers. Available online at: www.teachers.org.uk/resources/pdf/CostsofInclusion.pdf (Accessed 12/12/2017).

Mallett, R. and Slater, J. (2014) Language. In Cameron, C. (ed.), *Disability studies: A student's guide*. London: Sage.

Mitra, S. (2006). The capability approach and disability. *Journal of Disability Policy Studies (Sage)*, 16(4), pp. 236–247.

Mittler, P. (2000). *Working towards inclusive education: Social contexts*. London: David Fulton.

Norwich, B. (2009). Dilemmas of difference and the identification of special educational needs/disability: international perspectives. *British Educational Research Journal*, 35(3), pp. 447–467.

Ofsted (2006). *Inclusion: Does it matter where pupils are taught?* Available online at: http://dera.ioe.ac.uk/6001/1/Inclusion%20does%20it%20matter%20where%20pupils%20are%20taught%20%28pdf%20format%29%20.pdf (Accessed 07/06/2018).

Open University (2008). *Personal blogs*. Available online at: https://learn1.open.ac.uk/mod/oublog/viewpost.php?post=70707 (Accessed 12/04/2018).

Riddick, B. (2012). Labelling learners with SEND: The good, the bad and the ugly. In Contemporary Issues in Special Educational Needs, edited Squires A. 25–34. Maidenhead: Open University Press.

Rose, R. (ed.) (2010). *Confronting obstacles to inclusion: International responses to developing inclusive education*. London: Routledge.

Round, P., Subban, P.K. and Sharma, U. (2016). 'I don't have time to be this busy': Exploring the concerns of secondary school teachers towards inclusive education. *International Journal of Inclusive Education*, 20(2), pp 185–198.

Shakespeare, T.W. (2006). *Disability rights and wrongs*. London: Routledge.

Smeltzer, S.C. (2007). Improving the health and wellness of persons with disabilities: A call to action too important for nursing to ignore. *Nurs Outlook*, 55, pp. 189–195.

Telegraph (2005) *Warnock-U-turn-on-special-schools*. Available online at: www.telegraph.co.uk/news/uknews/1491679/Warnock-U-turn-on-special-schools.html (Accessed 05/05/2018).

Thomas, G. and Loxley, A. (2007). *Deconstructing special education and constructing inclusion*. 2nd ed. Berkshire: Open University Press.

Trussler, S. and Robinson, D. (2015). *Inclusive practice in the primary school: A guide for teachers*. London: SAGE publications.

Union of the Physically Impaired Against Segregation (UPIAS) (1976). *Fundamental principles of disability*. London: UPIAS.

Wilson, J. (2000). Doing justice to inclusion. *European Journal of Special Needs Education*, 15(3), pp. 297–304.

6 Introducing developmental diversities

Introduction

In whichever SEND context you are likely to be working, there is a fundamental need to be conversant with a range of perspectives, research and theoretical explanations for human growth, development and behaviour. This chapter will provide a foundation of knowledge within the frameworks of biology, sociology and psychology and a range of theories spanning the stages in life relevant to the focus of this book. It aims to:

- relate the nature or nurture debate in relation to SEND

- outline Carol Dweck's view of fixed IQ versus untapped potential in relation to SEND

- discuss the notion of disability and impairment with respect to development

- identify how typical and atypical development might proceed in relation to the concept of milestones

- discuss attachment theory and the impact that early experience has on the process of attachment

- relate difficulties in attachment to Attachment Disorder (AD) and Reactive Attachment Disorders (RAD)

- examine ways we can support pupils with AD, in the classroom

- outline Erikson's Psychosocial Development Theory and how it might relate to the area of SEND

- discuss the impact that adolescence might have on individuals with SEND

- outline the theories of Piaget, Vygotsky and Bruner and relate them to the inclusive classroom.

Nature or nurture: echoes of models of SEND?

The nature versus nurture debate occupies centre ground within a number of discourses in education, such as personality, intelligence and in particular special needs. On the one hand, nature suggests that who we are (and who we will become) is a result of our genes, our physiology and biology – characteristics we were born with. Nurture, on the other hand, states that who we are (and who we will become) is a result of the environment, for example, our parents, our culture, our landscape, economic circumstances, ethnicity, history, predominant attitudes and our peer group. Working out the extent to which nature or nurture impacts how we develop is challenging as development is most likely to be influenced by a range of factors and variables in an interactionist way.

The principle of the child as an active learner is that there are certain periods during early development when experiences have a more significant effect than others. These sensitive periods are thought of as windows of opportunity during which certain types of experience have a foundational effect on the development of skills or competencies (Fox and Rutter, 2010). Data from twin studies provided estimates of heritability of specific human personality traits or cognitive processes and, at the same time, attempted to model the effects of shared and non-shared experience on the developing child. This work has been useful in maintaining a voice in the debate as to whether development was more influenced by 'nature' versus nurture; however, this may no longer be valid as the interactionist approach is the one which is mostly accepted.

 Activity

Many of the chapters in this book relate to the nature or nurture debate within SEND.

- Identify where the debate is identified and what is your opinion on where the issue stands in relation to SEND?

- What arguments are put forward by both sides in the nature versus nature debate in relation to a specific difficulty or disability such as Attention Deficit Hyperactivity Disorder (ADHD), Autism or dyslexia?

- Review the models of disability, outlined in Chapter 5 and suggest which model(s) supports which side of the debate.

Fixed IQ and untapped potential

One interesting approach to this debate is offered by Dweck (2008) who suggests that pupils are divided into two main groups, with approximately 15 per cent of students falling in the middle of these and the remainder divided between the two theories. Fixed IQ theorists believe that their ability is fixed, probably at birth, and there is very little if anything they can do to improve it. They believe ability comes from talent rather than from the slow development of skills through learning. Either you can do it with little effort, or you will never be able to do it, so you might as well give up in the face of difficulty, for example, 'I can't do maths'. Untapped Potential theorists believe that ability and success are due to learning, and learning requires time and effort. In the case of difficulty, one must try harder, try another approach, or seek help.

Activity

- How might this idea relate to a pupil with SEND and their approach to the curriculum studied and their attribution of the causes of difficulty?

- How might this approach be utilised by teachers who hold the medical and social model attitudes towards SEND?

Disability and impairment

The Union of Physically Impaired against Segregation (UPIAS, 1976) adopts a social model and suggest that it is normal for a society to contain individuals with mental and physical impairments. Disability is a consequence of society's failure to recognise and respond to these as norms. Impairments may not lead to serious disabilities in some contexts (for example, dyslexia in a world where there is no literacy, short-sightedness in a world where spectacles are freely available to all). However, not all of the problems faced by individuals with impairments are within the power of society to abolish (Shakespeare, 2006). Impairments vary greatly and cannot generalise but types of impairment include learning, motor and sensory. Comparing children with and without impairments may reveal pathways of development that include diversity in terms of rate, sequence and structure of development. Concepts of development have historically favoured linear progressions that oversimplify and tend to homogenise development. In contrast to these linear models, Ayoub and Fischer (2008) pose that a person develops along a web of multiple strands and that different people develop along different pathways or webs. A further area of disagreement concerns the question of the significance of the earliest years of life and whether what happens during this period influences the whole life course.

Development is the gaining of skills in all aspects of the child's life (Bulman and Savory, 2006). It is important to be aware of the usual ages for developmental milestones in different areas (social, emotional, communication, cognitive, perceptual and physical) and to monitor children's emerging skills to make sure that they are developing as expected (the age band given is always an average). Typical development follows a recognised sequence in most children and children have to acquire certain skills before being able to move on to the next skill (for example, the development of head control is a prerequisite for sitting). Almost all children follow the same patterns of development, even if the timing is different. The four key areas that tell us whether a child is following the normal pattern of development are motor, social and emotional language, cognition and understanding.

It is important to remember that the rate of development varies from child to child and within each child. This means that not only do children develop at different rates, but they may develop more quickly in some of the areas mentioned and be slower to develop in other areas. Children's difficulties and disabilities will disrupt their development, which could be delayed, in which the child will reach developmental milestones in the same order as typically developing children, but their progress is significantly slower than expected in one or more areas of development. Or, disordered in that some difficulties or disabilities change the order of a child's developmental progress in one or more developmental areas. The child will gain developmental skills with the support of specialised teaching, and/or adapted classrooms or resources.

 Activity

There are many reasons why children are born with disabilities and/or health needs. These can include difficulties during the pregnancy, including infections in the mother, trauma during or shortly after birth, genetic disorders, for example. Any of the following can affect development:

Before birth
1. infections and toxins, including alcohol

2. ischaemia (interrupted blood flow to the brain)

3. nutrition

4. genetic factors: chromosomal disorders, single gene defects

After birth
1. social environment

2. personality

3. emotional factors including interaction with caregivers

4. cultural factors

5. nutrition

6. parenting

7. physical health

- From reading the chapters in this book and your own practice, can you give any specific examples of how the impact of these factors might be evidenced in a child with SEND?

Although people often talk about child development as though it is a simple series of ages and stages, it is more complex than this. At any point, children may also be using strategies from earlier stages of their development and learning develops in overlapping waves with children altering their approach in different situations (Evangelou et al., 2009). Some children develop differently and do not follow the expected pattern of development. Delayed or atypical development is recognised through comparison with the following typical milestones:

1. Typical development: a mainstream or 'normal' pattern.

2. Delayed development: follows the typical pattern, but at a much slower pace. The developmental milestones will be reached in the right order, but later than most children.

3. Atypical/disordered development: the usual sequence of milestones is not followed; there is something different about the way in which the child develops.

4. Borderline development: this lies between the typical and atypical.

 Activity

Lancashire County Council has published a guide to developmental milestones covering the following: Child Development Stages; Physical Development; Language and Speech Development; Social and Emotional Development and Cognitive Development. It can be accessed online via the website of Lancashire County Council (2018).

▪ Taking each of the areas described in the handout, identify how a child with a specific issue such as autism might show atypical development at any of the stages.

Attachment theory

Attachment is a bond between a baby or young child and an adult or caregiver, where security and protection are provided within a safe environment (Prior and Glaser, 2006). This forming a concrete, secure attachment, normally during the first three months following birth, albeit continues further during attachment patterns up to the age of 48 months. This is vital for a secure attachment to occur. During the early stages following birth, lack of fundamental stimulus by the parent or caregiver, described as insensitive love and care, can prevent normal development of the baby's brain (Bomber, 2008). Bowlby (1969) defined attachment as a deep and enduring emotional bond that connects one person to another and which does not need to be reciprocal. The 'internal working model' describes how attachment behaviour is adaptive and evolving and so encourages human survival through ensuring safety, forming emotional relationships and creating a platform for exploration, imperative for cognitive and social development. Schaffer and Emerson (1964) claimed that it was the 'quality of interaction' that was a key to the attachment formation. Furthermore, they proposed that attachment to more than one caregiver was possible and was not an exclusive relationship between a mother and a child.

 Pause for reflection

There are four types of attachment:

1. Secure attachment: where parents are emotionally available, perceptive and responsive to infant's needs and mental states. The internal working model of these infants is likely to be one that expects that their needs will be known and met, that they will be attuned to and emotionally regulated and that they can freely explore their environment with safety.

2. Avoidant attachment: where parents are emotionally unavailable, imperceptive, unresponsive and rejecting. Responsive interactions could be very dismissive and non-responsive when the infant was emotionally needy, frustrated or angry. These infants often expressed random aggression and could be clingy and demanding. The internal working model is likely to result in infants protecting themselves from this difficult situation by dissociating from contact with their normal need for connection and repress their emotions more generally.

3. Ambivalent attachment: where parents are inconsistently available for the infant, and when available she was often preoccupied and unattuned to the infant in her responses. These infants were the most anxious, clingy and demanding at home. The likely internal working model is that although the parents are present, they are not likely to comfort them.

4. Disorganised attachment: this is not used as a primary classification, but rather an additional descriptor, where there may be psychologically disturbed parents, and/or parents with substance abuse. The inner working model of this relationship is not functional and is one where the supposed comforter is a source of soothing and also the source of danger, leaving their mind state and behaviour very disorganised.

● Think about how these types of attachment might be shown in a classroom.

Attachment issues

The following four categories are proposed diagnoses or clusters of AD:

1. Anxious Attachment Disorder

2. Avoidant Attachment Disorder

3. Ambivalent Attachment Disorder

4. Neurologically Disorganised Attachment Disorder

Children with milder forms may be described as having attachment issues or attachment insecurities (the mildest form would be a child with separate anxiety), with the most severe being a child with Attachment Disorder (AD). Attachment issues fall on a spectrum, from mild problems that are easily addressed to the most serious form, known as Reactive Attachment Disorder (RAD). RAD is a condition in which a child is unable to establish healthy attachment with their parent or primary caretaker. This can lead to difficulty connecting with others and managing their emotions, resulting in a lack of trust and self-worth, a fear of getting close to anyone, anger and a need to be in control. A child with an AD feels unsafe and alone. RAD is common in children who have been abused, bounced around in foster care, lived in orphanages or taken away from their primary caregiver after establishing a bond (Malchiodi and Crenshaw, 2010).

Common signs and symptoms in young children include:

1. An aversion to touch and physical affection. Children with RAD often flinch or laugh rather than producing positive feelings, and touch and affection are perceived as a threat.

2. Control issues. Most children with RAD go to great lengths to remain in control and avoid feeling helpless, when they can be disobedient, defiant and argumentative.

3. Anger problems. Anger may be expressed directly, in tantrums or acting out, or through manipulative, passive-aggressive behaviour.

4. Difficulty showing genuine care and affection. For example, children with RAD may act inappropriately affectionate with strangers while displaying little or no affection towards their parents.

5. An underdeveloped conscience. Children with RAD may act like they do not have a conscience and fail to show guilt, regret or remorse after behaving badly.

As children with RAD grow older, they often develop either an inhibited or a disinhibited pattern of symptoms. Inhibited symptoms of RAD include the child becoming withdrawn, emotionally detached and resistant to comforting. They may push others away, ignore them or even act out in aggression when others try to get close. Disinhibited symptoms of RAD show when the child seeks comfort and attention from virtually anyone. They may be anxious, extremely dependent and act much younger than their chronological age.

Shi (2014) states that babies are biologically programmed to seek comfort from their carers and that AD has historically been largely seen as a product of dysfunctional provision of care from adult to child (Ainsworth, 1979). However, recent research on twins (Minnis et al., 2007) suggests a strong genetic link which may account for some cases of AD, particularly in boys. Genes identified as having possible involvement in AD include the dopamine D4 receptor gene (DRD4) (Gervai, 2009). Barry, Kochanska and Philibert (2008) identified that some children were more genetically susceptible to AD than others. The quality of early care influenced the severity of the disorder and the genetic makeup of the child either enhancing or offsetting that severity. The serotonin transporter gene (5-HTTLPR) has also been implicated, with children with long alleles likely to establish secure attachments even with poor quality of care, and those with short alleles only attached securely when the quality of care was sensitively responsive.

Bosman (2016) initially refers to a child's natural biological system producing the required care by communicating needs, which if unmet results in an unsecure attachment. Ashton et al. (2016) and Shea (2015) all suggest that AD is a neurological disorder that develops by repeated neglect or abuse where basic needs, within early childhood, are mismanaged or not met. The right hemisphere of the brain, is affected following trauma, consequently the way in which the brain responds to trauma, and creates an unhealthy attachment. Shea (2015) implies that there is evidence of neurochemicals, which are produced following trauma, affecting the way in which a child can self-regulate their emotions. Archer, Drury and Hills (2015) suggest that the central and autonomic nervous system, also known to be neuroplasticity, creates new pathways of development, therefore enabling the ability to repair the damage. Zeanah and Gleason (2015) and Archer et al. (2015) also express that an inadequacy of care can create emotional and sociable phenotypes, particularly within RAD.

Bademci, Karadayi and Zulueta (2015) suggest that AD is a social psychological disorder caused by negative social experiences, thereto causing negative relational distress, effecting the normal regulation and development of the brain. Colonnesi et al. (2013) suggest that without basic trust between a baby or child and a parent, insecure attachment could result. An impairment of cognitive, social and emotional development regression following neglect or abuse causes inconsistent signalling to develop, thus resulting in a deprived understanding and knowledge of the social world and a flight or fight response could then kick in. If a child has been unable to form a secure attachment, a fight (hyperarousal), flight (hypervigilance) or freeze (dissociation) effect could follow. This process, known as affect dysregulation, occurs in an individual with attachment issues, when faced with a threatening situation (Downey, 2007).

When in fight mode, a child who is in a constant state of stress may overreact or over-respond to stimuli by fending off threat using physical strength. When in flight or hypervigilance mode, the child responds to the environment as if it poses imminent threat or danger and therefore is on constant alert and may run away from the threat. Freeze occurs when a child learns to take their focus away from the threatening situation or 'block it out', switching off from their physical sensations causing them to 'disassociate'. Dissociation is a form of withdrawal from others and their surroundings. It causes the child to become numb, unfeeling or unaware and a child may subconsciously implement this absence of sensation to avoid being overwhelmed by fear. A child who has experienced negativity in the form of rejection, criticism or abuse will have an internal working model which reflects this negativity (Crittenden, 1992). The securely attached child eventually intuitively learns to achieve affect regulation and achieve a positive internal working model of themselves. This enables them to self-regulate their feelings to help cope with potential threats without going into fight, flight or freeze.

Classroom support for attachment disorder

Estimates suggest that there are 30 per cent–35 per cent of young people experiencing attachment difficulties, the majority do not have a formal diagnosis (NICE, 2015), with the prevalence of more severe RAD of approximately 1.40 per cent (Minnis et al., 2013), with estimates as high as 80 per cent in areas of severe deprivation, in areas where there is also a high rate of adolescent mothers. A child with attachment issues may present social behaviours such as being superficially charming, being indiscriminately affectionate with strangers and/or being overly demanding or clingy or displaying pseudo maturity. In a school environment, the child may also chatter incessantly or persistently ask nonsense questions, and may also have poor peer relationships, due to poor theory of mind.

A lack of thinking which predicts cause and effect may also be evident in the child with attachment issues, and some experience poor impulse control, lack of self-organisation and executive function. Some physically harmful behaviours include abnormal eating patterns, destructive behaviour and lying and stealing are also evident among some insecurely attached children. Difficulties relating to low self-esteem may include lack of eye contact and an overriding feeling of shame. In addition, the fight, flight or freeze response may result in these children struggling to cope with the interpersonal demands of school life and lead to poor peer/staff interactions, exclusions and detention.

Activity

A concise overview of how we can support pupils with AD can be accessed online via the SEN magazine website (SEN magazine, 2018).

- What strategies might the children adopt in response to early trauma?

- What strategies might a teacher or support member of staff adopt during a Maths or English lesson, for example?

Erikson's life stages

Erikson developed his 'Stages of Psychosocial Development' to explain growth and development from birth (Erikson, 1994), claiming that development is a continuous process and lasts throughout the life of an individual. He proposed a theory that described eight separate stages of development in which people would face new challenges at each stage. Erikson's theory posits that every human being passes through several distinct and qualitatively different stages in life, from birth to death. According to him, the stages are universal, and the ages at which one is said to have passed from one to another stage are also fairly universal.

The key idea in Erikson's theory is that the individual faces a conflict at each stage, which may or may not be successfully resolved within that stage. For example, he called the first stage 'Trust vs Mistrust'. If the quality of care is good in infancy, the child learns to trust the world to meet her/his needs. If not, trust remains an unresolved issue throughout succeeding stages of development. According to Erikson's stages of development, tasks which must be mastered at each stage may be short circuited by the intrusion of a disability. Lack of mastery of certain tasks at particular stages leads to non-mastery or the negative counterpart of each stage, thus the SEND child may suffer more from the lack of mastery of certain tasks than from the disability itself. Erikson proposed desirable outcomes for different stages of development in life (the first six stages are relevant to this chapter):

 Activity

From the stages outlined below, identify one that is appropriate to the age group you are working with, for example, Stage 4.

▨ What characteristics or behaviour might you see in the classroom, if the child or young person had not resolved the conflict at this stage?

▨ What obstacles might stand in the way of achieving these outcomes for:

1. An individual with a sensory impairment

2. An individual with a learning impairment

3. An individual with a motor impairment?

Stage 1 – Trust versus Mistrust (0–1 year): Infants trust in the environment and are entirely dependent on adults for needs such as warmth, comfort and food. If their custodians meet these requirements, the infants would get emotionally attached to them and develop a sense of security.

Stage 2 – Autonomy versus Shame and Doubt (1–2 years): Toddlers have a sense of autonomy and self-esteem. The ability to initiate activities gain independence and acquire skills such as dressing themselves. Depending on how they handle these challenges, they may grow up with a sense of shame or autonomy.

Stage 3 – Initiative versus Guilt (3–6 years): A sense of accomplishment and achievement. Children at this stage learn how to control their emotions and become self-confident.

Stage 4 – Industry versus Inferiority (6–12 years): The ability to see oneself as a consistent and integrated person. Infants should be competing with their peers in preparation for taking adult roles.

Stage 5 – Identity versus Role Confusion (Adolescence): The ability to experience love and commitment to others. At the end of this stage, they are required to be wholly transformed and identify their role in society.

Stage 6 – Intimacy versus Isolation (Young adulthood): The ability to be concerned about others in the wider sense.

Stage 7 – Generativity versus Self-absorption (Middle adulthood): A sense of satisfaction with one's life and accomplishment.

Stage 8 – Integrity versus Despair (old age): Evaluating your life.

Adolescence

Adolescence is recognised by many psychologists as a distinct and important period of an individual's life, during which significant physiological changes take place and when key developmental shifts occur in cognitive, emotional and social development.

 Pause for reflection

For many of us, adolescence was a time of significant growth and development. The following might have been relevant to our own lives:

1. We may have been striving to find our identity (as a social being, an employee, a member of a family)

2. We may have been striving for independence

3. We may have fallen in love for the first time

4. We may have become aware of changes in our bodies and of sexual feelings

5. We may have felt intensely shy and self-conscious

- What do you remember about adolescence and your experiences of it?

- What do you think that adolescence is a time for and what is the role of parents, practitioners and wider society in that?

Though there are patterns of development that we might be able to identify, it is impossible to make universal claims about what adolescence is and how everyone experiences it…. However, searching for patterns has brought insight and understanding. For example, 'teens' are emotionally unstable and pathic. It is the age of natural inebriation without the need of intoxicants, which made Plato define youth as spiritual drunkenness. It is a natural impulse to experience hot and perfervid psychic states and is characterised by emotionalism (Hall, 1904). He put forward the notion of 'storm and stress' by referring to the notion that adolescence is a particularly turbulent time for many individuals. Adolescents are likely to have increased conflict with parents, have mood disruptions and undertake risky behaviour. Erikson (1968) claimed that, for adolescence, the crisis was one of identity versus identity confusion. During this period, they explore possibilities and begin to form their own identity based on the outcome of their explorations. In response to role confusion or identity crisis, an adolescent may begin to experiment with different lifestyles (for example, work, education or political activities), while simultaneously wanting to secure a fixed or secure identity. The tension is between transformation and stability.

Identity formation is thus presented by Erikson as something that should be achieved. However, the concept of identity formation has evolved to the understanding that it is a process and that it varies between stages of change and stability (Kroger, 2007). Researchers have also established that this process often needs more time, and therefore, some have extended the adolescent period and refer to the emerging adulthood stage (Arnett, 2004).

Knowing who one is and developing a clear sense of identity are crucial aspects of healthy psychosocial development, and they can have an impact on many different facets of one's life. Adolescents in particular face considerable pressure to form a sense of who they are and to decide on what they are going to do with their lives (Kroger, 2007). One of the main reasons for this is that, by the end of this developmental stage, they are required to transition successfully from school to the world of work, where they are expected to become active members of society and make an economic contribution.

If adolescence is a period of stress and turmoil, all the more so for children with SEND and their families, parents, along with the young person, experience a great amount of stress in trying to help decide a career pathway or vocational option for their child. According to Lindsay et al. (2012), young adults with disabilities find the transition to adulthood and seeking employment a challenge because they lack marketable skills. They face discrimination, problems with accommodation and a lack of training when they look for job opportunities.

Activity

Identify two areas covered in this book, for example, ADHD, Autism Spectrum Disorder, Profound and Multiple Learning Difficulties, and Speech and Language Difficulties.

◾ What specific issues might an individual have when trying to secure employment?

◾ What barriers might they come up against?

◾ If you were in charge of a Skills for Working Life module, what specific content would you add to support the young person with SEND?

Three of the most influential educational theorists are Piaget, Vygotsky and Bruner. It is useful for practitioners working in the area of SEND to be familiar with their approaches and how we can adapt them with specific reference to working with pupils with additional needs.

Piaget

For Piaget, cognitive development was an aspect of children's adaptation to their physical and social environment in order to survive. Over time, exposure to new features of the environment led to further adaptation. Piaget understood children's cognitive development as linear, progressing through four increasingly complex stages towards mature (formal operational) thinking.

Stages of cognitive development

Sensorimotor: birth to two years. The child receives sensory information through physical exploration. From only reflex responses at birth, babies become goal orientated with experience, gain understanding of object permanence, and cause and effect; they begin to use symbols in play (for example, objects that stand for something else) and in language (words that stand for objects).

Preoperational: ages 2–7. Children's thinking is intuitive, based on what they sense and experience. They are egocentric, gradually developing an awareness of others' perspectives.

Concrete operational: ages 7–11. Children are capable of organising information (for example, categorising, sorting and ordering), and begin to use numbers and understand conservation. They can reason based on a present situation, but cannot generalise or think abstractly.

Formal operational: ages 12 and up. Children can reason from abstracts, allowing them to use concepts and generalisations and to think flexibly. They can solve problems and act based on extrapolations of what they know.

Although criticised in later research, for Piaget, children are born with a basic mental structure allowing them to learn, with them being the active 'lone scientist' or thinker. Piaget proposed that we construct knowledge into schemes or schemas. Schemas are prototypical associations of perceptions, ideas and actions which we use to interpret and understand the world. New knowledge is either assimilated (associated with existing schemas) or accommodated: associated with a new schema. Through the process of equilibration – the need to make meaning of our experiences – schemas which are negated by new information are abandoned. For many children with special educational needs, particularly those with profound and multiple learning disabilities, caregivers will need to help them to assimilate and accommodate their experiences through the exploitation of touch, taste and smell (Tilstone et al., 2004).

Piaget emphasised children play for enjoyment rather than to further their development and different stages of play are linked cognitively (Jarvis and Chandler, 2001). Development is a continuous process. As a child learns new skills, these are added to pre-existing skills enabling the child to progress intellectually, and the child would essentially complete one stage before progressing to the next. He believed it is essential that learners of all ages have concrete material experiences and one should form their own ideas from this. In learning through play, children build knowledge and adapt to situations around them. He promoted child centeredness and advocated that learning should not be dependent on attainment. In primary school practice, his theories are applied to classroom situations; it helps teachers and learning support assistants maximise the control children have over their own education through listening, sharing power and responsive actions (Thompson, Kilbane and Sanderson, 2008). Notwithstanding criticisms, educators of children with SEND find some of Piaget's principles helpful, including the notion of the child as an active learner; the importance of independent activity and the role of exploratory activity, including object manipulation, in promoting cognitive activity and development.

 Activity

Research findings suggest that there is a delay in cognitive development of learning-disabled children during primary school years, which corresponds to preoperational, concrete operational, and transition to formal operational stages.

■ You are working with a group of pupils aged seven to nine years in an inclusive primary school classroom. Identify what cognitive tasks typical children of these ages might be capable of engaging with, then suggest ways in which pupils with SEND might be supported in the same tasks. It might be useful to think of an activity which is focussed in a particular curriculum area.

Vygotsky

Vygotsky emphasised that children's learning is socially and culturally mediated through interactions with adults and peers with the higher skill level. He described the process of cognitive development as a transfer of social and cultural understanding from a more experienced adult (teacher) or peer. This transfer included existing knowledge in the mind of teacher; co-construction of meaning in the minds of the teacher and learner based on their interaction (including resources), which became internalised knowledge in the mind of the learner, who can then apply it independently and build on it. For Vygotsky, this process was fundamental to all learning including voluntary attention, logical memory, formulation of concepts and development of volition and without social interaction, a child would not receive experiences to produce effective learning. Children develop tools for thinking the first tools being physical ones which help children to expand attention, memory and thought: these may include tangible objects, pictures of the objects and physical actions. Later tools are internalised, including language, numbers, signs, plans, etc. and these cultural tools help children acquire 'higher mental functions (Bodrva and Leong, 2007).

Vygotsky's zone of proximal development is 'the gap between what a child can do alone and what they can do with the help of somebody more skilled or experienced' (Pound, 2008). Smidt (2009) explains that, as the child's developmental journey begins, the support of the teacher will be frequent and obvious. However, as the child's journey progresses, the help will become sporadic and less formal. Focussing on the zone for teaching is 'a means of capturing both developed and developing abilities' of the child. By intervening to support developing skills, the adult allows the child to externalise those skills, so they can be shaped by adult and child together and then internalised by the child for effective, independent use. Unlike summative assessment, dynamic assessment is not a snapshot of a child's level of attainment at a particular time. It goes beyond formative assessment, which identifies a child's next step in learning. Dynamic assessment encompasses the process of gaining the next developmental step and identifies a child's current skill level, their ultimate goal, the skills needed to develop onto the next step and ways the teacher will structure the learning (Poehner, 2011).

Vygotsky developed his theories in relation to children with learning difficulties. For example, they have provided guidance for teachers in structuring sensory experiences to help children making sense of the world, especially for children with sensory impairment; supporting children to gain skills based on their current capabilities and developing peer mentoring among children with SEND (Chalaye and Male, 2011). Peer Mediated Learning is an umbrella term, which describes a procedure, during which one student/tutor provides to another student/tutee a learning experience, under teacher supervision. It can also be referred to as peer-mediated instruction, peer-assisted learning strategies (PALS), classwide peer tutoring (CWPT), buddying programmes, paired reading and peer mentoring. As far as children with special needs are concerned, they can be benefited both academically and in self-esteem matters, when acting as tutors, especially in the early years of their education. Benefits from peer-mediated learning on the academic and cognitive progress of children have been evaluated through research more than on the social benefits (Ladd, Herald-Brown and Kochel, 2009).

One of the most popular strategies that use peer-mediated learning in interventions is CWPT. It is a strategy that requires no materials to be implemented and very little teaching when introduced in any subject. Children are paired to practise the skills taught or pin point errors. The pair discuss, find solutions, trade roles and the activities are then repeated. According to research, CWPT is a strategy that can improve academic performance, reduce disruptive behaviours and promote relations between classmates, whether these are typically developing children or children with special needs (Maheady and Gard, 2010). Another strategy that retrieves from CWPT is the PALS, which follow more or less the same organising as CWPT, but involve frequent and repeated feedback and discussions between the pairs (Fuchs et al., 2001). These strategies that occupy peer-mediated learning do promote inclusion of all children, as the needs of every child are met individually through the peer tutor (Mitchell, 2008).

 Activity

Chaleye and Male (2011) use two case studies on applying Vygotsky's zone of proximal development and peer collaboration to pupils with profound and multiple learning difficulties and severe learning difficulties. The successful peer mentoring case study between a child with Severe Learning Difficulties (SLD) and her peer, Gary, with Profound and Multiple Learning Difficulties (PMLD), led to both children extending their skills across many activities.

▨ Based on Vygotsky's mediated learning, consider how you could set up peer mentoring for a child that you work with. Draw up a plan, including the details of what will happen, and how the outcomes will be recorded.

Activity

The Integrated Play Group Model, based on Vygotsky's social constructivist theory, aims to improve the social and symbolic play skills of children with autism spectrum disorders of ages 3–11. An article on 'Play Time: An Examination of Play Intervention Strategies for Children with Autism Spectrum Disorders' can be accessed from the University website (2018):

- How does this approach support a pupil with SEND?

Bruner

Bruner's interest in the process of how children form concepts led him to extend Piaget and Vygotsky's thinking. His main focus was on the importance of culture, social interaction, language and external resources as the media of cognitive development. For him, adults create the conditions for learning, in supporting thinking and problem-solving, using scaffolding to support children to extend their skills and become independent (Lindon, 2010).

Bruner proposed three modes (each with four stages) used for representing and organising knowledge: the Enactive mode in which child understands the world by physically interacting with it (0–18 months); the Iconic mode in which the child begins to develop sensory memory and can learn from sensory presentation, for example, pictures (from 18 months) and the Symbolic mode in which knowledge and thought are represented as words, mathematical symbols, etc. (from six years). However, the modes do not represent a progression, and earlier modes of representation may be selected by a child. Associated with these modes, Bruner conceived of amplifiers which are used to extend the human abilities, these include amplifiers of human motor capacity: for example, tools for everyday human activities (cutlery, weapons, writing implements, computer mouse); amplifiers of human sensory capacity: tools that enhance or extend sensory experience (loud hailers, magnifying glasses, radars) and amplifiers of symbolic thought: tools such as language systems and theories. For example, in Sherborne Developmental Movement, the bodies of those supporting movement become a motoric 'amplifier' for children, enabling them to experience different movements (Tilstone et al., 2004). Shared movement also becomes the scaffold for developing interactive relationships (Hill, 2006; Marsden and Egerton, 2007).

A key concept originated by Bruner is that of scaffolding which takes place within the child's zone of proximal development. A more experienced adult or peer supports the extension of a child's skills, behaviour or performance by, for example by directing attention, offering guidance through visual and verbal prompts and reviewing and adjusting performance and support. Learning should be through inquiry/exploration, with the teacher providing guidance to accelerate children's thinking. Children adapt based on this guidance and finally become able to use the skill independently and subsequently the curriculum should revisit the inquiry and repeatedly build upon basic ideas until the child fully understands them.

 Activity

In their article: 'Clarifying teacher and teaching assistant roles for children with special educational needs', Radford et al. (2014) discuss a model on scaffolding learning for independence: It sets out the three roles and makes suggestions regarding who should take responsibility, to clarify how teachers can offer support to the Teaching Assistant.

The article entitled 'Scaffolding learning for independence: Clarifying teacher and teaching assistant roles for children with special educational needs'.

Radford et al. (2014) can be found online.

- Taking the three roles of repair, model and heuristic, identify how these could be utilised in an inclusive classroom to support pupils with SEND.

Summary

It is important to view developmental stages and the focus on milestones, as indicators to the interaction of genes and the environment. We may not refer as much to the terms 'normal' and 'abnormal' when working in the area of SEND, replacing them with terms such as '(neuro)typical' or '(neuro)atypical'. We refer to the concept of continuum when discussing issues such as autism, ADHD, etc., and so is the case with developmental diversities. It is useful for practitioners to be familiar with the work of theorists such as Piaget, Vygotsky and Bruner, but it is also important to relate these to the practice of working with pupils with SEND. The impact of delayed milestones, early life experiences and interaction with family and peers might have a propound influence on the developmental trajectory, but it is important to recognise that we need to relate these to the uniqueness and diversity of such individuals.

References

Ainsworth, M.D.S. (1979). Infant-mother attachment. *American Psychologist*, 34, pp. 932–937.
Archer, C., Drury, C. and Hills, J. (2015) *Healing the hidden hurt*. London: Jessica Kingsley Publishers.
Arnett, J.J. (2004). Emerging adulthood: The winding road from the late teens through the twenties. New York: Oxford University Press.

Ashton, C., O'Brien-Langer, A. and Silverstone, P. (2016). The CASA trauma and attachment group (TAG) program for children who have attachment issues following early developmental trauma. *Journal of the Canadian Academy of Child and Adolescent Psychiatry*, 25(1), pp. 35–42.

Ayoub, C. and Fischer, K. (2008). Developmental pathways and intersections among domains of development. In McCartney, K. and Phillips, D. (eds.), *Blackwell handbooks of developmental psychology. Blackwell handbook of early childhood development*. Malden: Blackwell Publishing.

Bademci, H., Karadayi, E. and Zulueta, F. (2015). Attachment intervention through peer-based interaction: Working with Istanbul's street boys in a university setting. *Children and Youth Services Review*, 49, pp. 20–31.

Barry, R.A., Kochanska, G. and Philibert, R.A. (2008). G · E interaction in the organization of attachment: mothers' responsiveness as a moderator of children's genotypes. *Journal of Child Psychology and Psychiatry*, 49(12), pp. 1313–1320.

Bodrova, E. and Leong, D.J. (2007). *Tools of the mind*. 2nd ed. Columbus: Merrill/Prentice Hall.

Bomber, L.M. (2008). *Inside I'm hurting: Practical strategies for supporting children with attachment difficulties in schools*. London: Worth Publishing.

Bosmans, G. (2016). Cognitive behaviour therapy for children and adolescents: Can attachment theory contribute to its efficacy? *Clinical Child and Family Psychology Review*, 19(4), pp. 310–328.

Bowlby, J. (1969). *Attachment and loss, Vol. 1 attachment*. New York: Basic Books and Hogarth Press.

Bulman, K. and Savory, L. (2006). *BTEC first children's care*. Oxford: Heinemann.

Chalaye, C and Male, D. (2011) Applying Vygotsky's zone of proximal development and peer collaboration to pupils with profound and multiple learning difficulties and severe learning difficulties: Two case studies. *SLD Experience*, 61, pp. 13–18.

Colonnesi, C., Wissink, I.B., Noom, M., Asscher, J.J., Hoeve, M., Stams, G., Polderman, N.G. and Kellaert-Knol, M. (2013). Basic trust an attachment-oriented intervention based on mind-mindedness in adoptive families. *Research on Social Work Practice*, 23, pp. 179–188.

Crittenden, P.M. (1992). Quality of attachment in the preschool years. *Development and Psychopathology*, 4, pp. 209–241.

Downey, L. (2007). *Calmer classrooms – a guide to working with traumatised children*. Melbourne: State of Victoria, Child Safety Commissioner, Australia.

Dweck, C. (2008). *Mindset: The new psychology of success*. New York: Random House.

Erikson, E.H. (1968). *Identity: youth and crisis*. Oxford: Norton & Co.

Erikson, E.H. (1994). *Insight and responsibility*. 1st ed. New York: W.W. Norton.

Evangelou, M., Sylva, K., Wild, M., Glenny, D. and Kyriacou, M. (2009). *Early years learning and development: Literature review*. Nottingham: DCSF Publications.

Fox, N.A. and Rutter, M. (2010). Introduction to the special section on the effects of early experience on development. *Child Development*, 81(1), pp. 23–27.

Fuchs, D., Fuchs, L.S., Thompson, A., Svenson, E., Yen, L., Al Otaiba, S. and Saenz, L. (2001). Peer-assisted learning strategies in reading extensions for kindergarten, first grade, and high school. *Remedial and Special Education*, 22(1), pp. 15–21.

Gervai, J. (2009). Environmental and genetic influences on early attachment. *Child and Adolescent Psychiatry and Mental Health*, 3, Article ID 25. pp 1–12.

Hall, G.S. (1904). *Adolescence: Its psychology and its relation to physiology, anthropology, sociology, sex, crime, religion, and education.* Vols. I & II. Englewood Cliffs: Prentice-Hall.

Hill, C. (2006). *Communicating through movement: Sherborne developmental movement – towards a broadening perspective.* Clent: Sunfield Publications.

Jarvis, M. and Chandler, E. (2001). *Angles on child psychology.* Cheltenham: Nelson Thornes.

Kroger, J. (2007). *Identity development: Adolescence through adulthood.* 2nd ed. Thousand Oaks: Sage Publications, Inc.

Ladd, G.W., Herald-Brown, S.L. and Kochel, K.P. (2009). Peers and motivation. In K.R. Wenzel and A. Wigfield (eds.), *Educational psychology handbook series. Handbook of motivation at school.* New York: Routledge/Taylor & Francis Group, pp. 323–348.

Lancashire County Council (2018). *Handout – child development.* Available online at: www3.lancashire.gov.uk/corporate/web/viewdoc.asp?id=127243 (Accessed 12/03/2018).

Lindon, J. (2010). *Understanding child development.* 1st ed. London: Hodder Education.

Lindsay G., Dockrell, J., Law, J. and Roulstone, S. (2012). *The better communication research programme: Improving provision for children and young people with speech, language and communication needs.* London: Department for Education.

Maheady, L. and Gard, J. (2010). Classwide peer tutoring: Practice, theory, research, and personal narrative. *Intervention in School and Clinic*, 46(2), pp. 71–78.

Malchiodi, C. and Crenshaw, D. (2014). *Creative arts and play therapy for attachment problems.* New York: Guilford Press.

Marsden, E. and Egerton J. (eds.) (2007). *Moving with research: Evidence-based practice in sherborne developmental movement.* Clent: Sunfield Publications.

Minnis, H., Reekie, J., Young, D., O'Connor, T., Gray, A. and Plomic R. (2007) Genetic, environmental and gender influences on attachment disorders behaviours. *British Journal of Psychiatry*, 190, pp 90–95.

Minnis, H., Macmillan, S., Pritchett, R., Young, D., Wallace, B., Butcher, J., Sim, F., Baynham, K., Davidson, C. and Gillberg, C. (2013). Prevalence of reactive attachment disorder in a deprived population. *British Journal of Psychiatry*, 202, pp. 342–346.

Mitchell, D. (2008). *What really works in special and inclusive education using evidence-based teaching strategies.* London: Routledge.

NICE (2015). *Children's attachment. Attachment in children and young people who are adopted from care, in care or at high risk of going into care.* Available online at: www.nice.org.uk/guidance/ng26/documents/childrens-attachment-full-guideline2 (Accessed 21/04/2018).

Poehner, M.E. (2011). Validity and interaction in the ZPD: Interpreting learner development through L2 dynamic assessment. *International Journal of Applied Linguistics*, 21(2), pp. 244–263.

Pound, L. (2008). *How children learn.* London: Step Forward Publishing.

Prior, V. and Glaser, D. (2006). *Child and adolescent mental health series. Understanding attachment and attachment disorders: Theory, evidence and practice.* London: Jessica Kingsley Publishers.

Radford, J., Bosanquet, P., Webster, R. and Blatchford, P. (2014). *Scaffolding learning for independence: Clarifying teacher and teaching assistant roles for children with special educational needs learning and instruction 36.* Available online at: http://maximisingtas.co.uk/assets/content/scaffolding-1.pdf (Accessed 12/03/2018).

Schaffer, H.R. and Emerson, P.E. (1964). The development of social attachments in infancy. *Monographs of the Society for Research in Child Development*, 29(3), serial number 94.

SENmagazine (2018). *Attachment, trauma and education.* Available online at: https://senmagazine.co.uk/articles/articles/senarticles/examining-the-severe-challenges-facing-those-with-attachment-issues-and-how-to-support-these-children-in-the-classroom (Accessed 20/05/2018).

Shakespeare, T.W. (2006). *Disability rights and wrongs.* London: Routledge.

Shea, S. (2015). Finding parallels: The experiences of clinical social workers providing attachment-based treatment to children in foster care. *Clinical Social Work Journal*, 43(1), pp. 62–76.

Shi, L. (2014). Treatment of reactive attachment disorder in young children: Importance of understanding emotional dynamics. *American Journal of Family Therapy*, 42(1), pp. 1–13.

Smidt, S. (2009). *Introducing Vygotsky.* London: Routledge.

Thompson, J., Kilbane, J. and Sanderson, H. (2008). *Person centred practice for professionals.* 1st ed. Maidenhead: Open University Press/McGraw-Hill.

Tilstone, C., Layton, L., Williams, A., Mason, S., Anderson, A. and Morgan, J. (2004). *Child development and teaching the pupil with special educational needs.* 1st ed. London: RoutledgeFalmer.

University of Indiana (2018). *Play time: An examination of play intervention strategies for children with autism spectrum disorders.* Available online at: www.iidc.indiana.edu/pages/Play-Time-An-Examination-Of-Play-Intervention-Strategies-for-Children-with-Autism-Spectrum-Disorders (Accessed 12/08/2018).

UPIAS. (1976). *Fundamental principles of disability.* London: Union of the Physically Impaired Against Segregation.

Zeanah, C. and Gleason, M. (2015). Annual research review: Attachment disorders in early childhood - clinical presentation, causes, correlates, and treatment. *Journal of Child Psychology and Psychiatry*, 56(3), pp. 207–222.

Profound and multiple learning disabilities and difficulties

Introduction

Pupils with profound and multiple learning disabilities/difficulties (PMLD) have complex learning needs. In addition to very Severe Learning Difficulties (SLD), pupils have other significant difficulties such as physical disabilities, sensory impairment or a severe medical condition. Pupils require a high level of adult support, both for their learning needs and also for their personal care. They are likely to need sensory stimulation and a curriculum broken down into very small steps. Some pupils communicate by gesture, eye pointing or symbols, others by very simple language. Their attainments are likely to remain in the early P scale range (P1–P4) throughout their school careers (that is below level 1 of the National Curriculum).

Pupils with profound intellectual and multiple disabilities may have the highest levels of care needs in our communities, but are taught both in special and mainstream schools. They have a profound intellectual disability (an IQ of less than 20) and, in addition, they may have other disabilities such as visual, hearing or movement impairments, or they may have autism or epilepsy. Most people in this group need support with mobility and many have complex health needs. They may have considerable difficulty communicating, doing so non-verbally, and characteristically have very limited understanding. In addition, some people may need support with behaviour that is seen as challenging. It has taken a long period of time to move from the medical model of disability surrounding approaches to PMLD pupils, towards an inclusive social approach, identifying the strengths of individuals. This chapter cannot cover such a wide and diverse spectrum of categories under the umbrella of PMLD, that would take a book in itself. Instead, it aims to:

- provide an overview of the historical perspective of PMLD

- outline where PMLD is identified within the SEND Code of Practice (2015)

- offer alternative definitions of the term PMLD

- describe Rett´syndrome as an example of a PMLD

- discuss the aetiology of PMLD

- examine the move from P scales, towards the assessment of seven aspects of cognition and learning

- review a number of teaching, learning and assessment methods such as Programmes of Learning, Routes for Learning, Quest for Learning and the use of Thematic Units.

Historical perspective of PMLD

Prior to 1970 in the UK, children, who were classed then as mentally handicapped (of which children with PMLD were a subgroup), were the educational responsibility of the Department of Health, reflecting a notion that these children were indeed uneducable. This policy changed with the passing of the 1970 Education (Handicapped Children) Act (Legislation.gov.uk., 2018), which marked a significant change in policy, which was intended to reflect a belief that this group of learners were educable and had a right to attend a school. In the 1980s, the World Health Organization defined pupils with PMLD as those who have an IQ under 20; it described a range of impairments, including a range of cognitive functions: perception, attention, memory and thinking. Thus, for a time definitions of PMLD were dominated by the medical model with pupils presenting a list of impairments and deformities (Orelove and Sobsey, 1996). Ware (1994) talks about children with PMLD having several disabilities in an extreme degree, including profound intellectual impairment, while Lacey and Ouvry (1998) state that they have more than one disability and that one of these is profound intellectual impairment.

The Warnock Report (Warnock, 1978) talked about the notion of a continuum of learning difficulties, with pupils with PMLD being a small part of the 2 per cent of pupils requiring specialist provision, normally in a special school. The definition offered by the School Curriculum and Assessment Authority (SCAA) stated that pupils with PMLD appear to be functioning at the earliest levels of development and who additionally have physical or sensory impairments. Some of these pupils may be ambulant and may behave in ways that either challenge staff and other pupils or result in their isolation making it difficult to involve them in positive educational experiences. Most experience difficulties with communication (SCAA, 1996). The definitions of special educational need proposed in the Department for Education and Skills DfES consultation paper (2003) placed PMLD into one category. Pupils that fell within this category had a greater degree of intellectual impairment and more than one significant disability requiring one-to-one support for their learning and personal needs.

Lacey and Ouvry (1998) offer a different approach to defining PMLD that reflects the views of parents, carers and professional staff. Such a collaborative approach looks at the abilities of, as well as appreciating the extensive difficulties encountered by, those young people. Such an approach offers an example of a paradigmatic shift towards a more holistic and positive view of this group of pupils and a move away from a view that concentrates solely on a range of inabilities in the young person. More recently, the World Health Organization has adopted a classification of disability that embraces a more social model of disability: a classification that acknowledges individual strengths and also the environmental barriers that may compound a disability (WHO, 2001), these two views representing a move away from the medical model towards a social model of disability.

Activity

▮ Using another category under the SEND umbrella such as Autism Spectrum Disorder (ASD), Down's syndrome or dyslexia, trace the historical development of how the perceptions held about this issue has changed over the past 40 years.

Currently, the SEND Code of Practice 0–25 (2015) (DfE, 2015b) identifies four broad areas of special educational need and support: communication and interaction; cognition and learning; social, emotional and mental health and sensory and/or physical needs.

Activity

PMLD is within section 6.30 of the SEND Code of Practice 0–25 (2015) (DfE, 2015b):

Support for learning difficulties may be required when children and young people learn at a slower pace than their peers, even with appropriate differentiation. Learning difficulties cover a wide range of needs, including moderate learning difficulties and SLD, where children are likely to need support in all areas of the curriculum and the associated difficulties with mobility and communication, through to PMLD, where children are likely to have severe and complex learning difficulties as well as a physical disability or sensory impairment.

▮ What are the advantages and issues of using this continuum as an indicator of where children and young people are placed within education?

▮ What do you think would be the key factors involved in placing such pupils within an inclusive classroom?

▮ What is your experience of working with this group of pupils?

Definition(s) of the term PMLD

There are a number of definitions of the term PMLD, not the least in whether to refer to difficulty or disability. Learning disability and learning difficulty are the most commonly used terms in the UK and are sometimes used interchangeably.

The term learning difficulty is often used in educational settings in the UK to include those individuals who have 'specific learning difficulties', such as dyslexia, but who do not have a significant general impairment of intelligence. However, the social model would support the term learning difficulty over the term learning disability as it helps to focus on capabilities rather than deficits.

The term intellectual disability is growing in usage across and may be favoured by professional groups in the UK, parts of Europe, the USA and Australia as part of a shared language and approach to supporting people. In 2010, a report by Professor Jim Mansell, for the Department of Health, called Raising our sights: services for adults with profound intellectual and multiple disabilities used the term intellectual disability instead of learning disability (Mansell, 2010). The term learning disability covers a broad range of individuals, each with different strengths and capabilities, as well as needs. In the UK, we have used the terms profound, severe, moderate and mild to describe people with learning disabilities, but there are no clear dividing lines between the groups. Furthermore, there is no clear cut off point between people with mild learning disabilities and the general population and you may hear the term borderline learning disability being used.

The term Profound and Multiple Learning Difficulties (or Disabilities) (PMLD) is a description rather than a clinical diagnosis. While there is no definitive set of characteristics for PMLD, it is widely acknowledged that there are a heterogeneous/diverse group of people with learning disabilities who have a complex range of difficulties. Children and adults with PMLD have more than one disability, the most significant of which is a profound intellectual disability. These individuals all have great difficulty communicating, often requiring those who know them well to interpret their responses and intent. They frequently have other, additional, disabling conditions which may include, for example:

- physical disabilities – that limit them in undertaking everyday tasks and often restrict mobility; risk to body shape
- sensory impairments
- sensory processing difficulties
- complex health needs (for example, epilepsy, respiratory problems, dysphagia and eating and drinking problems)
- 'coping behaviours' (to their communication or other difficulties, for example), which may present as challenging
- mental health difficulties.

The World Health Organization provides the following definition: the IQ in this category is estimated to be under 20, which means in practice that affected individuals are severely limited in their ability to understand or comply with requests or instructions. Mostly such individuals are immobile or severely restricted in mobility, incontinent, and capable at most of only very rudimentary forms of non-verbal communication. They possess little or no ability to care for their own basic needs and require constant help and supervision (WHO, 1992). Lacey (1988) suggests that the term PMLD implies that the individual can be described as having both profound intellectual impairment and additional disabilities, which may include sensory disabilities (for example, visual impairment or hearing loss), physical disabilities and/or autism or mental illness; challenging or self-injurious behaviour may also be present.

In the past, diagnosis of a learning disability and understanding of a person's needs were based on IQ scores; today the importance of a holistic approach is recognised, and IQ testing forms only one small part of assessing someone's strengths and needs. Assessments of adaptive function focusses on how people can manage their daily living skills and what support they may need; this form of assessment is considered more useful in assessing the impact of any learning disability on a person than an intelligence test.

Activity

Read the following two accounts of the characteristics of people with PMLD. They:

- have more than one disability
- have a profound learning disability
- have great difficulty communicating
- need high levels of support
- may have additional sensory or physical disabilities, complex health needs or mental health difficulties
- may have behaviours that challenge us.

(NHS, 2018b)

People with PMLD:

- have extremely delayed intellectual and social functioning
- may have limited ability to engage verbally but respond to cues within their environment (e.g. familiar voice, touch, gestures)
- often require those who are familiar with them to interpret their communication intent
- frequently have an associated medical condition which may include neurological problems, and physical or sensory impairments.

They have the chance to engage and to achieve their optimum potential in a highly structured environment with constant support and an individualized relationship with a carer.

(Bellamy et al., 2010).

■ What are the similarities and differences between these two views?

■ Why do you think there are so many definitions of the term?

■ Would accepting any of the two views change your practice?

The lack of agreement about the definition of PMLD means that it is hard to find accurate or recent statistics. Research by Emerson (2009) estimated the number of adults with profound intellectual and multiple disabilities in England to be 16,000. This number was anticipated to increase by, on average, 1.8 per cent each year. From a survey undertaken in Scotland (*The Keys to Life*, 2013) (Gov.scot., 2013), it is estimated that the prevalence of PMLD in the general population is 0.05 per 1,000. This estimate would lead to a figure of 2,600 people with PMLD in Scotland. This is possibly an underestimate and a useful working figure would be 3,000. The Department for Education figures demonstrate the significance of this rise, in England, based on their annual data collection. For example, in 2009, statistics identified those with PMLD to be 9,400 aged between 5 and 16 years and recent figures note that 10,032 pupils aged 5–16 years are identified with PMLD as their primary need (DfE, 2018) and these numbers will increase with better survival rates.

In 2014, there were 26,786 adults known to local authorities across Scotland. This equates to 6.0 people with learning disabilities per 1,000 people in the general population (Scottish Consortium for Learning Disability, 2015). Estimates suggest that the prevalence of people with mild to moderate learning disabilities in Scotland is approximately 20 in every 1,000, and for people with PMLD in the region, it is 3–4. The Royal College of Speech and Language Therapists (2003) estimates that approximately 80 per cent of people with severe learning disabilities never acquire effective speech. People with PMLD are among those with learning disabilities who are most likely to have some form of communication difficulty.

 Pause for reflection

Individuals with PMLD have a profound Learning Disability D (IQ < 20), have more than one disability (sensory/physical), have complex health/mental health difficulties (may have behaviours that challenge), have great difficulty communicating and need high levels of support with most aspects of daily life (Mansell Report, 2010).

■ Using the above definition of PMLD and applying any additional knowledge you have about these pupils, what can you infer about the impact of PMLD on someone's communication skills?

■ What do you think are the main issues faced when working with pupils with PMLD?

■ What strengths do you think that pupils with PMLD bring to the 'life of a classroom'?

Children and adults with PMLD have more than one disability, the most significant of which is a profound intellectual disability. All people who have profound and multiple intellectual disabilities will have great difficulty communicating. Many people will have additional sensory or physical disabilities, complex health needs or mental health difficulties. The combination of these needs and/or the lack of the right support may also affect behaviour. Some other people, such as those with autism and Down's syndrome, may also have PMLD. All children and adults with PMLD will need high levels of support with most aspects of daily life.

The term PMLD is also used to include a number of pupils who may not appear to have profound learning difficulties. They may have established self-care skills and possess simple understanding of cause and effect. These pupils may have additional learning difficulties such as autism, but will not generally have the physical and multiple disabilities, or the 'M' in PMLD (Ware, 2004). However, the intellectual and cognitive impairments of this group will restrict their development to around P4 and below. There are examples conditions and syndromes usually associated with PMLD throughout this book, including Down's syndrome and ASD. Another syndrome under the umbrella term PMLD is Rett syndrome (RS).

Rett syndrome

RS is a pervasive neurodevelopmental disorder that affects girls almost exclusively. It is characterised by normal early growth and development followed by a slowing of development, loss of purposeful use of the hands, distinctive hand movements, slowed brain and head growth, problems with walking, seizures and intellectual disability (Skotko, Koppenhaver and Erickson, 2004). It affects approximately one in every 10,000–15,000 girls (Bird, 2001; Rapp, 2006). The severity and outcome of the disorder varies from person to person, which may vary from ambulatory to dependence on a wheelchair for mobility. Cognitive ability, however, tends to be significantly delayed across the majority of affected individuals.

RS is characterised by a specific set of symptoms and behaviours including regression and loss of hand skills, apraxia, deceleration of head growth, and increasing spasticity and scoliosis (Mount et al., 2003). According to Pizzamiglio et al. (2008), children with RS may also have other problems such as cognitive delays, stereotypical hand mannerisms, breathing difficulties, teeth grinding, trouble sleeping and seizures. Children with RS often exhibit autistic-like behaviours in the early stages. There are four stages of RS:

Stage I: early onset. Signs and symptoms are subtle and easily overlooked during the first stage, which starts between 6 and 18 months of age and can last for a few months or a year. Babies in this stage may show less eye contact and start to lose interest in toys. They may also have delays in sitting or crawling.

Stage II: rapid destruction. Starting between one and four years of age, children lose the ability to perform skills they previously had. This loss can be rapid or more gradual, occurring over weeks or months. Symptoms of RS occur, such as slowed head growth, abnormal hand movements, hyperventilating, screaming or crying for no apparent reason, problems with movement and coordination, and a loss of social interaction and communication.

Stage III: plateau. The third stage usually begins between the ages of two and ten years and can last for many years. Although problems with movement continue, behaviour may have limited improvement, with less crying and irritability, and some improvement in hand use and communication. Seizures may begin in this stage and generally do not occur before the age of 2.

Stage IV: late motor deterioration. This stage usually begins after the age of ten years and can last for years or decades. It is marked by reduced mobility, muscle weakness, joint contractures and scoliosis. Understanding, communication and hand skills generally remain stable or improve slightly, and seizures may occur less often (Mayoclinic, 2018).

Almost all cases of RS are caused by a mutation in the MECP2 gene, which is found on the X chromosome. The MECP2 gene contains instructions for producing a particular protein (MeCP2), which is needed for brain development. The gene abnormality prevents nerve cells in the brain from working properly. There is usually no family history of RS, which means that it is not passed on from one generation to the next. Almost all cases (over 99 per cent) are spontaneous, with the mutation occurring randomly (NHS, 2018). Males may also have a mutation on the MECP2 gene, but it usually expressed through a diagnosis of Klinefelter syndrome, Angelman syndrome or possibly a somatic mosaic pattern.

Aetiology of PMLD

Just as there is a range of difficulties experienced by the heterogenous group identified as PMLD, there are a range of causes which can be subdivided into those conditions that arise at conception and those that arise during pregnancy, labour and after birth, however, the cause of learning disabilities cannot be determined in 40 per cent–80 per cent of cases.

Conception

Some of the primary causes of learning disabilities are genetic. Genetic abnormalities may be subdivided into chromosomal, single gene disorders and multifactorial disorders.

Chromosomal disorders include Down's syndrome, Edwards' syndrome and Patau's syndrome. Edwards' syndrome as trisomy 18 (three copies of chromosome number 18, instead of two) is a rare but serious genetic condition that causes a wide range of severe medical problems, typically including heart and kidney problems and breathing difficulties, alongside intellectual disability. Patau's syndrome or trisomy 13 is another serious rare genetic disorder caused by having an additional copy of chromosome 13 in some or all of the body's cells, resulting in a low birth weight, severe heart defects, a smaller than normal head size (microcephaly) and ear malformations, alongside intellectual disability.

Single gene disorders include phenylketonuria (PKU), Prader-Willi syndrome (a rare genetic condition caused by faulty genes on chromosome 15, which cause a wide range of physical symptoms, learning difficulties and behavioural problems), Fragile X syndrome and Tuberous Sclerosis.

Multifactorial disorders include neural tube defects such as spina bifida and occur when both genetic and environmental factors combine.

Pregnancy

Chemicals (such as radiation, cigarette smoke and alcohol), drugs (including 'recreational' and prescription) and diseases (such as rubella and measles) can interfere with the normal development of the embryo or foetus that leads to conditions associated with learning disability.

Prenatal alcohol exposure can lead to the occurrence of foetal alcohol syndrome. Although not a common condition, it is regarded as the leading known cause of non-genetic learning disabilities.

Labour and after birth

Oxygen deprivation (during or after birth) can cause learning disability, as can traumatic birth, meningitis or head injury. Low birth weight and prematurity are strongly correlated with the later development of learning disabilities.

Learning disabilities are not inevitable but can occur as a result of the brain damage that has caused cerebral palsy. Cerebral palsy is caused by damage to the brain, which normally occurs before, during or soon after birth. Other causes of cerebral palsy include infections such as meningitis or encephalitis, while the child is young and the brain is still developing.

Congenital hypothyroidism which appears from birth is a cause of learning disabilities. Causes of congenital hypothyroidism are:

- abnormalities in the development of the thyroid gland while the baby is in the womb
- genetic abnormalities that interfere with thyroid hormone production
- iodine deficiency
- problems with the pituitary gland (which regulates the thyroid gland).

Goodbye P scales

In the academic year 2018/2019, P scales will continue to be used as Statutory assessment of pupils not engaged in subject-specific learning, including PMLD pupils. In 2019/2020, subject to recommendations being accepted following a pilot, assessment against seven areas of engagement for cognition and learning will replace P scales.

Following the Rochford Review (2015) (DfE, 2015) in September 2017, the DfE made the following recommendations for pre-scale standards. These were:

R3. Schools assess pupils' development in all four areas of need outlined in the SEND Code of Practice, but statutory assessment for pupils who are not engaged in subject-specific learning should be limited to the area of cognition and learning.

R4. There should be a statutory duty to assess pupils not engaged in subject-specific learning against the following seven aspects of cognition and learning and report this to parents and carers: responsiveness, curiosity, discovery, anticipation, persistence, initiation and investigation.

R5. Following recommendation 4, schools should decide their own approach to making these assessments, according to the curriculum that they use and the needs of their pupils DfE (2107).

 Activity

The DfE (2017) response to the Rochford Review Primary school pupil assessment: Rochford Review recommendations and government consultation response can be accessed online via the (DfE, 2018) website.

Read Recommendations 1 and 2.

◼ Why does it call for the removal of the statutory requirement to assess pupils using P scales?

◼ What is the justification for making the interim pre-key stage standards permanent and extending them to cover all pupils engaged in subject-specific learning?

Read Recommendations 3, 4 and 5, which specifically relate to PMLD pupils.

◼ What is the justification in making cognition and learning the focus of statutory assessment for pupils?

◼ What justification is there for the seven areas of engagement and how will they be assessed

Teaching, learning or assessment?

Activity

In a recent article in the SEN magazine (Lacey 2018), a curriculum for pupils with PMLD is described with the emphasis upon four areas: cognition, communication, physical, and self-care and independence. The article can be accessed online.

Read how the curriculum in this school is focussed on Programmes of Learning in each of the four curriculum areas, with an emphasis on learning rather than on assessment, so that the pupils can demonstrate what they can do and understand, rather than being taken step by step through a list of pre-decided behaviours.

▨ If you are working with PMLD pupils, how is this approach different, or similar to your context?

▨ What are the advantages and issues of such a curriculum, with its focus on learning rather than on assessment?

▨ Identify an activity under any of the four curriculum areas from this article and identify how it could be used within your own practice.

An approach to the curriculum which does focus on assessment is the Routes for Learning from the Welsh Assembly updated in 2015 (Learning.gov.Wales., 2015a), which advocates that learning for those with a PMLD is best done holistically, rather than as a series of separate skills chained together, using real-life events in which the pupil with PMLD is an essential part of that enactment. Using the ubiquitous Specific, Measurable, Attainable, Relevant and Timely (SMART) targets is often limiting the progress of pupils, in that defined SMART targets are often not achieved and do not promote learning. Where targets are relevant, they will more than likely be Student-led, Creative, Relevant, Unspecified, Fun, For Youngsters) (SCRUFFY (Lacey, 2010).

Activity

Routes for Learning: a resource for assessment
The Routes for Learning (RfL) assessment materials were produced in Wales for learners with profound learning difficulties and additional disabilities created by the Qualifications and Curriculum Group, Department for Education, Lifelong Learning and Skills Wales (Welsh Assembly, updated 2015). It provides details of typical infant development applied to older children and young people who are functioning at this level. The Routemap contains early development behaviours in the areas of communication and early cognition, and

these can guide teachers on the precise nature of what they should be teaching pupils. The assessment booklet clearly shows how and what to assess, and what to look for during the assessment, and then gives teaching strategies for a particular behaviour.

The materials focus on the early communication, social interaction and cognitive skills that are crucial for all future learning, leading from very basic 'notices stimuli' to 'contingency awareness', 'object permanence', 'early problem solving', 'expresses preference for items not present via symbolic means' and 'initiates actions to achieve desired result', and look at the relationship between the pupils and their environment. They are part of the resources for Routes to Literacy and Numeracy.

There is no hierarchical or predetermined order to achievement of the steps in the Routemap and that pupils may follow a range of pathways. Also, the Routemap is not a curriculum for pupils with PMLD. However, the strength lies in the possibilities of recording significant developments and suggesting possible next steps.

The materials can be accessed online via the Learning.gov.Wales. (2015b) website.

■ Familiarise yourself with the Routes for Learning approach.

■ By referring to an actual or fictitious pupil, use an assessment area and identify the relevant RfL milestones and map onto the learning outcomes for each of the areas. Use a One-Page Profile template as the first step in setting the learning intentions for this pupil.

Mittler (2000) points out that to be specific about the needs of distinct groups is not to undermine inclusion. Providing equal opportunities is about meeting individual needs – not treating everybody in the same way. Moreover, the development of specific programmes for the distinct group of PMLD learners provides an opportunity to build key skills in communication, cognition and social interaction, which allow for more inclusive experiences when these skills can be generalised. With this view in mind, the Northern Ireland Curriculum (2018) has produced a comprehensive Guidance and Assessment pack of materials for PMLD called Quest for Learning, based on Routes to Learning. A similar focus is on skills and capabilities rather than 'working towards' subject-related targets, which may not be priorities for the individuals concerned. This flexibility should allow for pupil-centred planning and assessment, which puts the needs of learners first. Planning, teaching, learning and assessment should be built around these needs.

 Activity

Quest for learning
These assessment materials focus on the following key learning priorities for learners with PMLD using an individually structured sensory approach under the headings of communication, social interaction and early cognitive development.

There are extensive strategies, references to milestones, resources and tracking documents within these materials.

The materials can be accessed online via the Northern Ireland Curriculum (2018) website.

■ Familiarise yourself with the Quest for Learning approach.

■ By referring to an actual or fictitious pupil, use an assessment area and identify the relevant strategies, milestones and resources which would support this individual.

Another useful strategy when working with PMLD pupils is to use a thematic approach to the curriculum.

 Activity

The use of thematic units

These activities adopt a process-based interactive approach with the aim of best supporting learners in acquiring, practising and establishing the early skills of communication and active involvement in everyday experiences. An example of such an approach is the use of thematic units produced by the Council for the Curriculum, Examinations and Assessment, in Northern Ireland. These thematic units provide activities and resources to support the curriculum for learners aged 3–19 with PMLD. Although these units are aligned with the Northern Ireland Curriculum, they provide useful materials for any context. The units help embed information technology, along with communication and assistive technologies.

The materials can be accessed online via the Council for the Curriculum, Examinations and Assessment (2018) website.

www.nicurriculum.org.uk/curriculum_microsite/SEN_PMLD_thematic_units/

■ Familiarise yourself with the thematic approach to the PMLD curriculum.

■ By referring to an actual or fictitious pupil/group of pupils, use a theme which they would be able to access and enjoy and identify how you would use this within your practice.

Summary

Pupils with PMLD have more than one disability. These may entail profound developmental delay, learning difficulties, physical disabilities, sensory impairments, mental and health problems as well as ASD. Due to the severity of these disabilities and complex medical health needs, people with PMLD often have a number of healthcare needs of support and assistance, alongside the educational support. Their disabilities can present challenges for them and those who support them. Pupils with PMLD are a diverse group of individuals with their own personalities, preferences and ways of communicating. The abilities of those described as having PMLD vary considerably. They are one of the most marginalised groups, but hopefully attitudes towards inclusivity, personalisation, the SEND Code of Practice 0–25 (2015) (Dfe, 2015) and the role of EHC plans will support their access to opportunities afforded to other groups of SEND learners.

References

Bellamy, G., Croot, L., Bush, A., Berry, H. and Smith, A. (2010). A study to define: Profound and multiple learning disabilities (PMLD). *Journal of Intellectual Disabilities*, 14(3), pp. 221–235.

Bird, A. (2001). The Rett syndrome research foundation. *Exceptional Parent*, 31(6), pp. 93–96.

Council for the Curriculum, Examinations and Assessment (2018). Available online at: www.nicurriculum.org.uk/curriculum_microsite/SEN_PMLD_thematic_units/ (Accessed 12/08/2018).

Department for Education (2015a). *Final report of the commission on assessment without levels*. Available online at: www.gov.uk/government/uploads/system/uploads/attachment_data/file/483058/Commission_on_Assessment_Without_Levels_-_report.pdf (Accessed 27/05/2018).

Department for Education (2015b). *Special educational needs and disability code of practice: 0 to 25 years*. Department for Education. Available online at: https://www.gov.uk/government/publications/send-code-of-practice-0-to-25 (Accessed 12/04/2018).

Department for Education (2017). *Rochford Review recommendations Government consultation response*. Available online at: https://assets.publishing.service.gov.uk/government/uploads/system/uploads/attachment_data/file/644729/Rochford_consultation_response.pdf (Accessed 21/07/2018).

Department for Education (2018). *Special educational needs in England: January 2017.* Information from the school census on pupils with special educational needs (SEN), and SEN provision in schools. Available online at: www.gov.uk/government/statistics/special-educational-needs-in-england-january-2018 (Accessed 12/02/2018).

Department for Education and Skills (2003). *Report of the special schools working group.* London: DfES.

Emerson, E. (2009). *Estimating future numbers of adults with profound multiple learning disabilities in England: CeDR research report 2009 (1)*. Working Paper. Centre for Disability Research, Lancaster: Lancaster University.

Gov.scot. (2013). *Keys to life*. Available online at: https://keystolife.info (Accessed 12/02/2018).

Lacey, P. (1988). People with profound and multiple learning disabilities. A collaborative approach to meeting complex needs. In Lacey, P. and Ouvry, C. (eds.), *People with profound and multiple learning disabilities*. London: David Fulton. pp 29–38

Lacey, P. (2010). SMART and SCRUFFY Targets. *SLD Experience*, 57, 16–21

Lacey, P. (2018). *A profound challenge*. Available online at: https://senmagazine.co.uk/articles/articles/senarticles/designing-a-curriculum-for-pmld-a-profound-challenge (Accessed 14/08/2018).

Lacey, P. and Ouvry, C. (1998). *People with profound and multiple learning disabilities*. London: David Fulton.

Learning.gov.Wales. (2015a). Available online at: http://learning.gov.wales/resources/browse-all/routes-for-learning-additional-guidance/?lang=en (Accessed 12/03/2018).

Learning.gov.Wales. (2015b). *Routes to literacy and numeracy*. Available online at: http://learning.gov.wales/resources/collections/routes-to-literacy-and-numeracy?lang=en (Accessed 12/03/2018).

Legislation.gov.uk. (2018). *Education (Handicapped Children) Act 1970*. Available online at: www.legislation.gov.uk/ukpga/1970/52/enacted (Accessed 14/04/2018).

Mansell, J. (2010). Raising our sights: Services for adults with profound intellectual and multiple disabilities. *Tizard Learning Disability Review*, 15(3), pp. 5–12.

Mayoclinic. (2018). *Rett syndrome*. Available online at: www.mayoclinic.org/diseases-conditions/rett-syndrome/symptoms-causes/syc-20377227 (Accessed 07/02/201).

Mittler, P. (2000). *Working towards inclusive education: Social contexts*. London: David Fulton.

Mount, R.H., Charman, T., Hastings, R.P., Reilly, S. and Cass, H. (2003). Features of autism in Rett syndrome and severe mental retardation. *Journal of Autism and Developmental Disorders*, 33, pp. 435–442.

NHS (2018a). *Rett syndrome*. Available online at: www.nhs.uk/conditions/rettsyndrome/ (Accessed 12/04/2018).

NHS (2018b). *Top tips for supporting and meeting the needs of people with Profound and Multiple Learning Disabilities (PMLD)*. Available online at: www.mencap.org.uk/sites/default/files/2016-06/NHS%20EM%20-%20PMLD.pdf (Accesssed 12/04/2018).

NICurriculum.org.uk. (2018). *Quest for learning*. Available online at: www.nicurriculum.org.uk/docs/inclusion_and_sen/pmld/quest_guidance_booklet.pdf (Accessed 01/08/2018).

Orelove, F.P. and Sobsey, D. (1996). *Educating children with multiple disabilities: A trans-disciplinary approach*. 3rd ed. London: Paul H Brookes.

Pizzamiglio, M.R., Nasti, M., Piccardi, L., Zotti, A., Vitturini, C., Spitoni, G., Nanni, M.V., Guariglia, C. and Morelli, D. (2008). Sensory-motor rehabilitation in Rett syndrome. *Focus on Autism and Other Developmental Disabilities*, 23, pp. 49–62.

Rapp, C.E. (2006). Rett syndrome: A brief update and special features in adults. *Exceptional Parent*, 36(5), pp. 78–82.

Royal College of Speech and Language Therapists (2003). *Speech and language therapy provision for adults with learning disabilities*. Available online at: www.rcslt.org/docs/free-pub/position_paper_ald.pdf (Accessed 23/06/2018).

Schools Council Assessment Authority (SCAA) (1996). *Planning the curriculum for pupils with profound and multiple learning difficulties*. London: SCAA.

Scottish Consortium for Learning Disability (2015). *Learning disability statistics Scotland, 2014*. Available online at: www.scld.org.uk/wp-content/uploads/2015/08/Learning-Disability-Statistics-Scotland-2014-report.pdf Accessed 15/06/2018).

Skotko, B.G., Koppenhaver, D.A. and Erickson, K.A. (2004). Parent reading behaviors and communication outcomes in girls with Rett syndrome. *Exceptional Children*, 70, pp. 145–166.

Ware, J. (1994) *Educating children with profound and multiple learning difficulties.* London: David Fulton.

Ware, J. (2004). Ascertaining the views of people with profound and multiple learning disabilities. *British Journal of Learning Disabilities*, 32, pp. 175–179.

Warnock, M. (1978). *House of commons - education and skills - third report.* [online] Publications.parliament.uk. Available online at: www.publications.parliament.uk/pa/cm200506/cmselect/cmeduski/478/47805.htm (Accessed 11/03/2018).

World Health Organization (1992). *International statistical classification of diseases and related health problems, tenth revision (ICD-10).* Geneva, Switzerland: Author.

World Health Organization (2001). *International classification of functioning, disability and health (ICF).* Geneva, Switzerland: Author.

8 Autism spectrum disorder

Introduction

The behaviours that we see in the classroom by pupils with Autism Spectrum Disorder (ASD) are a result of complex and interacting factors and as a practitioner it is important to be able to have the knowledge to dispel statements such as 'He will grow out of it' and 'They can help it'. Using evidence from research, along with case studies it offers suggestions which practitioners could use within their context to support such individuals. It does not aim to go into detail about the range of strategies which could be utilised in supporting pupils (they are discussed in depth in a number of other texts and Internet searches). Rather, it seeks to get you to reflect upon your own thoughts and practice around the issues discussed and as such it aims to:

- review the impact of the notion of Refrigerator Mothers from a historical perspective

- define the term Autism Spectrum Disorder

- outline two approaches in the classification of autism (DSM-V and ICD-10) and the debate between a triad and dyad of impairment

- use research findings to evaluate the standing of the role of genetics on autism

- use research finding to evaluate the standing of the role of neurobiology on autism

- examine the role of environmental and risk factors on the development of autism

- discuss cognitive theories relating to autism (Theory of Mind, Weak Central Coherence (WCC) and Executive Dysfunction, Monotropism)

- outline the General and Unique Differences approach to Special Educations Needs (SEN) and autism

- suggest that there are four key areas of difference in relation to autism

- discuss the use of Social, (or Narrative) Stories, Comic Strip Conversations, Power Cards and Token Economy Strategies (TES), in working with pupils with ASD.

The term autism was first used by Bleuler in 1911 to try and describe a type of what was then called 'childhood schizophrenia'. His descriptions, however, only show a passing resemblance to how autism is thought of today:

> The schizophrenics who have no more contact with the outside world live in a world of their own. They have encased themselves with their desires and wishes...they have cut themselves off as much as possible from any contact with the external world. This detachment from reality with the relative and absolute predominance of the inner life, we term autism.
>   (Bleuler, 1911, cited in Parnas, Bovet and Zahavi, 2002, 131)

In the 1940s, two psychiatrists Kanner and Asperger were both studying small groups of children deemed as having some form of 'childhood schizophrenia'. Both found that in the groups of children with whom they were working, a set of distinct symptoms were being identified that were markedly different from schizophrenia as it was conceived of at the time. Definitions of what autism is and what causes an autistic developmental pattern in children have been hotly contested ever since, including an unfortunate era where autism was thought to be a reaction to 'refrigerator mothers'.

Refrigerator mothers

As early as 1943, Kanner argued that he saw a lack of parental warmth and attachment contributing to autism in children and attributed a genuine lack of maternal warmth to the development of autism. It is more likely that any lack of attachment he saw between the parents and their autistic children was due to the lack of social reciprocity in the children. Bettleheim in the 1950s and 1960s popularised the idea that autism was caused by maternal coldness towards their children – ignoring, as Kanner did, that these same mothers had other children who were not autistic. In 1964, Rimland, a psychologist with an autistic son, produced the book *Infantile Autism: The Syndrome and its Implications for a Neural Theory of Behavior*, which attacked the 'Refrigerator Mother' hypothesis directly. In a direct response to Rimland's book, Bettleheim wrote *The Empty Fortress: Infantile Autism and the Birth of the Self*, in which he compared the autistic child to a prisoner in a concentration camp (casting the parents as the Schutzstaffel

(SS) guards). Although the concept of Refrigerator Mother is now widely disputed, other debates still exist within the area, including not allowing their child to receive routine vaccinations with products that contain thimerosal (a mercury-containing preservative) preservative or a combination measles, mumps, and rubella vaccines and the search for 'cures' to eradicate autism.

Pause for reflection

■ Why do you think that these debates are still relevant today?

■ If you were a parent with a child living with autism, how would you go about gaining evidence for and against these views?

Definition of autism spectrum disorder

ASD is a lifelong complex neurodevelopmental disorder, typically identified within the first three years of a child's life, its aetiology remaining unclear (Boucher, 2017). It is a permanent disorder beginning in childhood affecting one in ten (Ornoy, Weinstein-Fudim and Ergaz, 2015), or as current estimates suggest, 1 in 80 children presenting individuals with impairments and difficulties in social, communication interactions and repetitive behaviours and difficulties (National Institute of Neurological Disorders and Stroke, 2018).

These characteristics are referred to as the triad of impairments. According to Wing (1996), the severity of autism varies for everyone affecting their abilities, communication, behaviour, sensory problems and social interactions. It is a widely accepted concept that autism lies within a complex trajectory with its origin emerging from genetic blueprint, further determined by phenotypic variability, neuroanatomy and connectivity of the brain, manifesting in cognitive behaviours, associated with the triad of impairment (Just et al., 2007).

Triad or dyad of impairment?

Wing and Gould (1979) largely created the contemporary definition of autism as a 'triad of impairments' in: social communication, social interaction and imagination (repetitive interests/activities). ASD is a collective term for a group of heterogeneous disorders characterised by impairments in social interaction and verbal and non-verbal communication, and repetitive and stereotyped behaviours, the triad of impairment (van Wijngaarden-Cremers, 2014). DSM-V American Diagnostic and Statistical Manual of Mental Disorders (DSM) published in 2013 saw the triad of impairment changing to a dyad with two core areas: social communication and repetitive restricted interests, which now also includes sensory behaviours. As a result of this, rather than identifying communication, interaction and imagination as the three main areas that children face difficulty, DSM-V removes impaired imagination and creates a dyad of the final two components. DSM-V uses the term 'autism spectrum disorders' (ASDs), rather than being included in a subset under the umbrella of Pervasive Disorders. However, the World Health International Classification of Diseases (ICD) classification ICD-10 used in the UK and parts of

Europe (Boucher, 2017) retains the diagnostic classifications of Asperger's Childhood Autism, High-Functioning Autism and 'Pervasive Disorders'. However, the revised ICD-11 classification (WHO, 2018) has changed this to 6A02 ASD.

 Activity

ICD-11 can be accessed via the WHO website (WHO, 2018).

DSM-V classification for Autism Spectrum Disorder can be accessed via the Autism-speaks (2018) website.

▓ How do they compare? What are the similarities and differences?

▓ Why do you think that there are two different classification systems?

▓ Does this make a difference for parents in obtaining a diagnosis?

Abnormalities in the genetic code for brain development

Autism is one of the most heritable of psychiatric disorders with a monozygotic concordance rate of 60 per cent 91 per cent and a family recurrence risk of 20 per cent (Muhle, Trentacoste and Rapin, 2004). There are a large number of chromosome abnormalities associated with autism, with familial clustering of autism well above the normal population prevalence. Chromosomes 2, 7, 5, 15 and 17 have all been linked to autism. Hereditability (how much of the variation in a trait is due to variation in genetic factors) is approximately 90 per cent (schizophrenia and major depression is approximately 40 per cent–50 per cent), but it is not a simple genetic transmission. Bourgeron (2016) explores the link between genetics and ASD and explains that due to the high concordance rates of 45 per cent found for monozygotic twins, a genetic link exists to some degree. Bailey et al. (1995) also show a high concordance rate of 69 per cent in monozygotic twins, and conclude that ASD is largely genetically determined, and therefore, while there may be some contribution from other factors, genetics has the greatest impact. Bourgeron (2016) goes on to state that evidence is consistent to highlight twin and familial studies contributing to 45 per cent heritability of autism, with de novo mutation a possibility to causing autism by suggesting that 10 per cent of autistic individuals are carriers of de novo copy number variants (CNV) with monozygotic twins having an heritability of 74 per cent (Yeh and Weiss, 2016).

Recent studies have suggested that autism is even more complex and complicated than the clinical variation might suggest. For example, we have realised for decades that ASD runs in families with concordance rates, for example, being 47 per cent–96 per cent in monozygotic twins for ASD and 0 per cent–36 per cent in dizygotic twins for autism and wider ASD phenotypes. Genetic studies link 'hundreds of susceptibility loci' to ASD. Broadly, however, 2.6 per cent of ASD cases seem to arise from rare de novo mutations, 3 per cent from rare inherited variants and 49 per cent from common inherited

Table 8.1 Families and autism

Simplex family	Multiplex family
Only one member of extended family has a diagnosis of ASD	More than one member of extended family has a diagnosis, or several members have very high levels of autistic traits
Might be due to 'de novo' changes in DNA sequence (for example, rare sequence variant or a CNV)	Might never have a formal diagnosis
One off-change during formation of gametes can account for approximately 10 per cent of all people diagnosed with ASD	Specific genetic variations passed down through generations

variants. However, twin studies suggest that the environment accounts for between 10 per cent and 55 per cent of the risk.

The genetic map of the individual can also be linked to the atypical development of the brains of individuals with ASD. Fahim et al. (2011) explains that enlarged brain volume is a consistent biological finding for ASD and that this is a prominent feature along with atypical connections within the brain. It has also been suggested that there may be two types of families in relation to ASD, those of simplex and complex families (Table 8.1).

Scientists are now suggesting a new way to classify ASD based on its genetic foundations – mild with little impairment of motor skills or IQ, moderate impairment mainly to motor skills and severe impairment affecting both (McRae, 2018).

Abnormal mechanisms of brain development leading to structural and functional abnormalities of brain

Neuroimaging and Magnetic Resonance Imaging (MRI) have assisted in detecting abnormalities between Autism, brain development and function, particularly within the cerebral cortex. Zielinski et al. (2014) found that children with ASD had abnormally large head circumferences along with increased temporal lobe grey matter, suggesting overgrowth of the brain. Laidman (2014) suggests that cell organisation within the frontal temporal cortex is disorganised especially within the communication area of the brain, giving the reason for communication difficulties found in autism. Supporting this are findings that displaced activity within the frontal cortex, suggesting rigidity of thinking, and obsessions are caused by this irregular connectivity.

Neural pathways may be affected during crucial stages of prenatal development between the brainstem and the cerebellum, resulting in deficits of inter-modal attention shifting, clumsiness and imitation difficulties. The dysregulation of cell migration, synaptic pruning, insufficient apoptosis and problems with myelination are also contributing factors to the development of ASD (Carper and Courchesne, 2000).

Table 8.2 Possible areas of the brain linked to ASD

Areas of possible difficulty	Functions
Prefrontal cerebral cortex	Social thinking
Hypothalamus	Attachment behaviours
Amygdala	Emotional learning; decode emotional facial expressions
Fusiform gyrus	Face recognition
Mid-temporal gyrus	Recognition of facial expression

More recent research, such as mirror neuron signals, may also be linked to ASD impacting an individual's cognitive and social interaction and processing skills. An increased total of grey and white matter brain volume is observed in those with autism. This study speculates that this excess is due to diminished regression or pruning in cortical and subcortical parts of the brain. The study further suggests that it may be due to a mutation in specific genes involved in pruning and/or a lack of socio-emotional environmental experience during a critical developmental period (Fahim et al., 2011) (Table 8.2).

Research suggests that people with autism display unique synchronisation patterns (Hahamy, Behrmann and Malach, 2015). Functional magnetic resonance images, while participants were at rest, the time when patterns emerge spontaneously, revealed several differences in brain activity between healthy volunteers and people with ASD. For instance, the regions in healthy volunteers showed high connectivity between the brain's hemispheres (such as the sensory-motor and occipital cortices), while those in people with ASD showed reduced connectivity. In contrast, regions that typically showed low levels of connectivity between the hemispheres (for example, frontal and temporal cortices) in controls tended to have increased connectivity in people with ASD. In addition, healthy brains showed 'substantially similar connectivity profiles, and, for those with ASD, they were much more unique. The researchers dubbed the synchronisation patterns in healthy controls and ASD patients' 'conformist' and 'idiosyncratic', respectively.

Just et al. (2007) view autism as being a complex information-processing disorder, intact or enhanced simple information processing, but poor complex/higher order processing. fMRI and EEG studies suggest that adults with ASD have local over connectivity in the cortex and weak functional connections between the frontal lobe and the rest of the cortex. Under connectivity is mainly within each hemisphere of the cortex and thus autism is a disorder of the association cortex. In many autistic people, the brain develops too quickly beginning at approximately 12 months but by age ten, their brains are at a normal size, but 'wired' atypically. There is accelerated growth at the wrong time, and that creates havoc; the consequences, in terms of disturbing early development, include problems within the cortex and from the cortex to other regions of the cortex in ways that compromise language and reasoning abilities. While social and communication skills may be compromised by the unique wiring in the brain, other abilities are actually enhanced. Autistic people have a really stellar ability to use the visual parts of the right side of the brain to compensate for problems with language processing. This may be the basis for detail-orientated processing and may be a decided advantage!

Risk factors

There are a number of risk factors which research suggests might be implicated in the development of autism. Ward (1990) suggests that prenatal exposure to encountered stressful events is associated with an increased risk of ASD, concluding that mothers of children with ASD reported having experienced significant family discord during pregnancy. Beversdorf et al. (2005) found a higher rate of ASD in children born to those mothers who had encountered stress such as a job loss or the death of a husband. Shelton et al. (2010) cited in Sealey et al. (2016) suggests that the chances of having a child with ASD are much higher for mothers who are older when giving birth and that 51 per cent of mothers older than 40 are more liable to give birth to an autistic child than mothers aged between 25 and 29. Additionally, it was found that the paternal age only had an adverse impact when the mother is younger than 30 and the father older.

Newschaffer et al. (2007) speculate that exposure to varying toxicants including pesticides, polychlorinated biphenyls (PCBs) and polybrominated diphenyl ethers (PBDEs) bring detrimental consequences to developmental processes, specifically to genetically susceptible individuals. Furthermore, they argue that PCBs and PBDEs have endocrine-disrupting and neurological effects, concluding that both also persist in the environment, bioaccumulating through the food chain, with many neurotoxic compounds suspected to interfere with neurotransmitter systems implicated in ASD.

Perinatal foetal distress could also play a major part in a child having an ASD diagnosis and suggests that postnatal respiratory infection could impact normal brain development. Parental antigens have also been reported as a potential cause of ASD as they pass to the foetus freely, with proteins being found within a foetus's brain. Distress during the birth, long durational births and oxygen deficiency along with premature births have been suggested as factors causing brain damage relating to an element of ASD, with prematurity being a higher risk factor for ASD along with further difficulties and disabilities. Their findings suggested that environmental factors were associated more with parental stress than any other factor.

According to Brown and Derkits's (2010) debate, if maternal viral infections such as influenza, virus rubella and bacterial (urinary tract) can be prevented in pregnancy, it could reduce the number of schizophrenia cases by 30 per cent, which has already been linked to an Autistic condition. However, there did not appear to be any figures to support the evidence and the conclusion, is that there is no overall association between all infections and an ASD throughout pregnancy suggesting, the timing of the infection was the significant risk factor.

It would appear that journey into understanding the aetiology of autism may start with a genetic susceptibility where mutations to either chromosomes or genes set the path for neuroatypical brain development. Thus, the functioning of particular parts of the brain may be impaired, or indeed enhanced by atypical neural connections. How might this manifest itself in the classroom, in relation to cognitive processes, for example?

Pause for reflection

■ How would you respond to the statement from a colleague that 'Autism is learned and used as an excuse for not working hard enough in class and using excuses'?

Theory of Mind

One of the most enduring psychological theories concerning autism has been the assertion that the key universal core 'deficit' found in autistic spectrum conditions is an impaired 'theory of mind' (Baron-Cohen, Leslie and Frith, 1985). 'Theory of Mind' refers to the ability to empathise with others and imagine their thoughts and feelings, in order to comprehend and predict the behaviour of others (also called 'mind-reading' and 'mentalising'). They found that 80 per cent of autistic children between the ages of 6 and 16 failed at false-belief tasks, such as in the 'Sally-Ann' test. However, task failure on false-belief tasks could be due to difficulties in language processing or memory, or a lack of motivation to deceive. 'Theory of mind' deficit as a general theory has been subsequently revised in order to differentiate between an ability to ascertain the feelings of others, and the development of 'affective' empathy once those feelings are recognised.

Later studies by Baron-Cohen (2001) and Happé and Happé (1994) also found that the ability to successfully complete theory of mind tasks increased with age and IQ, suggesting a delayed 'mentalising' capacity. It has also been argued that a deficit in 'social functioning' cannot be solely located within an individual, and that what is being seen as a 'theory of mind' deficit is more to do with a breakdown in communication between two people who process information very differently. Frith and Happé (1994) highlight a limitation with the theory in that although ToM has been successful at predicting impairments in socialisation, imagination and communication in autism, it cannot explain other non-triad features of ASD including excellent rote memory and Islets of ability. As a result, Baron-Cohen modified his theory by proposing that ToM was in fact a delay rather than a deficit.

Executive dysfunction

Rajendran and Mitchell (2007) define Executive Function (EF) as an umbrella term for functions including: initiating, sustaining, shifting and inhibition/stopping and an umbrella term used for brain functions such as planning, impulse control, initiation and monitoring of action, shifting set, as well as working memory. The central executive part of the brain may be responsible for attention and planning and may be impaired in autism. EF also refers to the ability to maintain an appropriate problem-solving strategy in order to attain a future goal. Evidence from first-hand accounts suggest that autistic people have 'difficulties' with switching attention, and adverse reactions to interference with attention (Tammet, 2006). However, there is also evidence that individuals diagnosed with Asperger syndrome have performed well on executive functioning tests such as the 'Tower of London' test, and that other clinical groups can struggle with such tests, suggesting a lack of specificity to people diagnosed autistic. Dawson et al. (2007) found that autistic people can often do very well at non-verbal IQ tests and problem-solving tasks that do not require verbal processing. This would suggest that executive planning for non-verbal tasks is separable in brain functioning from verbal tasks, or that this weakness in verbal response tests is not due to an executive functioning deficit. It could be suggested that rather than such evidence suggesting an overarching deficit in executive processing, there is a difference that exists within the way autistic executive processing operates, yet rather than an impairment or deficiency, this is better articulated by the theory of Monotropism (see below).

Weak central coherence

'Theory of Mind' and EF tend to focus on deficit approach to Autism. Attempting to address the assets seen in ASD, the 'weak central coherence' account proposes that people with ASD show a bias in cognitive style. Specifically, coherence refers to the tendency to integrate information in context for higher level meaning or gestalt, often at the expense of attention to or memory for featural information. People with ASD appear to show 'weak' coherence, attending preferentially to details, apparently at the expense of meaning and gist, which are perhaps essential for social cognition. Weak coherence is postulated to lie at the root of characteristic ASD symptoms such as insistence on sameness, attention to parts of objects and uneven cognitive profile, including savant skills (Happé and Frith, 2006). Central coherence is the ability to derive overall meaning from a mass of details. A person with strong central coherence, looking at an endless expanse of trees, would see 'the forest'. A person with WCC would see only a whole lot of individual trees.

It was Frith's belief that other theories might account for the core deficits of individuals with ASD, but could not account for their amazing strengths. For instance, some individuals with ASD have 'savant' skills – a remarkable ability in areas such as music, memory or calculation. People on the spectrum tend to excel at focussing on extreme detail, and so are able to pick out a tiny element from a mass of complex data or objects. The notion of 'weak central coherence' could explain both deficits and strengths.

Morgan et al. (2003) suggest that children with autism demonstrate WCC, or a bias towards 'local' cognitive processing, meaning that children with autism focus on individual pieces of information rather than the 'global' context. WCC can be seen as a reduced ability with processing and an increased ability with processing distinctive detail. Research suggests that individuals are impaired in achieving local coherence, as they prefer not to strive for coherence unless informed to do so. WCC now seen as a cognitive style or preference in terms of some may be inclined to pay attention to detail, yet may be able to extract overall meaning with the concept of a deficit in global processing being recast as superior local processing and a cognitive style rather than a dysfunction or deficit.

Activity

Taking each of the cognitive theories:

- What behaviours have you witnessed in the classroom which might support the theory?

- If we accept that there is evidence to support the theory, how would you go about reducing the impact of these 'deficits' in practice?

Monotropism: a different cognitive style?

In the theory of Monotropism, Murray, Lesser and Lawson (2005) argue that the central core feature in autism refers to an atypical strategy being employed in the distribution of attention, which is suggested to be the basis of the 'restricted range of interests' criteria inherent in the diagnostic criteria for autism and further found in the testimonies of subjective experience from autistic people themselves (Williams, 1994; Grandin, 1995; Lawson, 1998). Monotropism suggests that the amount of attention available to an individual at any one time is necessarily limited, as can be found among numerous cognitive studies. Thus, many cognitive processes depend on a competition between mental processes for this scarce resource. Murray, Lesser and Lawson (2005) propose that strategies for the way attention is used is normally distributed, and to a large degree genetically determined, between those with a broad use of attention, and those who concentrate attention on a small number of interests. Social interaction, the use of language, and the shifting of object attention are all tasks that require a broad attention and are inhibited by a narrow use of attention.

Monotropism also suggests a reason for the sensory integration difficulties found in the accounts of autistic people, as they suggest that there is a 'hyper-awareness' of phenomena within the attentional tunnel, but hypo-sensitivity to phenomena outside of it. For example, the recognition of others may only occur if connected to the fulfilling of interests that the autistic individual has, otherwise the existence of others may not be registered at all. A monotropic focus leads to a fragmented view of the world, and from such a viewpoint, it is exceptionally hard to make sense of social interactions, potentially leading to both apparent and real 'theory of mind' difficulties. Rather than being a 'core deficit' however, this is described as a tendency produced as a consequence of a monotropic interest system.

Models of disability

We covered models of disability in Chapter 5 and introduced the terms medical, social and biopsychosocial models. The medical model locates difficulties within the individual's impairment. In other words, the cause of learning 'difficulty' is innate (nature rather than nurture) and lies within the individual. In teaching practice, adoption of this model may lead to pedagogy that focusses on that impairment to the exclusion of other possible factors that might undermine learning. The extent to which impairment is disabling to the learner depends on barriers in the environment. Impairment is acknowledged, awareness that the disabling impact of impairment is diminished or amplified by the social and physical environment (attitudes, culture, the built environment, curricula, teaching style and organisation).

Connors and Stalker (2007) found, in a two-year study of 26 disabled children aged 7–15, that 'barriers to being' (impairment, difference, other people's behaviour towards them and material barriers) were particularly significant to children with SEND, affecting self-worth and confidence. Thus, the environment (including attitudes and beliefs) is the barrier to learning and the impairment may be the least relevant factor in making determinations about pedagogy. The biopsychosocial model (Grinker, 1964) advocates a holistic, idiographic approach to defining and responding to learning and development, disability and, more specifically, SEND. He further argues that biological, psychological and social factors must be considered and that barriers to learning cannot, and should not, be reduced to any single illness or condition.

Pause for reflection

■ How could each of these models be applied in relation to professional practice?

■ What discourses are used in each of the models?

How should we teach someone living with ASD: specialist pedagogy?

A common assumption is that Child X has condition Y; therefore, the teacher needs to use the teaching approach on the list of prescription strategies for condition Y and it will all be fine...and it will work.... However, it may be unhelpful to believe that lists of specialist, condition specific pedagogies (in themselves) are the answer because the list of teaching strategies for condition Y may be irrelevant to child X; the list of teaching strategies for condition Y may be as relevant to other learners as they are to child X; the list of teaching strategies for condition Y may not be relevant tomorrow or the next day as the child develops etc. Also, the list of teaching strategies might lead practitioners to believe that this learner is entirely different from all other learners ('othering') and the idea that there is a specialist pedagogy that only experts understand which could lead practitioners to feel that they cannot be and should not be responsible for learners with autism.

Examples of specialist strategies include:

- applied behaviour analysis
- intensive interaction
- social stories
- sensory integration
- TEACCH – Treatment and Education of Autistic and Communication Handicapped children
- REACh – Relationship Education for the Autistic Child
- objects of recognition.

Lewis and Norwich (2005) conceptualise two possible positions that are taken in the field of SEN, specifically in terms of pedagogy and argue that there is a lack of evidence to support the general differences position 'which may be surprising since there is a persistent sense that special education means special pedagogy' (p. 5) and, where there is evidence, this tends to support the unique differences position (Table 8.3).

Table 8.3 What is your position?

The general differences position	The unique differences position
Practitioners who adopt this frame of reference would believe that teaching approaches are informed by needs that are specific or distinctive to a group that shares common characteristics. The needs of all children and of individuals are important, but are in the background. The specific needs of a subgroup of those with disabilities and difficulties are in the foreground. Here, terms like Moderate Learning Difficulties (MLD), Severe Ledraning Difficulties (SLD) and Social, emotional and mental health needs (SEMH) are seen as relevant to the selection of pedagogies. The belief that the needs of a subgroup can be met by pedagogies that are specific to that group is regarded as valid.	This is a position that assumes that while all learners are in one general sense the same, they are also all different. Differences between individuals are accommodated within this position, not in distinct groups or subgroups. From this perspective, terms like 'MLD' and 'SLD' are less relevant; the phrase, 'Good teaching is good teaching for all' is attributable to this position. From this perspective, the generally effective teacher has the skills and expertise necessary to understand all children's needs because teaching for SEN is not qualitatively different from teaching for children without SEN.

Activity

■ Take each of the two positions and suggest how a teacher might support a pupil living with autism.

■ How would they justify each of the approaches?

One additional approach might be to use the Waves Model, identified in Chapter 5, by using a teaching strategy that is inclusive to the whole group, and then utilising specialist pedagogy when needed.

■ What is the advantage of such an approach?

Supporting pupils in the classroom

Activity

Before we look at some examples of how we can support pupils living with ASD, read the following brief case studies.

Case study: James
James is 12 years old. He has a diagnosis of autism and attends a mainstream secondary school. He enjoys art and ICT and has been provided with a classroom assistant for 20 hours per week. He finds it difficult to organise himself and his belongings, as well as meet deadlines. He is reluctant to acknowledge help from others as he thinks it makes him stand out from the class. He spends most of his time alone despite wanting to make friends, but not knowing how to. His parents have said that he is becoming increasingly withdrawn and spends large amounts of time alone, usually online. James has indicated that he is aware that he has autism, but will not talk to anyone about it. Staff feel that it is possible that his difficulty in establishing and maintaining friendships has had a negative impact on his self-esteem. His difficulties with planning and organisation mean that he gets into trouble for forgetting homework, which also damages his perception of school.

Case study: Mia
Mia is a ten-year-old girl who attends a mainstream primary school and has a diagnosis of Asperger's syndrome. She has difficulties with emotional regulation, resulting in outbursts of challenging behaviour at times. She enjoys art and loves reading about Disney films. Mia has difficulty regulating emotions when faced with certain situations in school, for example, losing at games, taking turns or engaging in

group work. These situations typically lead to a build-up of anxiety, which results in emotional outbursts and disruptive. She feels unable to use strategies when feeling anxious and is unaware of consequences of actions on herself and others.

Case study: Mohammed

Mohammed is a ten-year-old boy who lives with his mum and dad. He is very happy and has a wonderful sense of humour and it is a pleasure to be around. He has adapted well to primary school, but realises that he will be moving onto secondary school very soon and both he and his parents are concerned about how he will manage the transition. He attends mainstream classes for most of the curriculum, but is supported on a one-to-one basis for English, Maths and Science and does not receive SEN support. Mohammed can understand instructions as long as they are in the form of visual information, such as a visual timetable, or the sequencing of activities, and is able to understand and use Makaton signs and symbols. He does tend to work in isolation and is unable to cope with transitions between classes, unexpected changes to his familiar routine and non-supervised breaks.

For each of the case studies outlined:

■ Identify what are the key issues for these pupils in relation to their schooling?

■ Outline one strategy you could use to support each of these case studies in which it could be used.

■ Plan an activity which incorporates an appropriate strategy to support the case study.

Four key areas of difference

Every child on the autism spectrum will have a range of abilities within each of these areas. Many pupils on the spectrum have high levels of anxiety. Pupils on the autism spectrum have differences in interacting, processing information, communication and sensory processing

 Activity

■ Using examples from your practice identify any specific behaviours you have seen in the classroom could correspond to each of the key areas of difference.

Activity

The Autism Education Trust publishes a range of educational resources to support your practice.

These can be accessed via the Autism Education Trust (2018) website.

An autism competency framework for people working with pupils from ages 5 to 16
This is presented as a self-evaluation tool that practitioners can use to rate their current practice and understanding against a set of descriptors (knowledge, skills and personal qualities), which provides a clear structure against which you can reflect upon and evaluate your practice. It is designed to be used as an ongoing self-reflection tool to help focus on which aspects of your autism practice require further development. It enables you to rate your knowledge, skills and personal qualities against a set of descriptors outlining best practice that is recognised and valued by individuals on the autism spectrum, their families and professionals. The competencies are arranged under the individual pupil, building relationships, curriculum and learning and enabling environments.

■ Using the competencies, carry out an audit of your own practice and how this may inform future professional development.

Schools Autism Standards is a set of standards from the Autism Education Trust (AET) to enable educational settings to evaluate your practice in addressing the needs of pupils on the autism spectrum which reflect good practice for those on the autism spectrum. These standards have been written for all schools and educational settings for pupils with autism aged between 5 and 16 years. This includes mainstream schools; special and specialist schools and colleges, autism-specific units, alternative educational settings and programmes.

■ Using the standards, evaluate the extent to which each standard is in place within the school/setting using the ratings: Not appropriate; Not yet developed; Developing; Established; Enhanced.

■ Depending on your context, there are competencies and standards for both Early Years and Post 16. Using the one most appropriate to your setting, carry out an audit of your own competencies and evaluation of your own practice.

We covered general inclusive and personalised pedagogical approaches in previous chapters, specifically in relation to the Pathognomonic and Interactionist Perspectives, as well as the Graduated Response and Quality First Teaching. This next section focusses on some examples of specific strategies that you may encounter when working with pupils.

The characteristics of autism vary from one person to another, but in order for a diagnosis to be made, a person will usually be assessed as having had persistent difficulties with social communication and social interaction and restricted and repetitive patterns of behaviours, activities or interests since early childhood, to the extent that these limits impair everyday functioning.

 Activity

Complete the table below, using evidence from your own practice, or an Internet search.

What are the issues?

	Social communication and social interaction	Repetitive patterns of behaviours, activities or interests
Example of the issue		
How it may impact on the individual		
Example of a specific strategy which could be used in support		

Here are four examples of specific practices which could be used within a classroom or other settings.

Token economy strategies

TES are a form of behaviour modification that uses positive reinforcement to engage children to achieve tasks, improve academic performance or increase desirable behaviours. This is achieved by collecting tokens after desired behaviour occurs, and tokens are later exchanged for back-up reinforcers or rewards; an activity, item or privilege at a chosen time. TES are very effective approaches to modify behaviour (Kazdin and Azrin, 1977). This can be a positive intervention that can be successfully used in all educational settings to aid practitioners to support children on the autistic spectrum, for maintaining appropriate behaviours in individuals.

How does TES work in practice?
Desired behaviours are set and once the child displays the behaviour they are reinforced with tokens (secondary reinforcers), which are then exchanged for rewards (primary reinforcers). This strategy increases the frequency of desired behaviours and reduces undesired behaviours. Tokens could be objects that such as; marbles, counters, stickers or printed cards with pictures on (Educate Autism, 2016) and charts/boards could be used for visual reinforcement.

■ 'I am working for...' Think about a goal a pupil may be working towards such as playing a game for half an hour on my iPad, or an extra ten minutes on a break. Identify how you would go about incorporating a TES?

■ A parent feels that your token economy is bribery. How do you respond to this parent?

More information can be accessed via the Autism Education Trust (2018) website.

Social Stories (narratives)

A Social Story describes a situation, skill or common concept in relation to relevant social cues, perspectives and common responses in a specifically defined style and format (Gray, 2004).

Social stories are a method of teaching social skills to those with autism. These stories describe specific settings, activity or experience. The aim of a social story is to explain to the child what to anticipate in the setting and why.

Social Stories may be used to:

■ develop self-care skills, social skills and academic abilities

■ teach children how to cope with changes to their routine and unexpected circumstances

■ teach children how others might behave or respond in a particular situation, and how they could react to this appropriately

■ teach a behavioural strategy.

Social Stories provide:

■ details for the child to understand what is expected of them

■ specific behaviours and actions the child may expect in a given situation

■ relevant social cues that a child may miss if not directly taught.

More information can be accessed via the website: Gray (2018).

Power cards

Using Power Cards is a strategy to help with social situations, and it supports communication and appropriate behaviour. The aim of the Power Card is to teach and maintain appropriate strategies for social behaviour by relating the problem and solution to someone or something the child can relate to. Power Cards are based around an important character, super hero, special interest or obsession the child has and obsessions form part of the characteristics of autism along with repetitive behaviour. A narrative is then written, normally in first person (as if the character is speaking), going through different scenarios, explaining how even superheroes and special people sometimes need help and support, by relating it to the child's behavioural issue.

This is an effective way of using visual aids to promote the special interests of a child and the introduction of social expectations (Daubert, Hornstein and Tincani, 2014) and the intervention can be used for a number of social and communicational situations encouraging the child to be the same as their hero (Spencer et al., 2008). The technique has been successful in reducing the ritualistic behaviour and decreasing obsessional behaviour, promoting social behaviour, and encouraging self-belief and self-esteem.

- ▓ Although Power Cards are more often used with children and young people, can you think of a situation where a Power Card approach might be useful for an older child or adult, given that they may not have a superhero?

More information can be accessed via the ErinoakKids (2018) website.

Comic Strip Conversations

A Comic Strip Conversation is an approach, developed by Carol Gray in 1994 that uses visual aids in the form of cartoons which help portray the thoughts and feelings of others in different social situations. Bogdashina (2005) suggests that a comic strip conversation is a drawing representing an interaction between two or more people, and that these drawings illustrate an ongoing communication, identifying what people say, do and think in certain situations. It uses simple line drawings of people, speech bubbles and thought bubbles to show how individuals in the same situation may have different thoughts and feelings and therefore act differently (Clements and Zarkowska, 2000). Comic Strip Conversations are based on the belief that visual supports are useful in structuring the learning of children with autism and may also improve their comprehension and understanding of conversation. In addition, Comic Strip Conversations illustrate social skills which can be abstract and difficult for children with autism to comprehend and help individuals with autism recognise the motivations and beliefs of others.

- ▓ 'It is rude to interrupt...'. Produce a one-page worksheet, incorporating a Comic Strip Conversation to support a child who keep on interrupting the teacher in class, incorporating what interrupting means, when it is ok to interrupt and the polite way to interrupt.

More information can be accessed via the Derby City Council (2018) website.

Summary

There is evidence to support the view that autism is a disorder of the association cortex and the problems of connectivity and only secondary as a behaviour disorder. A chromosome mutation results in atypical nerve cells, and biological irregularities then occur in the genetic code for brain development. Consequently, abnormal functioning of brain development creates structural and operational abnormalities of the brain, and an issue of impaired blooming and pruning such that there is a reduced connectivity in the social part of the brain and a hyperconnectivity in the parts of the brain that are involved in the attention to detail. The outcome of this is an atypical cognitive or psychological profile resulting in impairments of theory of mind, EF and central coherence evident in the behaviours such as anxiety, rigidity of thought, and language and communication issues. However, there are also islets of superiority for someone living with autism, involving visual processing and attention to detail. In the classroom, there are reasons as to why pupils with autism behave the way that they do, it is up to all of us working in this area to recognise that there are alternative ways to thinking about autism as a deficit and the consequences this has for classroom practice.

References

Autism Education Trust (2018). Available online at: www.autismeducationtrust.org.uk/shop/p16-cf/ (Accessed 21/03/2018).

Autismspeaks (2018). *DSM-5 Diagnostic criteria*. Available online at: www.autismspeaks.org/what-autism/diagnosis/dsm-5-diagnostic-criteria (Accessed 12/07/2018).

Bailey, A., Le Couteur, A., Gottesman, I., Bolton, P., Simonoff, E., Yuzda, E. and Rutter, M. (1995). Autism as a strongly genetic disorder: evidence from a British twin study. *Psychological Medicine*, 25 (1), pp. 63–77.

Baron-Cohen, S. (2001). Autism and pervasive developmental disorders. *Journal of Applied Research in Intellectual Disabilities*, 14(1), pp. 72–74.

Baron-Cohen, S., Leslie, A. and Frith, U. (1985). Does the autistic child have a "theory of mind"? *Cognition*, 21(1), pp. 37–46.

Beversdorf, D., Manning, S., Hillier, A., Anderson, S., Nordgren, R., Walters, S., Nagaraja, H., Cooley, W., Gaelic, S. and Bauman, M. (2005). Timing of Prenatal Stressors and Autism. *Journal of Autism and Developmental Disorders*, 35(4), pp. 471–478.

Bogdashina, O. (2005). *Theory of mind and the triad of perspectives on autism and asperger syndrome, a view from the bridge*. London: Jessica Kingsley Publishers.

Boucher, J. (2017). *Autism spectrum disorder*. Los Angeles: SAGE.

Bourgeron, T. (2016). Current knowledge on the genetics of autism and propositions for future research. *Comptes Rendus Biologies*, 339, pp. 300–307.

Brown, A.S. and Derkits, E.J. (2010). Prenatal infection and schizophrenia: A review of epidemiologic and translational studies. *American Journal of Psychiatry*, 167, pp. 262–280.

Carper, R.A. and Courchesne, E. (2000). Inverse correlation between frontal lobe and cerebellum sizes in children with autism. *Brain*, 123, pp. 836–844.

Clements, J. and Zarkowska, E. (2000). *Behavioural concerns and autistic spectrum disorders: Explanations and strategies for change*. London: Jessica Kingsley Publishers.

Connors, C. and Stalker, K. (2007).Children's experiences of disability: Pointers to a social model of childhood disability. *Disability and Society*, 22(1), pp. 19–33.

Daubert, A., Hornstein, S. and Tincani, M. (2015). Effects of a modified power card strategy on turn taking and social commenting of children with autism spectrum disorder playing board games. *Journal of Developmental & Physical Disabilities*, 27(1), pp. 93–110.

Dawson, G., Munson, J., Webb, S.J., Nalty, T., Abbott, R. and Toth, K. (2007). Rate of head growth decelerates and symptoms worsen in the second year of life in autism. *Biological Psychiatry*, 61, pp. 458–464.

Derby City Council. (2018) *Comic strip conversations.* Available online at: www.derby.gov. uk/media/derbycitycouncil/contentassets/documents/sendlocaloffer/comicstrip-conversations-booklet.pdf (Accessed 24/02/2018).

ErinoakKids. (2018). *Powercards.* Available online at: www.erinoakkids.ca/ErinoakKids/ media/EOK_Documents/Autism_Resources/Power-Cards.pdf (Accessed 07/02/2018).

Fahim, C., He, Y., Yoon, U., Chen, J., Evans, A. and Prusse, D. (2011). Neuroanatomy of childhood disruptive behavior disorders. *Aggressive Behavior*, 37, pp. 326–337.

Frith, U. and Happé, F. (1994). Autism: Beyond "theory of mind". *Cognition*, 50(1–3), pp. 115–132.

Grandin, T. (1995). *Thinking in pictures.* New York: Doubleday.

Gray, C. (2004). Social stories 10.0: The new defining criteria. *Jenison Autism Journal*, 15, pp. 1–21.

Gray, C. (2018). *Social stories.* Available online at: https://carolgraysocialstories.com/social-stories/what-is-it/ (Accessed 13/03/2018).

Grinker, R.R., Sr. (1964). A struggle for eclecticism. *American Journal of Psychiatry*, 121, pp. 451–457.

Hahamy, A., Behrmann, M. and Malach, R. (2015). The idiosyncratic brain: Distortion of spontaneous connectivity patterns in autism spectrum disorder. *Nature Neuroscience*, 8(2), pp. 302–309.

Happé, F. and Frith, U. 2006, The weak coherence account: Detail-focused cognitive style in autism spectrum disorders. *Journal of Autism and Developmental Disorders*, 36(1), pp. 5–25.

Happé , D. and Happé , F. (1994). *Autism.* Hoboken: Taylor & Francis Ltd.

Just, M.A., Cherkassky, V.L., Keller, T.A., Kana, R.K. and Minshew, N.J. (2007). Functional and anatomical cortical underconnectivity in autism: Evidence from an fMRI study of an executive function task and corpus callosum morphometry. *Cerebral Cortex*, 17, 951–961.

Kazdin, A. and Azrin, N. (1977). *Token economy.* 1st ed. Boston: Springer US. pp. 1–18.

Laidman, J. (2014). Disorganized brain cells help explain autism symptoms. Scientific American Mind 25, p. 20.

Lawson, W. (1998). *Life behind glass: A personal account of autism spectrum disorder.* London: Jessica Kingsley.

Lewis, A. and Norwich, B. (2005). *Special teaching for special children? Pedagogies for inclusion.* 1st ed. Maidenhead: Open University Press.

McRae, G. (2018). *This new autism genetics study could help explain why it's such a huge spectrum.* Available online at: www.sciencealert.com/de-novo-mutations-autism-spectrum-disorder-explain-reduced-iq-motor-skills (Accessed 12/05/2018).

Morgan, B., Maybery, M. and Durkin, K. (2003). Weak central coherence, poor joint attention, and low verbal IQ: Independent deficits in early autism. *Developmental Psychology*, 39, pp. 646–56

Muhle, R., Trentacoste, S.V. and Rapin, I. (2004). The genetics of autism. *Pediatrics*, 113, pp. 472–486.

Murray, D., Lesser, M. and Lawson, W. (2005). Attention, monotropism and the diagnostic criteria for autism. *Autism*, 9(2). pp. 139–56.

National Institute of Neurological Disorders and Stroke. (2018). *Autism spectrum disorders.* Available online at: www.nimh.nih.gov/health/publications/autism-spectrum-disorder/index.shtml (Accessed 12/03/2018).

Newschaffer, C.J., Croen, L.A., Daniels, J., Giarelli, E., Grether, J.K., Levy, S.E., Mandell, D.S., Miller, L.A., Pinto-Martin, J., Reaven, J., Reynolds, A.M., Rice, C.E., Schendel, D. and Windham, G.C. (2007). The epidemiology of autism spectrum disorders. *Annual Review of Public Health*, 28, pp. 235–258.

Ornoy, A., Weinstein-Fudim, L. and Ergaz, Z. (2015). Prenatal factors associated with autism spectrum disorder (ASD). *Reprod Toxicol*, 56, pp. 155–169.

Parnas, J., Bovet, P. and Zahavi, D. (2002). Schizophrenic autism: Clinical pathology and pathogenic implications. *World Psychiatry*, 1(3), pp. 131–136.

Rajendran, G. and Mitchell, P. (2007). Cognitive theories of autism. *Developmental Review*, 27(2), pp. 224–260.

Sealey, L.A., Hughes, B.W., Sriskanda, A.N., Guest, J.R., Gibson, A.D., Johnson-Williams, L., Pace, D.G. and Bagasra, O. (2016). Environmental factors in the development of autism spectrum disorders. *Environment International*, 88, pp. 288–298.

Spencer, V.G., Simpson, C.G., Day, M. and Buster, E. (2008). Using the POWER CARD strategy to teach social skills to a child with autism. *Teaching Exceptional Children Plus*, 5(1), pp. 1–10.

Tammet, D. (2006). *Born on a blue day.* London: Hodder & Stoughton.

van Wijngaarden-Cremers, P.J.M. (2014). Gender and age differences in the core triad of impairments in autism spectrum disorders: A systematic review and meta-analysis. *Journal of Autism and Developmental Disorders*, 44(3), pp. 627–635.

Ward, A.J. (1990). A comparison and analysis of the presence of family problems during pregnancy of mothers of "autistic" children and mothers of typically developing children. *Child Psychiatry and Human Development*, 20, pp. 279–288.

Williams, D. (1994). *Somebody somewhere.* London: Doubleday.

Wing, L. (1996). *The autistic spectrum.* London: Constable.

Wing, L. and Gould, J. (1979). Severe impairments of social interaction and associated abnormalities in children: Epidemiology and classification. *Journal of Autism and Developmental Disorders*, 9(1), pp. 11–29.

World Health Organization (2018). *6A02 Autism spectrum disorder.* Available online at: https://icd.who.int/browse11/l-m/en#/http%3a%2f%2fid.who.int%2ficd%2fentity%2f437815624 (Accessed 21/08/2018).

Yeh, E. and Weiss, L.A. (2016). If genetic variation could talk: What genomic data may teach us about the importance of gene expression regulation in the genetics of autism? *Molecular and Cellular Probes*, 30(6), pp. 346–356.

Zielinski, B.A., Prigge, M.B., Nielsen J.A., Froehlich, A.L., Abildskov, T.J., Anderson, J.S., Fletcher P.T., Zygmunt, K.M., Travers, B.G., Lange, N., Alexander, A.L., Bigler. E.D. and Lainhart, J.E. (2014). Longitudinal changes in cortical thickness in autism and typical development. *Brain*, 137(Pt 6), pp. 1799–1812.

9 Attention disorders (ADD and ADHD)

Introduction

Attention deficit hyperactivity disorder (ADHD) is a neurodevelopmental disorder present from childhood involving distractibility, impulsivity and excessive motor activity often leading to academic failure and social difficulties, or a syndrome characterised by a group of symptoms, which include hyperactivity, poor attention and impulsivity. ADHD is a term that is considered when a person's behaviour is persistently impulsive, inattentive and overactive, compared to other children of their age. It may affect a person's ability to function in a range of settings and the behaviours may include difficulty in listening, following instructions, organising and attention skills. Using evidence from research, along with case studies and suggestions for strategies designed to support individuals with Autism Spectrum Disorder (ASD), this chapter seeks to develop your understanding of the aetiology and the cognitive and behavioural impact on an individual living with Attention Disorder. It aims to:

- define the terms ADHD, Hyperkinetic Disorder (HKD) and ADD (Attention Deficit Disorder)

- outline two approaches in the classification of ADHD (DSM-V and ICD-10) and the similarities and differences between the two systems

- identify some of the characteristics associated with the core features of inattentiveness, hyperactivity and impulsivity

- use research findings to evaluate the standing of the role of genetics on ADHD

- use research findings to evaluate the standing of the role of neurobiology on ADHD

- examine the role of neurotransmitters, such as dopamine

- discuss cognitive theories relating to ADHD, including executive functioning

■ examine the importance of environmental risk factors in the development of ADHD

■ discuss the suggestion that ADHD is a Social Construct

■ discuss examples of pedogeological strategies to address Inattentiveness, Hyperactivity and Impulsivity.

Overview

O'Regan (2002) explains that ADHD exists if a group of specific behaviours cannot be explained by any other reasons or means. and for a diagnosis of ADHD, a child will have extreme symptoms for at least six months. Considerations will be given to the negative impact on the child's life at home and in school causing them difficulties in socialising. According to Spohrer (2002), children with ADHD have difficulty in auditory processing and following instructions; therefore, a child may feel confused of what is expected causing non-compliance and disruptive behaviour. However, Brown (2013) considers a change that renders this old definition of ADHD as a behaviour disorder no longer tenable. He takes the cartoon character 'Dennis the Menace' as the old paradigm of an individual with ADHD, often restless, impulsive and hyperactive, loveable but frustrating his parents and teachers. The new character is overwhelmed by a syndrome of chronic difficulties in focussing, starting a task, sustaining effort, utilising memory and regulating emotions that chronically impair their ability to manage everyday tasks of daily life. Kewley (2011) defines ADHD as a medical disorder affecting the brain's function, which impacts individuals' educational capabilities and performance. This disorder affects 5.3 per cent of children worldwide (Polanczyk et al., 2007), with 5 per cent of children in the UK having a diagnosis; males are more affected than females and the ratio is 3:1.

Pause for reflection

It is interesting that more males are also diagnosed with autism than females.

■ Can you suggest two reasons as to why this is the case?

Diagnosis and classification

The International Classification of Mental and Behavioural Disorders (ICD-10) refers to ADHD as HKD, a persistent and severe impairment of psychological development, characterised by the early onset of a combination of overactive, poorly modulated behaviour with marked inattention and lack of persistent task involvement. Moreover, the ICD-10 classification requires that all three features of inattention, hyperactivity and impulsivity are present, before a diagnosis of HKD is given. However, ICD-11 which was released in 2018 has fallen in line with DSM-V be referring to ADHD (International Statistical Class of Diseases, 2018) (WHO, 2018). The Diagnostic and Statistical Manual of Mental disorders (DSM-V, 2013) (APA, 2018) defines ADHD as a persistent inappropriate pattern of hyperactivity-impulsivity or inattention or both (Figure 9.1). According to Hughes and Cooper (2007), the characteristics are detailed as:

Inattention	Refers to the child's inability to sustain or inability to pay attention and focus.
Impulsiveness	Refers to a child who acts without thinking about the consequences. They may shout the answers and make quick decisions.
Hyperactivity	Refers to extreme activity rather than normal active behaviours. Child constantly 'on the go', touching or playing with everything or talking non-stop.

The Diagnostic and Statistical Manual of Mental Disorders (DSM-V) (APA, 2018) defines ADHD as a neurodevelopmental disorder with persistent patterns of inattention and/or hyperactivity and impulsivity that restrict an individual's functioning or growth, which can then have adverse influences on academic, social and professional functioning. According to American Psychiatric Association (2018), there are 18 symptoms used to diagnose ADHD, which are divided into two domains, these being inattention and hyperactivity/impulsivity. At least six symptoms in one area are required for an ADHD diagnosis. Behaviour must display six or more symptoms and be evident in two or more contexts consistently for six months or more, and emphasised before the age of 12. There are three presentations of ADHD as defined in DSM-V based on the predominant symptom pattern for the past six months:

- Combined presentation – all three core features are present, and ADHD is diagnosed when ≥6 symptoms of hyperactivity/impulsivity and ≥6 symptoms of inattention have been observed for ≥6 months

- Predominantly inattentive presentation – diagnosed if ≥6 symptoms of inattention (but <6 symptoms of hyperactivity/impulsivity) have persisted for ≥6 months

- Predominantly hyperactive/impulsive presentation – diagnosed if ≥6 symptoms of hyperactivity/impulsivity (but <6 symptoms of inattention) have been present for ≥6 months

In the USA in 2011, 11 per cent of four- to seven-year olds were diagnosed equating to 6.4 million children (Centre for Disease Control and Prevention, 2018), with an increase in diagnosis having been reported within the last decade resulting in between 2 per cent and 5 per cent of school-aged children having the label of ADD or ADHD (Saul, 2014) and in

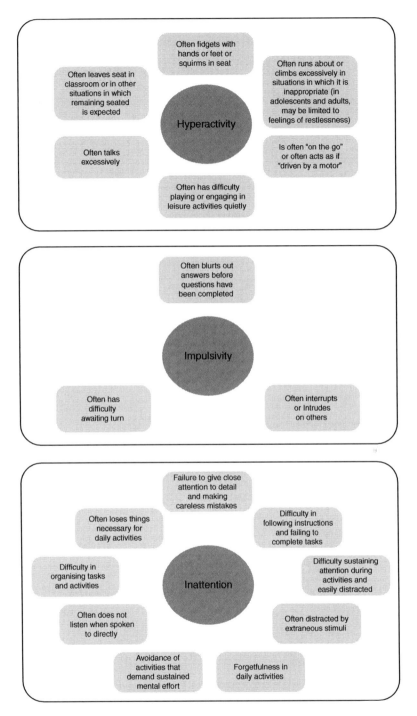

Figure 9.1 Examples of the behaviours associated with ADHD

2016 six boys were diagnosed to every girl (ADHD Institute, 2018). In the UK, HKD occurs in 1 per cent–2 per cent when diagnosed through ICD-10, compared to 3 per cent–9 per cent being diagnosed with ADHD, with Hughes and Cooper (2007), suggesting that the preferred diagnostic system is the DSM-V as it includes cognitive, physical and emotional difficulties among other behavioural symptoms when assessing children for ADHD traits, with the ICD-10 criteria omitting reference to social impairment.

Pause for reflection

■ Do you think the revisions made in ICD-11 will have any implications on how the disorder is viewed by both clinicians, teachers and parents?

Some common myths surrounding ADHD:

All ADD/ADHD children are hyperactive.	Some children with ADD/ADHD may be hyperactive. Children who are inattentive may appear 'spacey' and uninterested.
Children with ADHD never pay attention.	These children are often able to concentrate on activities that they enjoy. They do, however, find it difficult focussing on tasks they find boring or repetitive.
Children with ADHD 'choose' to be difficult and not to behave.	These children can try their best to be good, but find it hard to remain still, be quiet or focus.
Children will eventually grow out of their symptoms.	ADHD often carries on into adulthood. Treatments can help the child learn to deal with and minimise symptoms.
Medication is the only treatment for ADHD.	Medication is often prescribed but may not be in the best interest of the child. Education, behaviour therapy, support at home and school, exercise and proper nutrition are also options.
	(Adapted from Hyche and Maertz, 2014).

Pause for reflection

■ Why do you think that these myths still perpetuate?

The debate surrounding ADHD is not that the behaviours associated with it are evident in classrooms throughout the country, but what is the underlying cause of these and whether or not ADHD exists, or is a social construction? One main view is that it follows a similar aetiology as that of Autism Spectrum Disorder, discussed in Chapter 8, starting with genetic vulnerability.

Genetic factors

With a worldwide prevalence of approximately 5 per cent, ADHD has become one of the most common psychiatric disorders. Although the aetiology of ADHD is still incompletely understood, results from family, twin and adoption studies, as well as molecular genetic studies consistently indicate the strong genetic influence on ADHD with estimated heritability ranging from 75 per cent to 91 per cent. Kuntsi et al. (2003) found a correlation of 0.86 for Monozygotic (MZ) twins compared to 0.47 for Dizygotic (DZ) twins. The polygenetic nature of ADHD is widely acknowledged, implying that multiple genes have a moderate effect on ADHD. There is a risk to first-degree relatives when ADHD runs in families, with ADHD traits among children of parents with ADHD being in the order of 55 per cent (Brock, Jimerson and Hansen, 2009).

Adoption studies have unequivocally found that biological relatives of children with ADHD are more likely to have hyperactivity than adoptive relatives. Indeed, ADHD appears to be one of the most heritable psychiatric disorders, with a pooled analysis of 20 twin studies reporting a mean heritability estimate of 76 per cent. A more recent quantitative systematic approach, which considered possible biases of previous twin studies (such as lack of power to detect sibling interaction, and the correction used for contrast effects), concluded that genetic factors explained 60 per cent of the variance of ADHD. ADHD, schizophrenia and bipolar disease may have a common link.

Pause for reflection

■ If ADHD was wholly a result of genetics, concordance rates would be 100 per cent. As it is not, what factors do you think might influence the ADHD phenotype? If ADHD, schizophrenia and bipolar disorder share a common genetic link, what line of research do you think geneticists should embark upon in trying to identify the genes responsible?

Although the high heritability of ADHD suggests that it is a genetic disorder, to assert that any single gene causes the disorder would be inaccurate. Rather, many genes combine to increase the risk for ADHD. Thus, instead of declaring that genes cause ADHD, it is better to understand that, as with environmental risk factors, some gene variants boost one's susceptibility to the disorder. With the exception of very rare conditions, no single gene is either necessary or sufficient to cause ADHD. Linkage studies have implicated broad areas of chromosomes 5, 10, 12, 16 and 17. Currently, researchers are studying these chromosomal regions in more detail to determine which of the many genes in these regions are involved in ADHD.

An increasing number of studies have tried to gain insight into the specific genes involved in the aetiology of ADHD. By means of linkage association studies, chromosomal regions such as 5p13, 11q22e25 and 17p11 containing potentially implicated genes have been identified. A meta-analysis of these studies has revealed a region on chromosome 16 having the most consistent linkage evidence

(Franke et al., 2012). The identification of the exact genes is still challenging, chiefly due to methodological and technical limitations. Genome-wide association studies to potentially identify single genes involved in a disease have so far been inconclusive in the field of ADHD genetics research. The most recent meta-analysis of genome-wide association studies has found no genome-wide significant associations. This, of course, does not suggest that ADHD has no genetic underpinnings, but that there are several genes having a significant effect. Faraone, Biederman and Mick (2006) reviewed the candidate gene literature and examined pooled odds ratios for candidate genes implicating seven possible genes, many of which are involved in dopamine transmission. Perhaps, the most frequently studied of these genes is the dopamine D4 receptor (DRD4) gene.

Activity

You have been asked to present a talk at your school debating society to the motion that 'It is morally and ethically wrong to search for the genes implicated in the causation of ADHD and that it can lead to genetic selection'.

▨ What issues does this statement raise and how would you present a view to both sides of the debate?

Neurochemical factors

Cortese (2012) established that, within the frontal cortex, the neurotransmitter norepinephrine (noradrenaline) is affected by uncharacteristic dopamine signals, which, in turn, caused irregular self-control including impulsivity, hyperactivity and inattention, concluding that ADHD is a complex condition with multiple dysfunction and pathways irregularities. It has been suggested that individuals with ADHD have an imbalance in the neurotransmitter dopamine which influences attention, impulse control and activity level. At the chemical level of the brain, ADHD seems to involve dopaminergic and adrenergic systems with serotonergic and cholinergic systems also being involved. Individuals with ADHD have a reduction in the level of the neurotransmitter dopamine, which regulates the prefrontal cortex. This area of the brain is linked to the process of executive functioning which affects working memory, attention, reasoning and processing with low levels of dopamine, a key indicator for ADHD.

There are several distinct dopamine pathways in the brain, including the pathways associated with motor function and reward-motivated behaviour and, due to the imbalance of dopamine, neuronal transmission may be carried to the incorrect part of the brain. Furthermore, dopamine also acts as a reward pathway, ADDRC (2011) suggests that the body craves the feeling it gets when dopamine is released, as a result an individual will modify their behaviour in order to get this feeling and this is therefore reinforced. As a consequence, the brain seeks immediate reward that results in difficulties in executive functions.

The Moderate Brain Arousal Theory (Sikstrom and Soderlund, 2007) suggests that low dopamine levels cause a higher dopamine release in response to external stimuli. This results in a large boost in dopamine levels, which, in turn, results in hypersensitivity to the environment and as a consequence of this the body then becomes conditioned to seek out external stimuli because it is highly rewarding for them. Lower levels of dopamine may also cause issues such as inattention to work. However, Silkstrom and Soderlund (2007) suggest that this dysfunctional dopamine system allows higher levels of dopamine to be released when in response to an external stimulus, thus causing hyperactive and impulsive behaviour. Current research indicates that alterations in any single neurotransmitter system are unlikely to explain the complexity of ADHD neurobiology. Rather, ADHD is likely a consequence of the interplay between several dysfunctional neurotransmitter systems.

Pharmacotherapy

To assist with disruptive behaviour, drugs such as Ritalin (the brand name of methylphenidate (MPH)) can be used. In 2003, it was reported that Ritalin prescription increased by 25 per cent (The Economist, 2004). However, there is a divided opinion on the usage of such drugs; Ritalin can reduce the hyperactivity of a child while creating a flat behaviour but enabling learning to take place. This could be construed as removing their personality, also reported are side effects of suppressing appetite; therefore, weight loss can be a major concern (Mostafavi et al., 2012). Stimulant medication such as MPH targets dopamine (DA) imbalances (Volkow et al., 2009) and is highly effective in alleviating ADHD symptoms. Nowadays, parallel to the increased prevalence of ADHD over the past decade, stimulant medication prescription rates have risen strongly. Although the efficacy and safety of stimulants prescribed to children diagnosed with ADHD has been extensively documented (Faraone and Buitelaar, 2010), it is currently unclear whether these drugs induce long-term effects, especially when they are first given during sensitive periods of ongoing human brain development, as is the case for children and adolescents.

 Activity

- What do you think are the benefits and issues surrounding the use of drugs for 'controlling' the ADHD child?

- If you were a parent of an ADHD child, where might you go for advice?

Activity

In an international research project, Singh (2012) interviewed children with ADHD in the UK and the USA about their experiences of ADHD and stimulant medication. The research team observed that the intense focus on negative behaviours in UK state school classrooms may mean that behaviour, not learning or academic performance, becomes a child's primary concern.

■ Think about your own practice, is this statement correct and if so why do you think it may occur?

■ If you were responsible for supporting or teaching a child with ADHD, what would your primary focus be? Can behaviour and learning be separated?

Neuroanatomy

Structural brain MRI has greatly increased our knowledge of the details of brain anatomy in children with ADHD. A wealth of neuroimaging evidence exists to suggest the presence of structural abnormalities in the brains of children with ADHD. Initial investigations pinpointed significant differences in the frontostriatal circuitry of children with ADHD. However, it has since become clear that other regions of the brain may exhibit morphological alterations, including areas of the cerebellum and temporoparietal lobes, basal ganglia and corpus callosum (Valera et al., 2007).

Other research (Shaw et al., 2007) implicates the frontal lobe (prefrontal cortex), especially the orbital prefrontal cortex responsible for controlling attention and motor planning, and the basal ganglia found deep within the brain. The cerebellum, anterior cingulate cortex and the corpus callosum are underactive and caused by neurotransmitter dysfunction or missing synapses. MRI scans of the brain in 446 children diagnosed with ADHD showed underdevelopment of the prefrontal cortex, creating a lag in brain development in the area by three years compared to their peers. Thus, this cortical thinning of the brain, evidenced through MRI imaging, emerges as a potential neurobiological marker for ADHD with a corresponding decrease in volume within the brain by 3 per cent–5 per cent resulting in 10 per cent–25 per cent less activity in the right frontal lobe of prefrontal cortex.

According to Barkley (2014), there are three main networks which function differently in ADHD, these being the connection between the frontal lobes and the striatum which processes the way someone holds information, and maybe the reason why someone with ADHD will get distracted; the connection between frontal lobes and the cerebellum, which creates difficulties with time management and coordination; the final connection is between the frontal lobes and limbic system where the main issues of ADHD lie, that of hyperactivity, impulsiveness and, in some individuals, inattention.

Blood flow within the brain regions is also implicated with Buitelaar, Kan and Asherson (2011), suggesting that for a child who has ADHD, there is a lack of blood flowing towards the prefrontal regions of the brain leading to inattentiveness and a lack of focus. Their brains have smaller and less active regions including the orbital prefrontal cortex cerebellum with these functional differences persisting into adolescence and adulthood. Miller and Cummings (2007) suggest that there is lack of blood flow to the prefrontal cortex of the brain. This results in the inability to inhibit undesired behaviours or actions, leading to impulsivity. Chandler (2010) found that a decreased brain volume, along with a reduction in grey and white matter in the prefrontal cortex along the hypofunctional dopamine systems, were in evidence in the brains of individuals identified with ADHD. Furthermore, a decrease in the volume of white matter and decreased brain activity have also been found, along with less functional connectivity.

Attention disorders require three neural networks, within the limbic area of the brain, to coordinate together: alerting, orienting and executive control. Alerting supresses peripheral distractions to allow concentration, orienting prepares the input of required senses, and executive control, located within the cerebrum, directs the neural process required to respond to a learning situation (Sousa, 2001). A variation or error in messages will influence the way in which the child responds and affect the in-attention and impulsiveness, and may cause hyperactivity with Konrad and Eickhoff (2010) reviewing whether the brain of someone with ADHD is wired differently.

A recent study at the Radboud University Nijmegen Medical Centre found that overall brain volume and five of the regional volumes were smaller in people with ADHD, with similar differences in brain volume also being seen in other psychiatric disorders, especially major depressive disorder. Some researchers currently propose that ADHD is a disorder of the brain and suggest that delays in the development of several brain regions are characteristic of ADHD (Radbound University, 2017) and there is a shift towards a more complex theoretical framework that considers the clinical heterogeneity of ADHD.

Pause for reflection

■ How would you attempt to resolve the debate as to whether the brain abnormality and atypical development cause ADHD, or whether the ADHD causes the brain abnormality and atypical development?

Environmental and risk factors

Many environmental risk factors have been implicated into the aetiology of ADHD, including complications during pregnancy such as stress, and perinatal factors, such as smoking and alcohol consumption. Han et al. (2015) surveyed 19,940 people and found that the risk of ADHD was 1.55 times higher in children of mothers who consumed alcohol during pregnancy and 2.47 times higher in children of mothers who smoked. Another environmental factor which is believed to impact ADHD is exposure to greenhouse gases, with Fluegge (2016) finding an association between N_2O (nitrous oxide) and ADHD, especially in the dopamine receptors as N_2O may disrupt DR4 via the compound's oxidation of cobalamin and inhibition.

Other environmental factors such as lead poisoning, inadequate parenting, diet and allergies have been suggested as aetiologies, although no recent substantiated evidence has been put forward. Some suggest that sugar intake is linked to ADHD; however, sugar consumption is yet to be proven as a link to ADHD. Lewis-Morton et al. (2014) suggest that children witnessing domestic violence in the home and receiving inconsistent care and love are also susceptible to ADHD.

Cognitive explanations of ADHD

Individuals with ADHD often show cognitive difference compared to those without ADHD. Martinussen et al. (2005) found that individuals with ADHD had poorer memories and that more than one component of the working memory had some deficits that then caused problems with memory. This resulted in language learning disorders and a lower intellectual ability which could suggest why some individuals with ADHD often struggle with education. Anything that they get taught would not remain in their memory, so every day it could be like starting again at school. Eventually information might be stored in the memory, but it could take longer, this could be why they learn at a slower pace than individuals without ADHD.

When cognitive abilities in children with ADHD were researched, Paul (2008) found that as parts of the brain such as the frontal lobes were less active, this caused deficiencies in their executive functioning. Executive functioning is linked to many behaviours, such as decision-making, response control and planning. Therefore, if an individual has a deficiency in his/her executive functioning, it could mean that he/she is not able to act in an appropriate manner at all times and especially they may have difficulties in a social environment. Furthermore, having a lack of executive functioning can also cause problems, such as not being able to pay attention at all times and often shift attention, so they struggle to keep occupied. Additionally, pupils often portray repetitive behaviours and rigidity, therefore they may struggle to feel settled and relaxed in a classroom environment.

For a child living with ADHD, Klingberg et al. (2005) suggest that executive functions of the working memory model will have deficits and therefore influence the performance of the child. Although the working memory model has not been widely applied to ADHD, there is evidence that the central executive has an impairment, due to focussed attention, divided attention and switching at the subprocesses of the central executive. Therefore, rather than the phonological loop and visuospatial sketch pad working together, a person with ADHD will only be able to focus their attention on one subprocess rather than both.

Klingberg et al. (2005) conducted a randomised testing over a two-month period to investigate whether improvement can be made to a child's working memory. Different tasks were proposed to 53 children aged 7–12 working on the different subprocesses and found that working memory and response inhibition were improved.

The most widely recognised model of executive function impairment in ADHD is that proposed by Barkley (2012) who proposes an integrated model that suggests that neurologically based problems of response inhibition lead directly to problems in four major 'executive functions' of the brain that are essential for self-regulation, including working memory deficits, internalised speech and weighing up implications of behaviour; difficulties in motivational appraisal causing decision-making difficulties in planning an issue and reconstitution lead to an inability to plan new behaviours as a result of analysing past behaviours.

 Activity

In Chapter 8 on Autism Spectrum Disorder, issues with working memory and executive functioning were outlined. If a pupil in your class had a diagnosis of both autism and ADHD, identify an activity in a specific curriculum and suggest

■ What support might they need?

■ What strengths might they exhibit?

■ How would you avoid the 'double labelling' of such an individual?

An alternative view: ADHD as a social construct

The notion that ADD/ADHD existence is a social construct is supported by Saul (2014) suggesting that, although certain behavioural conditions exist, they are predominantly caused by underlying medical conditions such as iron deficiency. France and Italy do not classify ADD and ADHD as a disorder, but rather a medical condition with psychosocial issues, concentrating on the underlying problems causing the child distress rather than the disorder, and furthermore, child-rearing philosophies in France differ from many other cultures. These include: providing a firm, consistent structure; constraints on snack times and mealtimes at specific times each day; children learn self-control at an early age and a rule-based culture. If any problems have been seen within the social context, they treat it with psychotherapy or family counselling (Wedge, 2012).

As an alternative to the Medical Model of ADHD, some medical professionals view varying degrees of childhood behaviours as a function of psychological and behavioural development. Those following this ideology express concern and suspicion over the use of psychostimulants to medicate small children. This group of medical professionals sees the overdiagnoses of ADHD as a catchall when diagnosis cannot be established, and as a means of labelling and controlling children who exhibit difficult behaviours. The belief is that children are being given drugs unnecessarily to control their behaviours using medication as a means of social control (Norris and Lloyd, 2000).

Lewis-Morton et al. (2014) researched how families talk about and construct their ideas surrounding ADHD and their child. It found that most families dismissed psychosocial causes for behaviour leading to the only obvious diagnosis that it could only be ADHD. The report also found that families are more than willing to accept an 'illness' model as an explanation. The report suggests a theory surrounding attachment. If the child's attachment needs are not being met, this can lead to the child becoming inattentive as a self-protective strategy. It goes on to suggest that less attention should be paid to school work or peer relationships and focus should be on promoting attachment needs. A family's acceptance of the child's disability is crucial, so they can support their child.

A study conducted by Wolraich et al. (1985) found that the connection between hyperactivity and sugar to be a myth. In this study, they researched the placebo effect of sugar on behaviour. Their findings show that mothers who thought their child had sugar were found to have more hyperactive behaviour compared to the mothers who were told their child was given a sugar substitute. They concluded that a vast number of studies have been unable to establish behaviour changes due to sugar consumption.

 Activity

'ADHD may not exist in and of itself. Rather it represents our cultural preferences for learners who are attentive and passive rather than inattentive and impulsive. In an education system which requires sustained attentiveness, stillness and compliance, a personality type that does not "fit" can be seen as "wrong" and in need of diagnosis and correction'.

▨ You have been invited to give a talk to a local Parent and Teachers Association to respond to the above statement. What evidence would you put forward in response?

Classroom strategies to support individuals with ADHD

ADHD can affect all developmental areas (Hughes and Cooper, 2007) who believe by implementing specific strategies can influence and empower children to achieve normal milestones. Below are some specific strategies which may help to support individuals in the classroom. It is not an exhaustive list, but may help practitioners target a specific issue, but in reality, they could be used with any pupils.

Managing inattention

- sit pupils at the front of the class, and make sure they are away from any external distractions
- get them to sit with peers who can be positive role models for them
- break tasks down into small, manageable sections
- limit the number of task choices
- use positive reinforcement for staying focussed or completing tasks
- give clear, simple classroom rules and expectations
- provide brief instructions, giving one instruction out at a time
- provide fixed routines wherever possible
- gain attention before giving instructions; provide information verbally or in writing such as in the form of a checklist
- non-verbal prompts or a prearranged signal can be used to gain attention
- use first names which makes your instructions personal
- if you fail to get the desired response after the third request, rephrase your instruction. A child can construe repeated instructions as 'nagging'.

Adapted from Yarney (2013); Bloor (2013).

Managing hyperactivity

- provide short bursts of physical activity whenever possible during tasks
- make sure that activities are structured, easy and enjoyable
- provide pupils with a 'fiddly' as children with ADHD often need something to do with their hands. A key ring, a small cube, for example, can help
- if they find it hard to keep his legs and/or feet still, encourage them to wriggle his toes in their shoes
- try to avoid keeping them behind at break or lunchtime, they may need to 'let off steam'
- when outside the classroom pupils may struggle with queuing. Make sure they know the point of the queue and help them quantify how long they will be queueing for.

Adapted from Yarney (2013); Bloor (2013).

Managing impulsivity

■ help pupils be aware of how their behaviour can affect those around them

■ get them to explain what they have done and what is a more acceptable way of behaving in the future

■ help them to understand why those around them may have responded the way they did to their behaviour

■ allow processing time for answers, for example, waiting 20 seconds before answering. This will give sufficient time to process an answer, as well as avoid shouting out the first thing in their head

■ offer the support of a homework club and ensure that they record homework accurately.

Adapted from Yarney (2017); Bloor (2013).

Strategies for other situations around school:

■ See if their form tutor or a teaching assistant can 'check in' to make sure they know their timetable for the day. They can also advise him of any changes to the school day, and this will also help with lateness and disorganisation.

■ Use a hobby or interest as a reward for positive behaviour, and this could also be used as a diversionary tactic should they need to let of steam.

■ Build in breaks, every 10 or 20 minutes.

■ Use timers to monitor time passing.

■ Establish routines of where and when they hand homework in.

 Activity

Stephen gets on well with his mum; he loves his little brother and says he really likes learning. Even as a young child, Stephen was always described as being always on the go, 'a cross between a butterfly and a bull in a china shop'. However, when other children found activities that engrossed them, only one activity grabbed Stephen's attention: football. He loved playing it, watching it and following his favourite football team, Manchester United. At primary school, although he appeared to love learning, his teachers often said it was difficult to keep him on task: his attention would wander at the slightest distraction. Since moving up to secondary school, he is often late to lessons and disorganised. He spends most of the lesson looking out of the window or distracting other members of his class. He seems incapable of settling to any task for more than a few minutes and often needs to be refocussed several times in one lesson. Some of Stephen's teachers have described him as attention seeking. Stephen is moving up into your class in September.

■ Using two roles, that of a support member of staff and a class teacher, what strategies would you look at in helping Stephen adjust to the transition into a new class?

 Activity

'In my day, there was no such thing as ADHD, kids were just naughty. Nowadays, there is no opportunity to be naughty as they are tightly controlled by parents. When they come to school, they don't have this control'.

■ The above remark was one given by a long-established member of your school staff. Having read this chapter and carried out the activities, how would you respond to this statement? What evidence would you put forward in your discussion with this member of staff?

Summary

There are a number of issues and debates in relation to ADHD, beginning with the definition of the term. The widely accepted view is that ADHD is considered when a person's behaviour is persistently impulsive, inattentive and overactive, compared to other children of their age. The cause of this may involve genetic pathways, neurological and neurochemical differences, along with risk factors. However, there are others who ascertain that ADHD is a social construct. Whichever of these views gains further acceptance, the cognitive and behavioural aspects associated with factors of inattentiveness, impulsivity and hyperactivity are often seen in classrooms. Perhaps it may be more beneficial not to label and stigmatise individuals with ADHD, but to examine strategies to support children with these issues, whether they have a diagnosis or not.

References

ADD Resource Centre (2011). *ADHD, executive function and school success.* Available on-line at: www.addrc.org/executive-function-and-school-success/ (Accessed 21/02/2018).

ADHD Institute (2018). Available online at: https://adhd-institute.com (Accessed 13/04/2018).

American Psychiatric Association (2018). *Diagnostic and statistical manual of mental disorders.* 5th ed. Arlington: American Psychiatric Publishing.

Barkley, R.A. (2012). *Executive functions: What they are, how they work, and why they evolved.* New York: Guilford Press.

Barkley, R.A. (2014). *Attention-deficit hyperactivity disorder: A handbook for diagnosis and treatment.* 4th ed. New York: The Guilford Press.

Bloor, A. (2013). *Supporting pupils with ADHD: Whole-school training materials and resources for Sencos.* London: Optimus Education.

Brock, S., Jimerson, S. and Hansen, R. (2009). *Identifying, assessing, and treating ADHD at school.* New York: Springer.

Brown, T.E. (2013). *A new understanding of ADHD in children and adults: Executive function impairments.* Hove: Routledge.

Buitelaar, J., Kan, C. and Asherson, P. (2011). *ADHD in adults.* Cambridge: Cambridge University Press.

Centers for Disease Control and Prevention (2018). Available online at: www.cdc.gov/datastatistics/index.html (Accessed 10/02/2018).

Chandler, C. (2010). *The science of ADHD: A guide for parents and professionals.* Hoboken: Wiley-Blackwell.

Cortese, S. (2012). The neurobiology and genetics of attention-deficit/hyperactivity disorder (ADHD): What every clinician should know. *European Journal of Paediatric Neurology,* 16, pp. 422–433.

Economist (2004). *Behave, or else.* Available online at: www.economist.com/britain/2004/12/02/behave-or-else (Accessed 16/05/2018).

Faraone, S., Biederman, J. and Mick, E. (2006). The age dependent decline of attention-deficit/hyperactivity disorder: A meta-analysis of follow-up studies. *Psychological Medicine,* 36(2), pp. 159–165.

Faraone, S. and Buitelaar, J. (2010). Comparing the efficacy of stimulants for ADHD children and adolescents using meta-analysis. *European Child and Adolescent Psychiatry,* 19(4), pp. 353–364.

Fluegge, K. (2016). The possible role of air pollution in the link between ADHD and obesity. *Postgraduate Medicine,* 128, pp. 573–576.

Franke, B., Faraone, S.C., Asherson, P., Buitelaar, J., Bau, C.H., Ramos-Quiroga, J.A., Mick, E., Grevet, E.H., Johansson, S., Haavik, J., Lesch, K.P., Cormand, B., Reif, A.C. (2012). The genetics of attention deficit/hyperactivity disorder in adults, a review. *Molecular Psychiatry,* 17, pp. 960–987.

Han, J.H., Kwon, H.J., Ha, M., Palk, K.C., Lim, M.H., Sang, G.L., Yoo, S.J. and Kim, E.J. (2015). The effects of prenatal exposure to alcohol and environmental tobacco smoke on risk for ADHD: A large population-based study. *Psychiatry Research,* 225(1–2), pp. 164–168.

Hughes, L. and Cooper, P. (2007). *Understanding and supporting children with ADHD.* London: Paul Chapman Publishing.

Hyche, K. and Maertz, V. (2014). *Classroom strategies for children with ADHD, autism and sensory processing disorders: Solutions for behavior, attention and emotional regulation.* Eau Claire, WI: PESI Publishing & Media.

Kewley, G. (2011). *Attention deficit hyperactivity disorder.* 3rd ed. Milton Park, Abingdon, Oxon: Routledge.

Konrad, K. and Eickhoff, S.B. (2010). Is the ADHD brain wired differently? A review on structural and functional connectivity in attention deficit hyperactivity disorder. *Human Brain Mapping,* 31, pp. 904–916.

Kuntsi, J., Eley, T., Taylor, A., Hughes, C., Asherson, P., Caspi, A. and Moffitt, T. (2003). Co-occurrence of ADHD and low IQ has genetic origins. *American Journal of Medical Genetics*, 124B(1), pp. 41–47.

Lewis-Morton, R., Dallos, R., McClelland, L. and Clempson, R. (2014). 'There is something not quite right with brad…': The ways in which families construct ADHD before receiving a diagnosis. *Contemporary Family Therapy: An International Journal*, 36(2), pp. 260–280.

Miller, B. and Cummings, J. (2007). *The human frontal lobes*. 1st ed. New York: Guilford Press.

Mostafavi, S.A., Mohammadi M.R. and Hosseinzadeh, P. (2012). Dietary intake, growth and development of children with ADHD in a randomized clinical trial of Ritalin and Melatonin co-administration: Through circadian cycle modification or appetite enhancement? *Iran Journal of Psychiatry*, 7, pp. 114–119.

O'Regan, F. (2002). *ADHD*. London: Continuum.

Polanczyk, G., de Lima, M.S., Horta, B.L., Biederman, J. and Rohde, L.A. (2007). The worldwide prevalence of ADHD: A systematic review and metaregression analysis. *The American Journal of Psychiatry*, 164, pp. 942–948.

Radboud University Nijmegen Medical Centre (2017). *Brain differences in ADHD*. Available online at: www.sciencedaily.com/releases/2017/02/170216105919 (Accessed 12/02/2018).

Saul, R. (2014). *ADHD does not exist: The truth about attention deficit and hyperactivity disorder*. New York: HarperCollins.

Shaw, P., Eckstrand, K., Sharp, W., Blumenthal, J., Lerch, J.P., Greenstein, D., Clasen, L., Evans, A.J., Giedd, J. and J.L. Rapoport, J.L. (2007). Attention-deficit/hyperactivity disorder is characterized by a delay in cortical maturation. *PNAS*, 104(49), pp. 19649–19654.

Sikstrom, S. and Soderlund, G. (2007). Stimulus-dependent dopamine release in attention-deficit/hyperactivity disorder. *Psychological Review*, 114(4), pp. 1047–1075.

Singh, I. (2012). Brain-talk: Power and negotiation in children's discourse about self, brain and behaviour. *Sociology of Health and Illness*, 35(6), pp. 813–827.

Sousa, D. (2001). *How the brain learns*. 2nd ed. New York: Corwin Press.

Spohrer, K. (2002). *Supporting children with ADHD*. Birmingham: Questions Pub.

Valera, E., Faraone, V., Murray, K. and Seidman, L. (2007). Meta-analysis of structural imaging findings in attention-deficit/hyperactivity disorder. *Biological Psychiatry*, 61, pp. 1361–1369.

Volkow, N., Fowler, J., Logan, J., Alexoff, D., Zhu, W., Telang, F., Wang, G., Jayne, M., Hooker, J., Wong, C., Hubbard, B., Carter, P., Warner, D., King, P., Shea, C., Xu, Y., Muench, L. and Apelskog-Torres, K. (2009). Effects of modafinil on dopamine and dopamine transporters in the male human brain. *JAMA*, 301(11), p. 1148.

Wedge, M. (2012). Why French kids don't have ADHD. *Psychology Today*, 8 March (Blog: Suffer the Children).

Wolraich, M., Milich, R., Stumbo, P. and Schultz, F. (1985). Effects of sucrose ingestion on the behavior of hyperactive boys. *Journal of Pediatrics*, 106, pp. 675–682.

World Health Organization (2018). *ICD-11. 6A05 attention deficit hyperactivity disorder*. Available online at: https://icd.who.int/browse11/l-m/en#/http%3a%2f%2fid.who.int%2ficd%2fentity%2f821852937 (Accessed 21/08/2018).

Yarney, S. (2013). *Can I tell you about ADHD? A guide for friends, family and professionals*. London: Jessica Kingsley Publishers.

10 Dyslexia

Introduction

The term dyslexia originally came from the Greek terms 'dys', which meant impairment and 'lexis', which translated into the modern word 'dyslexia' (Brunswick, 2009). There are multiple definitions related to this learning difficulty, so dyslexia can be simply defined as a neurobiological impairment within the brain, which causes an individual to struggle more than their peers in reading, spelling and writing (Mather and Wendling, 2012). This, however, does not mean the individual struggles to learn but due to a lack of reading experience, it could potentially limit their vocabulary throughout their life. In addition to this, the brain receives information and cognitively processes this differently compared to someone who does not live with the learning difficulty. This chapter aims to:

- identify how dyslexia is viewed as a difficulty or a difference in learning
- identify some common misunderstandings applied to the concept of dyslexia
- review the characteristics of dyslexia
- discuss how DSM-V and ICD-11 view the classification and diagnosis of dyslexia
- outline the view that dyslexia is a deficit or difference in cognitive processing
- summarise the biological factors associated with dyslexia, including the role of genetics and neurobiology
- review the role of environmental and risk factors
- relate the characteristics of dyslexia to a number of theories and explanations relating to neuroanatomy
- introduce the contrasting views held by Snowling and Elliot and Gibbs, about the nature of dyslexia
- discuss the role of cognitive explanations of dyslexia

■ review a range of classroom strategies aimed at supporting the characterises of dyslexia

■ provide a list of websites to support practice when working with pupils in a range of SEND contexts.

Dyslexia spells trouble

The cause, and indeed the existence of dyslexia, is often debated (Knight and Hynd, 2002) with some forms of dyslexia occurring alongside other learning difficulties, such as Attention Deficit Hyperactivity Disorder (ADHD) or Autism (Hall, 2009). Dyslexia can be either acquired, where language skills have developed typically and injuries or illness affecting the brain has caused them to deteriorate, or developmental, where language difficulties are present from birth (Pumfrey, 2001). Dyslexia is a specific learning disability, primarily involving literacy skills, and lies at the opposite end of the Special Educational Needs (SEN)spectrum to Profound and Multiple Learning Difficulties and many would argue that it is not a deficit but a difference in the way the brain processes information. This is an important point when discussing the concept of dyslexia and will be discussed later in this chapter.

What is dyslexia? A disorder manifested by difficulty in learning to read despite conventional instruction, adequate intelligence and sociocultural opportunity (Critchley, 1970). There is discrepancy between students' evident oral abilities and their written language performance, the persistence of difficulties in acquiring the skills of reading, writing and/or spelling, and other patterns of difficulty (Klein, 1993, p. 7). However, there ia a view that dyslexia is a myth invented by education chiefs to cover up poor teaching methods (Stringer, 2009); dyslexia, as commonly understood, is a myth and a myth which hides the scale and scandal of true reading disability (Elliott, 2005).

A more recent approach is to use the term 'neurodiversity' thought to have been coined in the 1990s by Judy Singer (an autism activist), which was originally used by the autistic community, who were keen to move away from the medical model. The idea of neurodiversity has now been embraced by many other groups, who are using the term as a means of empowerment and to promote the positive qualities possessed by those with a neurological difference. It encourages people to view neurological differences such as autism, dyslexia and dyspraxia as natural and normal variations in the human genome. Further, it encourages them to reject the culturally entrenched negativity, which has typically surrounded those who live, learn and view the world differently (Armstrong, 2011). Thus, the traditional view of dyslexia as a 'problem' is being challenged. The fact that dyslexia causes difficulties in processing information is generally accepted. Some now suggest that the neurological differences found in people with dyslexia may confer advantages for some individuals. This may explain the apparent paradox that some individuals who have problems with elementary skills such as reading and writing can be highly gifted in other areas. Dyslexia is increasingly being recognised as a difference in cognition and learning rather than a deficit.

Pause for reflection

Common misunderstandings:

1. writing letters backwards is a flag for dyslexia

2. reading difficulties are caused by visual perception problems

3. if given enough time, students will outgrow it

4. more boys than girls are dyslexic

5. only affects English speakers

6. coloured overlays will benefit all pupil with dyslexia

7. dyslexia can be cured.

- Have you come across these or other comments within your practice?

- Where were such comments derived from?

Characteristics of dyslexia

There may be associated difficulties in such areas as phonological processing, short-term memory sequencing, number skills, motor function, organisational ability and visual disturbance (Snowling, 2006). The main characteristic that is most common in individuals living with dyslexia is that of reduced literacy skills, which can vary across a level of severity (Pavey, 2016), from mild to severe. However, Williams and Lynch (2010) state that other characteristics such as difficulty in learning to speak, confusion surrounding different vowels and struggling to determine which way letters and numbers face are other common characteristics of an individual with dyslexia. As well as there being many characteristics of dyslexia, there are also at least four different types of Specific Learning Difficulty/Disorder (SpLD) that a child or adult could be living with, such as dysgraphia, dyscalculia, orthographic dyslexia and phonological dyslexia. An individual may have one of these independently or they can coexist as part of a wider profile. We can divide the types of dyslexia into a number of categories, for example, by the sensory system implicated which includes auditory or visual dyslexia; by deficit which includes phonological, surface and deep dyslexia; by time of onset such as developmental and acquired dyslexia; and others including dyscalculia. Examples of the different types are given in Table 10.1.

Table 10.1 Specific learning difficulties

Specific learning difficulty	Characteristics
Dysgraphia	Dysgraphia is related to an individual's ability to write down words presented to them; a slower pace than their peers and often-inaccurate formation of the words presented usually accompanies this learning difficulty. Letters may not be fully formed, with uneven spaces between words and spelling and reading abilities may also be affected
Dyscalculia	Dyscalculia is based around mathematics, an individual living with dyscalculia will have the ability to read, write and spell but will struggle with the concepts that surround maths, such as number and calculations. The rules of mathematics may also be confusing
Phonological dyslexia	Phonological dyslexia, this is when a person struggles to isolate words within sentences and the sounds within the words (Jamieson and Morgan, 2008). It is concerned with auditory processing difficulties, as individuals find it difficult to link sounds and spellings of words
Orthographic dyslexia	Orthographic dyslexia relates to an inability to identify and work with spelling patterns due to issues of memory and coding difficulties (Rapcsak et al., 2009; Nordqvist, 2017).

Classification and diagnosis

In DSM-V, dyslexia is included in the category 'Specific Learning Disorder' (SLD) and is described as problems with accurate or fluent word recognition, poor decoding and poor spelling abilities, difficulties with reading comprehension or math reasoning (American Psychiatric Association, 2013). According to DSM-V, SpLD is a type of neurodevelopmental disorder that impedes a person's ability to learn and use specific academic skills, such as reading, writing and arithmetic, which serve as the foundation for most other academic learning. SLD is a clinical diagnosis and is not necessarily synonymous with 'learning difficulties' identified by the education system. DSM refers to three SLDs: impairment in reading, impairment in the written expression and impairment in mathematics, described by subskills – are now part of the DSM-V. Three subcomponents of the reading disorder are expressly differentiated: word reading accuracy, reading rate, and fluency and reading comprehension. Impaired subskills of the SLD with impairment in written expression are spelling accuracy, grammar and punctuation accuracy, and clarity and organisation of written expression. The diagnosis is based on a variety of methods, including medical history, clinical interview, school report, teacher evaluation, rating scales and psychometric tests. The IQ discrepancy criterion has been abandoned, though that of age or class discrepancy criterion was retained.

ICD-11 (WHO, 2018) refers to Developmental Learning Disorder with subsections. These include Developmental Learning Disorder with impairment in reading.

Dyslexia is included within this section which is characterised by significant and persistent difficulties in learning academic skills related to reading, such as word reading accuracy, reading fluency and reading comprehension. The individual's performance in reading is markedly below what would be expected for chronological age and level of intellectual functioning and results in significant impairment in the individual's academic or occupational functioning. Developmental Learning Disorder with impairment in reading is not due to a disorder of intellectual development, sensory impairment (vision or hearing), neurological disorder, lack of availability of education, lack of proficiency in the language of academic instruction or psychosocial adversity. The other subsections are:

■ developmental learning disorder with impairment in written expression

■ developmental learning disorder with impairment in mathematics

■ developmental learning disorder with other specified impairment of learning

■ developmental learning disorder, unspecified.

Pause for reflection

■ Do the differing classification systems have any impact on how practitioners and pupils might view dyslexia?

Difference or deficit?

Although there may be some difficulties, for example, learning to work with symbols such as letters or numerals, there are positive traits also associated with dyslexia (Table 10.2).

Table 10.2 Difficulties and strengths associated with dyslexia

Difficulties	Strengths
Reading	Problem-solving
Writing (expressive writing and actual style)	Art, design and creativity
Articulation	Computing
Spelling	Spatial awareness
Coordination	Lateral thinking
Difficulties in working memory and long-term memory	Learning from experience
Organisation and sequencing	Problem-solving
Visual difficulties (blurring of letters, missing lines or words when reading, distortion of letters and letters merging together)	Vocabulary
Phonological difficulties (mindfulness of sounds and the appearances of these sounds in words)	Critical thinking and reasoning
Comprehension	

Within the SEND Code of Practice 0–25 (2015) (DfE, 2015), dyslexia is identified in Section 6.31 as a SpLD, affecting one or more specific aspects of learning, encompassing a range of conditions such as dyslexia, dyscalculia and dyspraxia.

 Activity

Read the following definitions of dyslexia:

1. Dyslexia is a specific learning disability that is neurobiological in origin. It is characterised by difficulties with accurate and/or fluent word recognition and by poor spelling and decoding abilities. These difficulties typically result from a deficit in the phonological component of language that is often unexpected in relation to other cognitive abilities and the provision of effective classroom instruction. Secondary consequences may include problems in reading comprehension and reduced reading experience that can impede growth of vocabulary and background knowledge (International Dyslexia Association, 2002).

2. The British Dyslexia Association's (BDA) definition adopted in Sir Jim Rose's Report (2009) state that dyslexia is a learning difficulty that primarily affects the skills involved in accurate and fluent word reading and spelling. Characteristic features of dyslexia are difficulties in phonological awareness, verbal memory and verbal processing speed. It is best thought of as a continuum, not a distinct category, and there are no clear cut-off points and it occurs across the range of intellectual abilities; it is not a disease to be cured, nor do people 'grow out' of it (BDA, 2018a).

■ What model(s) of disability do these statements support?

■ What messages do these definitions relay to the individual living with dyslexia?

The BDA (2018a) identifies a general range or cluster of issues which might indicate dyslexia, including difficulty with learning to read and/or write despite intervention; slow speed of processing spoken and/or written language; poor word retrieval and left/right confusion. Miles and Miles (1990) in Riddick (2000) suggest that the following are the key indicators for primary age pupils:

■ confuses left and right

■ difficulty in saying long words

■ difficulty in mental subtraction

■ difficulty in learning tables

- difficulty in saying the months of the year

- confuses b and d for longer than most children

- difficulty in recalling a chain of events

- family history of similar difficulties

- difficulty in tasks involving reading, writing and spelling

- reading age behind chronological age.

Biological factors associated with dyslexia

Genetics

Developmental dyslexia runs in families, and twin studies have confirmed that there is a substantial genetic contribution to poor reading. The way in which discoveries in molecular genetics are reported can be misleading, encouraging us to think that there are specific genes that might be used to screen for disorder. However, dyslexia is not a classic Mendelian disorder that is caused by a mutation in a single gene. Rather, like many other common disorders, it appears to involve combined effects of many genes and environmental factors, each of which has a small influence, possibly supplemented by rare variants that have larger effects but apply to only a minority of cases.

According to the UK's Dyslexia Research Trust (BDA, 2018b), a non-profit organisation that supports research into learning disabilities, chromosomes 6 and 18 have been implicated in dyslexia. For example, they looked at 50 genetic markers within 15 brain-expressed genes located on chromosome 6, finding strong associations between one particular gene, named KIAA0319, and low performance in tests for reading, spelling, orthography and phonology.

Research is beginning to identify the contribution of genetics to dyslexia, for example, four genes which contribute to verbal communication, phonology and memory difficulties associated with dyslexia have been recently discovered (Becker et al., 2017). Mueller et al. (2014) suggest that there are nine loci, fixed positions on a chromosome, which have an impact in relation to the learning difficulty of dyslexia situated on chromosome 18. Twin studies have shown that 84 per cent 0f Monozygotic (MZ) twins had a history of a reading difficulty, while 29 per cent of Dizygotic (DZ) twins had a history of reading difficulties (Mather and Wendling, 2012). In support of this Snowling, Gallagher and Frith (2003) cited by Marinac and Harris (2008) stated that 61 per cent of children with a family history of reading difficulties had one themselves, whereas 13.8 per cent of children with no family history of a reading difficulty had one themselves, leading Swagerman et al. (2015) to conclude that genetics were the primary cause of dyslexia, and that environmental factors did not have any effect.

Neurobiological factors

There is now a great deal of evidence to support the theories that dyslexia is caused by the brain and neurobiology (Reid, 2011). One theory is that the cerebellum is involved. This is because it does not finish developing until after birth and is involved in an individual's ability to read. Another theory is that magnocellular neurons may develop atypically, affecting reading and causing words to look blurred as they are involved with visual processes. However, there is evidence to suggest that this may not be the case for all with dyslexia (Stein, 2008, cited in Reid, 2011). A theory that has been researched many times is that the brain develops differently in individuals with dyslexia, causing problems with phonology and processing systems (Galaburda et al., 2006). In order to analyse the structure of the brain, studies have been conducted through MRI scans and through looking at post-mortem brains. These studies have shown that individuals with dyslexia do have differently structured brains to those who do not have dyslexia, and that the difference occurs during the development of the brain (Knight and Hynd, 2002). Studies have also been carried out on individuals who have had brain injuries that have affected their speech and language abilities, to determine the processes within the brain that control the difficulties experienced by individuals with dyslexia (Young and Tyre, 1983). These studies have found that the brain consists of the left and right hemispheres, and each hemisphere has a specific function (Reid, 2011).

The right hemisphere controls visual processes and the left hemisphere controls language processes, such as those found to be difficult in individuals with dyslexia and is typically larger and more developed (Young and Tyre 1983; Reid 2011). Because of this, reading involves both hemispheres working together effectively (Robertson and Bakker, 2002). Individuals with dyslexia often have difficulty with functions of the left hemisphere, but excel in those of the right hemisphere, leading researchers to believe that these individuals are more reliant on their right hemisphere. However, there is much debate about whether this is due to incomplete development of the left hemisphere, or overdevelopment of the right hemisphere. Additionally, Breznitz (2008), cited in Reid (2011), suggests that individuals with dyslexia have difficulty passing information between the two hemispheres. This could be due to nerve cells forming in excess, leading signals to be sent down the wrong pathways. Protopapas and Parrila (2018) disagree with the theory that dyslexia is caused by the atypical development of the brain, as they believe the brain is not for reading, and that it is the over-reliance on reading in society that is the issue.

Brunswick (2011) suggests that the dyslexic brain could be viewed as functioning differently to neurotypical brain, as it is 'wired' differently. There are three differences in the brain of dyslexic individuals compared to the brains of non-dyslexic individuals: first, the dyslexic brain is almost perfectly symmetrical, opposed to a non-dyslexic brain, which will have one side of the brain larger than the other, although Hammond and Hercules (2007) state that individuals who are dyslexic tend to be right brain thinkers, which involves creativity. Second, there are smaller neurons in the thalamus, which affects the timing of how information is transmitted across all the networks in the brain. Finally, they stated that multiple nerve cells have been found in bundles in areas of the brain, which usually will not have nerve cell bodies. All of these changes alter the brain and how it is wired, meaning that the individual living with this learning difficulty will struggle with their reading, writing and spelling as a cause of this.

Theories relating to the neuroanatomy of dyslexia

There are a number of theories which aim to suggest how the neuroanatomy of the brain is linked to dyslexia. Below are a number of these, and while it is a comprehensive list, it does give a flavour of the development of research into the causes of dyslexia.

Rapid auditory processing theory (Tallal and Piercy, 1973)
This theory specifies that the primary deficit lies in the perception of short or rapidly varying sounds. Support for this theory arises from evidence that dyslexics show poor performance on a number of auditory tasks, including frequency and temporal order judgement. The failure to correctly represent short sounds and fast transitions would cause further difficulties in particular when such acoustic events are the cues to phonemic contrasts.

Phonological theory (Bradley and Bryant, 1983)
This explains that the origin of the disorder is a congenital dysfunction of left-hemisphere brain areas underlying phonological representations or connecting between phonological and orthographic representations. The phonological theory postulates that dyslexics have a specific impairment in the representation, storage and/or retrieval of speech sounds. Reading impairment evident in some dyslexic learners may be due to the fact that learning to read an alphabetic system requires the learning the grapheme–phoneme correspondence. If these sounds are poorly represented, stored or retrieved, the learning of grapheme–phoneme correspondences, the foundation of reading for alphabetic systems, will be affected accordingly.

Visual theory (Lovegrove et al., 1980)
This explains that the disorder is a visual impairment giving rise to difficulties with the processing of letters and words on a page of text. This may take the form of unstable binocular fixations, poor vergence or increased visual crowding. The visual theory does not exclude a phonological deficit, but emphasises a visual contribution to reading problems, at least in some dyslexic individuals. The magnocellular pathway is selectively

disrupted in certain dyslexic individuals, leading to deficiencies in visual processing, abnormal binocular control and visuospatial attention.

Cerebellar theory (Nicolson and Fawcett, 1990)

Here the claim is that the dyslexic's cerebellum is in motor control and therefore in speech articulation. It is postulated that retarded or dysfunctional articulation would lead to deficient phonological representations mildly dysfunctional and that a number of cognitive difficulties ensue. Evidence of poor performance of dyslexics in a large number of motor tasks in dual tasks demonstrating impaired automatisation of balance and, in time estimation, a non-motor cerebellar task, is shown by brain imaging studies, they have also shown anatomical, metabolic and activation differences.

The insula-disconnection syndrome (Paulesu et al., 1996)

The Wernicke's and Broca's areas of the brain works in isolation in dyslexic individuals, so instead of rapidly knowing what a written word sounds like, they have to think about each word they see and consciously translate it from one form to another. The insula-disconnection syndrome is related to the Wernicke's area linked to speech and understanding written and spoken words and Broca's area which is related to the production of language, but in people with dyslexia these two areas do not collaborate with each other. Therefore, compared to an a neurotypical brain, it does not know immediately what a written word sounds like and instead each word must be thought about and translated from one form to another.

Magnocellular theory (Stein and Walsh, 1997)

This is a unifying theory that attempts to integrate all the findings mentioned in the previous theories. A generalisation of the visual theory, the magnocellular theory postulates that the magnocellular dysfunction is not restricted to the visual pathways but is generalised to all modalities (visual and auditory as well as tactile). The theory proposes that the visual, learning and processing problems found in dyslexia may be caused by a deficit in the magnocellular pathway to the brain, and that dyslexia therefore it is not a processing disorder but a sensory one. This theory claims that the underlying cause of literacy problems in dyslexia is not language specific but a more general impairment of the visual/auditory magnocellular system. Through a single biological cause, this theory therefore manages to account for all known manifestations of dyslexia: visual, auditory, tactile, motor and, consequently, phonological.

Elliott and Grigorenko (2014) do not query whether biologically based reading difficulties exist, but rather how we should best understand and address literacy problems as one of the factors; the problem is the word itself and suggests that the term 'construct reading disability' is preferable.

Activity

The dyslexia debate

Snowling (2008) suggested that dyslexia is a major obstacle to success, which can result in educational failure and economic disadvantage. She reports that there is a consensus definition characterised by difficulties with accurate and/or fluent word recognition and by poor spelling and decoding abilities. These difficulties typically result from a deficit in the phonological component of language that is often unexpected in relation to other cognitive abilities and the provision of effective classroom instruction (International Dyslexia Association, 2002). Dyslexia is primarily a phonological impairment sometimes linked to short-term memory and poor phonological awareness, with evidence of visual and auditory processing difficulties.

With regard to the aetiology of dyslexia, she suggests that there seems to be a genetic link, but it is difficult to pin down given the influence of the environment. The plasticity of the brain means that some people may be compensate for cognitive or neurological deficits, so it is difficult to track down a link between brain structure and reading difficulty. Neuroscience has shown structural brain differences between people with dyslexia and controls with less activity in some regions (temporoparietal regions) although we do not know whether there is a direct causal link between brain differences and dyslexia due to brain plasticity.

She argues that the nature and consequences of dyslexia are well understood, but we need to know what causes it. We need to research the varied developmental trajectories that lead to reading impairment. We need to identify the dyslexic type earlier, so that we can research the genes and brains and children earlier. In adulthood, its consequences are reported to include unemployment and criminal behaviour, with dyslexia presented as a factor in a sad and tragic life that needs to be identified, treated and possibly eradicated early.

In contrast to this view, Elliott and Gibbs (2008) are sceptical about the value and validity of the dyslexia construct and they ask whether it has clinical (identification, observation and treatment) or educational value. They question whether it is a discrete, identifiable and diagnosable condition and argue that it might be more useful to remove the subgroup 'dyslexia' and consider all learners with reading difficulties equally. The authors raise concerns about the fairness of allocating resources to those with a label of 'dyslexia' in ways that might leave those with reading difficulties (and without the label) less supported. They are concerned about the lack of moral and theoretical justification for this and seek to expose the lack of scientific support for the specificity of dyslexia (in terms of its diagnosis, characteristics and teaching approaches).

For them, dyslexia is viewed as an arbitrarily and largely socially defined construct with no clear-cut scientific basis for differential diagnosis of dyslexia versus poor reader versus reader. At various times and for various reasons, it has been a social convenience to label some people as dyslexic, but consequences of the labelling include stigma, disenfranchisement and inequitable use of resources (perhaps this is most disadvantageous for poor readers not diagnosed as dyslexic). The social, cognitive and behavioural phenomena associated with the construct remain important and fascinating issues. Proper educational response is, however, hindered by the false dichotomy between dyslexia and non-dyslexia. Let us not ask, 'Does dyslexia exist?' Let us instead concentrate upon ensuring that all children with literacy difficulties are served.

- Which models of SEND (and hence discourses) do these authors adhere to?
- What do they suggest should be the way forward when working with pupils with literacy difficulties?
- What do they suggest is the potential impact of dyslexia on an individual's life-course?

Cognitive explanations of dyslexia

There are a number of cognitive abilities which individuals with dyslexia may struggle with, including phonology, speed of processing and working memory (Reid, 2011), and dyslexia is a condition that impinges strongly upon cognitive functioning, affecting performance across a wide range of domains. Dyslexic deficits in simple verbal memory span seem to suggest that not only do dyslexic people have problems with storing information in working memory, but also with processing that information and that this working memory issues continues into adulthood, even in high-achieving individuals (Smith-Spark and Fisk, 2007).

Executive functions allow self-regulation and the enactment of goal-directed behaviour, permitting the coordination of different cognitive processes over time. They include such higher-order cognitive abilities as planning, problem-solving, organising behaviour, sequencing, self-monitoring, inhibiting verbal and motor responses, accessing information in long-term memory in a controlled and flexible manner, adapting responses to changes in task or environmental demands, dual-task management, and ensuring that task-relevant information is retained over the duration for which it is needed (Pennington and Ozonoff, 1996; Andrés, 2003; Fisk and Sharp, 2004). Research also suggests that executive functioning impairments in dyslexia which are present in childhood continue into adulthood (Brosnan et al., 2002).

Environmental and risk factors

The home and school environment might also have an impact on the issues seen in dyslexia For example, reading aloud to young children so they can hear the words, rather than just reading them themselves, benefits the children with their reading development in the future. Children at family risk of dyslexia are exposed to more risks than children not at family risk with the home literacy environment being an important predictor of reading readiness, together with child health, and it also predicts attention and behaviour together with family stresses (Dilnot et al., 2017). One risk factor that has been discussed is glue ear, which is common is infants, caused by catarrh, which blocks passages within the ear. Treatment for this can lead an individual to have delayed speech and language development. Peer (2005) describes the symptoms of glue ear, one of which is that it can cause individuals to confuse letters within words; individuals with dyslexia may also experience this difficulty; however, there is no evidence to suggest that glue ear causes dyslexia.

In conclusion, there is little to no evidence pointing to environmental causes of dyslexia, such as drinking during pregnancy, contact with heavy metals, etc. Children raised in impoverished reading environments can present as dyslexic, but respond very quickly to intervention, as long as they are caught at a relatively young age. Acquired forms of dyslexia (trauma, stroke) could be considered environmental in origin, but are really a different reading problem altogether.

Classroom strategies

Key strategies to support pupils can be divided into the following areas:

- key strategies for reading
- key strategies for spelling
- key strategies for writing
- strategies to support working memory difficulties
- strategic planning (adapted from NASEN, 2018).

Reading

Pupils with dyslexia can become fluent readers, although the speed at which they read and their ability to comprehend long, complex texts can remain impaired. They may have to read a text several times to reach the same level of understanding as other students. These are not exhaustive lists; but strategies to support reading difficulties include:

- only ask a pupil to read aloud if you know they want to
- ensure that books are at the right level of difficulty for pupils
- use audio books when appropriate
- teach reading skills, such as skimming, scanning and closed reading, and when to use them

■ limit the quantity of reading they have to do by guiding pupils to relevant strategies

■ provide texts before the lesson so that pupils can prepare for them

■ encourage pupils to condense and make sense of what they read, for example, by making mind maps and drawing diagrams and flow charts

■ use paired reading approaches.

Spelling

Spelling will remain a persistent difficulty for pupils with dyslexia. It is important that spelling difficulties do not impede pupils' creativity and ability to demonstrate their knowledge. It is important to encourage the use of ambitious words and teach pupils to spell key curricular words.

■ provide subject-specific key words in classroom handouts

■ encourage the use of personalised dictionaries

■ encourage pupils to take risks with their spelling, suggesting that they underline these words

■ teach the spelling of key words in a multisensory way

■ encourage a metacognitive approach by asking pupils to: analyse the spelling mistakes and identify the learning required, decide what they will change to ensure that they spell that word correctly in future.

Writing

Writing is a difficult medium for pupils with dyslexia to demonstrate their knowledge, understanding and creativity. They find it hard to interpret the questions and understand how much to write and what to include. Other barriers to writing include spelling, sequencing ideas, grammar and remembering their ideas long enough to record them. The time, effort and lack of awareness make proofreading a challenging conclusion to the process.

■ check understanding of the task

■ use collaborative learning

■ use Information and Communication Technology (ICT) to improve written outcomes, for example, voice recognition software or mind-mapping software

- teach 'questioning the question' approaches, for example, isolating the topic area, limiting words and directives
- provide a glossary of directives
- break down a writing task into manageable chunks
- give specific feedback at each stage so the pupils know what to repeat or improve
- provide written and verbal feedback.

Working memory

A working memory deficit will impair a pupil's ability to engage in the lesson and to make progress. Research has consistently demonstrated the adverse academic consequences for pupils with a weak working memory. Teachers can reduce these difficulties by using the following strategies:

- Teach using an integrated multi-sensory approach throughout the lesson.
- Revisit previous learning at the beginning of the lesson, allowing pupils to recall and make associations with new learning.
- Give an overview of the lesson so the pupils can see the outcome and make sense of the content.
- Revisit learning at regular intervals throughout the lesson.
- 'Chunk' the information being taught and check understanding.
- Use a step-by-step approach to complete a task.
- Explain the steps and use pictures where needed.
- When giving instructions, limit the number, repeat them and provide notes and a checklist.
- Use simple, concise sentences.
- Omit unnecessary words so that the instruction is succinct.
- Where possible, use alternative words and give explanations of key words.
- Allow time for the pupils to process the information and answer.

(NASEN, 2018)

Activity

The BDA (2018) suggest that specific indicators around neurodiversity could include areas around written work and reading. These can be accessed via their website.

■ How many of the indicators have you seen in pupils who have a diagnosis of dyslexia and those who do not?

■ By adapting the SEND Code of Practice (2015) of Quality First Teaching, how might you begin to support pupils with these indicators? Would it make any difference if they have a label of 'dyslexia'?

 Activity

There are three types of provision we could make within the classroom:

1. accommodations such as changes to amount of time given to complete a task, additional resources, differing types of questioning, etc.

2. compensations such as personal dictionaries, screen readers, etc.

3. skills such as over teaching and over learning of specific basic skills.

   ● Can you give any specific examples from your practice, of how these may be used to support a pupil with dyslexia?

   ● Describe how they worked and what was the outcome?

There are a number of specific strategies, which aim to support classroom practice, including the following:

 Activity

Multisensory teaching
The use of visual, auditory and kinesthetic information to improve the reading and generally the learning ability has a long history (Thomson, 1990). The use of multisensory teaching can help dyslexic children become independent learners and boost their self-esteem and children are encouraged to believe in themselves and to become independent learners from an early age. A recording of how the use of multisensory teaching can help dyslexic children become independent learners and boost their self-esteem can be accessed via the TES (2018) website.

Repetition approach

Repetition, the implementation of multisensory techniques and the word identification strategies are the essential factors in order to acquire reading ability. The repetitive reading of a certain text with the guidance of a computer, an educator or even another auditor has proven effective at the early years of education. There are two ways of effective repetition, the echo reading where the student repeats what he/she hears from the teacher or a fellow student and the co-operative reading where the pupil reads paired with a non-dyslexic student. O'Shea, Sindelar and O'Shea (1987) found that pupils with dyslexia who read texts seven times in a row obtain more fluency than children who read it three times.

ARROW

The Aural-Read-Respond-Oral-Write (ARROW) approach is a multisensory learning system (Lane, 2007) who suggested that when someone hears his/her own voice reads comprehension is improved. During this programme, children with dyslexia record their voices on a computer while reading a small text and play them back. Then they write down exactly what they heard. The programme is advised to take part 30 minutes a day for a sum of ten hours (Nugent, 2010).

Information on the ARROW programme can be accessed via the Arrowtuition (2018) website.

Peer reading

Peer reading is an intervention model where the dyslexic student who has reading difficulties is paired to a non-professional, who reads to the student, reads simultaneously with him/her and then listens and guides the student. In this way, the student will understand the meaning of the text and enjoy the reading procedure (Reid, 2009) as pupils gain in confidence and fluency.

Information on this approach can be accessed via the Drgavinread (2018) website.

- Consider the usefulness of the strategies suggested by the differing approaches.

- Have you used any of these within your own practice?

The role of metacognition

Pupils with dyslexia may have difficulty with the metacognitive aspects of learning. This implies that they need to be shown how to learn, for example, through identifying connections and relationships between different learning tasks. This essentially means the emphasis should not only be on the content or the product of learning but also on the process – that is, how learning takes place.

Strategies for developing metacognition in reading include:

1. Teacher-modelling, in which the teacher demonstrates the application of a reading strategy, such as self-questioning or summarising, explaining both the procedure for implementing the strategy, and the purpose and utility of the strategy.

2. Think-alouds, in which the pupil verbalises his/her processing as they read a text.

3. Reciprocal teaching, in which the teacher and pupil(s) take turns at (a) asking questions during reading, (b) summarising the text at appropriate points, (c) clarifying what has been read, noting any inconsistencies and (d) predicting the next part of the text.

4. Semantic mapping, in which the pupil uses a teacher-made graphic representation or mind map as a guide to the organisation of the material in the text and how the ideas of the content are related. Later, the pupil learns to mind map the text's content while they read.

 Activity

The following links contain a wealth of resources and support for practitioners who work with dyslexic pupils.

▪ How could you use any of the resources to support both the pupils you work with and your own professional practice?

Dyslexia Style Guide 2018: Creating Dyslexia Friendly Content can be accessed via the BDA (2018c) website.

A new mobile site quality assured by the British Dyslexia Association (BDA) and the result of a project funded by the Department for Education contains a range of videos and other resources that can be accessed via the dyslex.io (2018) website.

As a committee of the BDA, BDAtech have been concerned with all aspects of technology and how they can assist dyslexic people. Its website is a wealth of information on accessibility and the different types of technology available and can be accessed via the BDAtech (2018) website.

The Train the Trainer: Teaching for Neurodiversity project was funded by the Department for Education and ran until 31 March 2017. It was led by the BDA in partnership with the Dyspraxia Foundation, Dyslexia Action, Helen Arkell, Manchester Metropolitan University and Patoss. The aim of the project was to provide training and quality-assured information about dyslexia and other SpLD for teachers and support staff, and for dyslexic individuals and their families. The materials are broken down into the following sections:

■ Seeing the whole picture

■ Understanding neurodiversity

■ Dyslexia Action: Understanding neurodiversity Post 16/FE

■ Dyslexia Action: Train the Trainer Classroom support strategies

■ Teaching for Neurodiversity, Classroom support strategies (Secondary)

■ Teaching for Neurodiversity Classroom support strategies (Post 16/FE)

The webinars and resources can be accessed via the BDA (2018d) website.

Summary

There are fewer areas within the SEND arena, where practitioners offer differing views about the origin and support given, than the discourses surrounding dyslexia. Many people who are said to living with or have lived with dyslexia, such as Albert Einstein, celebrity chef Jamie Oliver, businessmen Richard Branson and popular crime novelist Agatha Christie, are often held up as examples of individuals who despite having dyslexia, have 'overcome' the difficulties. However, there is no agreement among experts as to what dyslexia even is, nor is there a universal definition of dyslexia. Is it about the experience of having reading difficulties despite having normal cognitive abilities and access to high-quality, evidence-based interventions, or a synonym for 'poor reading'. People with dyslexia, according to this group, have reading abilities in the bottom 5 per cent–10 per cent of the population and for most people diagnosed with dyslexia, reading difficulties can cast a long shadow in their lives. Some authors have stopped using the word dyslexia altogether, while others refer to it as a 'learning difference'. Not only is there a debate around the definition of dyslexia, but one also surrounds the way in which we support pupils. The label of dyslexia may allow individuals to access additional support for their education, while others would argue that this diverts vital resources from early intervention for all children with reading problems.

References

American Psychiatric Association (2013). *Specific learning disorder*. Available online at: www.psychiatry.org/patients-families/specific-learning-disorder/what-is-specific-learning-disorder (Accessed 13/05/2018).

Andrés, P. (2003). Frontal cortex as the central executive of working memory: Time to revise our view. *Cortex*, 39(4–5), pp. 871–895.

Armstrong, T. (2011). *The power of neurodiversity: Unleashing the advantages of your differently wired brain*. Cambridge: DaCapo Lifelong/Perseus Books.

Arrowtuition (2018). Available online at: www.arrowtuition.co.uk/arrow-in-schools (Accessed 25/04/2018).

BDAtech (2018). Available online at: https://bdatech.org (Accessed 20/05/2018).

Becker, N., Vasconcelos, M., Oliveira, V., Santos, F.C.D., Bizarro, L., Almeida, R.M.M., Salles, J.F. and Carvalho, M.R.S. (2017). Genetic and environmental risk factors for developmental dyslexia in children: Systematic review of the last decade. *Developmental Neuropsychology*, 42(7–8), pp. 423–445.

Bradley, L. and Bryant, P. (1983). Categorizing sounds and learning to read: A causal connection. *Nature*, 301, pp. 419–421.

British Dyslexia Association (2018a). Available online at www.bdadyslexia.org.uk (Accessed 27/05/2018).

British Dyslexia Association (2018b). *Understanding neurodiversity: A guide to specific learning differences.* Available online at: www.bdadyslexia.org.uk/common/ckeditor/filemanager/userfiles/A_Guide_to_SpLD_2nd_ed.pdf (Accessed 13/07/2018).

British Dyslexia Association (2018c). *Dyslexia style guide 2018: Creating dyslexia friendly content.* Available online at: www.bdadyslexia.org.uk/common/ckeditor/filemanager/userfiles/Dyslexia_Style_Guide_2018-final.pdf (Accessed 21/04/2018).

British Dyslexia Association (2018d). *Train the trainer: Teaching for neurodiversity webinars.* Available online at: www.bdadyslexia.org.uk/about/projects/webinar-recordings (Accessed 26/06/2018).

Brosnan, M., Demetre, J., Hamill, S., Robson, K., Shepherd, H. and Cody, G. (2002). Executive functioning in adults and children with developmental dyslexia. *Neuropsychologia*, 40(12), pp. 2144–2155.

Brunswick, N. (2009). *Dyslexia.* Oxford: Oneworld Publications.

Brunswick, N. (2011). *Living with dyslexia: Contemporary issues.* 1st ed. New York: Rosen Publishing Group.

Critchley, M. (1970). *The dyslexic child.* London: Heinemann.

Department for Education (2015). *Special educational needs and disability code of practice: 0 to 25 years.* Department for Education.

Dilnot, J., Hamilton, L., Maughan, B. and Snowling, M.J. (2017). Child and environmental risk factors predicting readiness for learning in children at high risk of dyslexia. *Development and Psychopathology*, 29, pp. 235–244.

Drgavinread (2018). *Dyslexia: Teaching approaches.* Available online at: www.drgavinreid.com/free-resources/dyslexia-teaching-approaches/ (Accessed 12/06/2018).

Dyslex.io (2018). Available online at: http://dyslex.io (Accessed 09/05/2018).

Elliott, J.G. (2005). The dyslexia debate continues. *The Psychologist*, 18(12), pp. 728–729.

Elliott, J.G. and Gibbs, S. (2008). Does dyslexia exist? *Journal of Philosophy in Education*, 42(3–4), pp. 475–491.

Elliott, J.G. and Grigorenko, E.L. (2014). *Cambridge studies in cognitive and perceptual development. The dyslexia debate.* New York: Cambridge University Press.

Fisk, J. and Sharp, C.A. (2004). Age-related impairment in executive functioning: Updating, inhibition, shifting, and access. *Journal of Clinical and Experimental Neuropsychology*, 26(7), pp. 874–890.

Galaburda, A.M., LoTurco, J., Ramus, F., Fitch, R.H. and Rosen, G.D. (2006). From genes to behavior in developmental dyslexia. *Nature Neuroscience*, 9(10), pp. 1213–1217.

Hammond, J. and Hercules, F. (2007). *Understanding dyslexia. An introduction for dyslexic students in higher education.* Available online at: www.gsa.ac.uk/media/888133/understandingdyslexiaforweb-1-.pdf (Accessed 04/04/2018).

International Dyslexia Association (2002). Definition of dyslexia. Available online at: https://dyslexiaida.org/definition-of-dyslexia/ (Accessed 12/03/2018).

Klein, C. (1993). *Diagnosing dyslexia. A guide to the assessment of adults with specific learning difficulties.* Available online at: https://files.eric.ed.gov/fulltext/ED356398.pdf (Accessed 17/06/2018).

Knight, D.F and Hynd, G.W. (2002). The neurobiology of dyslexia. In Reid, G. and Wearmouth, J. (eds.), *Dyslexia and literacy: Theory and practice.* Chichester: Wiley.

Lovegrove, W.J., Martin, F., Blackwood, M. and Badcock, D. (1980). Specific reading difficulty: Differences in contrast sensitivity as a function of spatial frequency. *Science,* 210, pp. 439–444.

Marinac, J.V. and Harris, C. (2008). *Cracking the code: Making spelling make sense.* Rev. ed., Business and Community Engagement Unit, School of Health and Rehabilitation Sciences, University of Queensland, St Lucia, Qld.

Mather, N. and Wendling, B.J. (2012). *Essentials of dyslexia assessment and intervention.* Hoboken: John Wiley & Sons.

Mueller, B., Ahnert, P., Burkhardt, J., Brauer, J., Czepezauer, I., Quente, E., Boltze, J., Wilcke, A. and Kirsten, H. (2014). Genetic risk variants for dyslexia on chromosome 18 in a German cohort. *Genes, Brain and Behavior,* 13(3), pp. 350–356. doi:10.1111/gbb.12118.

NASEN (2018). Available online at: www.nasen.org.uk (Accessed 11/06/2018).

Nicolson, R.I. and Fawcett, A.J. (1990). Automaticity: A new framework for dyslexia research? *Cognition,* 30, pp. 159–182.

Nordqvist, C. (2017). *What is dyspraxia?* Available online at: www.medicalnewstoday.com/articles/151951.php (Accessed 28/05/2018).

Nugent, M. (2010). Teaching our traveller children to read: An action research project. *Support for Learning,* 25(2), pp. 55–62.

O'Shea, L.J., Sindelar, P.T. and O'Shea, D.J. (1987). The effects of repeated readings and attentional cues on the reading fluency and comprehension of learning disabled readers. *Learning Disabilities Research,* 2(2), pp. 103–109.

Paulesu, E., Frith, C., Snowling, M., Gallagher, A., Morton, J. and Frackowiak, R.S. (1996). Is developmental dyslexia a disconnection syndrome? Evidence from PET scanning. *Brain,* 119, pp. 143–157.

Pavey, B. (2016). *Dyslexia and early childhood.* Abingdon: Routledge.

Peer, L. (2005). *Glue ear: An essential guide for teachers, parents and health professionals.* Abingdon: Routledge.

Pennington, B.F. and Ozonoff, S. (1996). Executive functions and developmental psychopathology. *Child Psychology & Psychiatry & Allied Disciplines,* 37(1), pp. 51–87.

Pumfrey, P. (2001). Specific Developmental Dyslexia (SDD): 'Basics to back' in 2000 and beyond?' In Hunter-Carsch, M. (ed.), *Dyslexia: A psychosocial perspective.* London: Whurr, pp. 137–159.

Rapcsak, S.Z., Beeson, P.M., Henry, M.L., Leyden, A., Kim, E., Rising, K. (2009). Phonological dyslexia and dysgraphia: Cognitive mechanisms and neural substrates. *Cortex,* 45(5), pp. 575–591.

Reid, G. (2009). *The Routledge companion to dyslexia.* London: Routledge.

Reid, G. (2011). *Dyslexia.* 3rd ed. London: Continuum.

Riddick, B. (2000). An examination of the relationship between the labeling and stigmatization with special reference to dyslexia. *Disability and Society,* 15(4), pp. 653–667.

Robertson, J. and Bakker, D.J. (2002). The balance model of reading and dyslexia. In Reid, G. and Wearmouth, J. (eds.), *Dyslexia and literacy: Theory and practice*. London: Wiley, pp. 99–114.

Rose, J. (2009). Identifying and teaching children and young people with dyslexia and literacy difficulties. Available online at: www.thedyslexia-spldtrust.org.uk/media/downloads/inline/the-rose-report.1294933674.pdf (Accessed 25/05/2018).

Smith-Spark, J.H. and Fisk, J.E. (2007). Working memory functioning in developmental dyslexia. *Memory*, 15(1), pp. 34–56.

Snowling, M.J. (2006). *Dyslexia, speech and language*. Chichester: John Wiley.

Snowling, M.J. (2008). *State of science review: SR-D2 dyslexia*. London: The Government Office for Science.

Stein, J. and Walsh, V. (1997). To see but not to read; the magnocellular theory of dyslexia. *Trends in Neurosciences*, 20, pp. 147–152.

Swagerman, S., van Bergen, E., Dolan, C., Geus, E., Koenis, M., Pol, H. and Boomsma, D. (2015). Genetic transmission of reading ability. *Brain and Language*, 172. pp. 3–8.

Tallal, P. and Piercy, M. (1973). Defects of non- verbal auditory perception in children with developmental aphasia. *Nature*, 241, pp. 468–469.

Thomson, M. (1990) *Developmental dyslexia*. 3rd ed. London: Whurr.

Times Educational Supplement (2018). *Teachers TV: Teaching the dyslexic child*. Available online at: www.tes.com/teaching-resource/teachers-tv-teaching-the-dyslexic-child-6049239 (Accessed 01/08/2018).

Williams, J. and Lynch, S. (2010). Dyslexia: What teachers need to know. *Kappa Delta Pi Record*, 46(2), pp. 66–70.

World Health Organization (2018). Available at: www.who.int/classifications/icd/en/ (Accessed 19/07/20180).

Young, P. and Tyre, C. (1983). *Realising the right to read*. Milton Keynes: Open University Press.

Understanding and managing speech, language and communication difficulties

Introduction

Speech, Language and Communication skills are crucial in the development of children and young people and individuals with Speech, Language and Communication Needs (SLCN) often exhibit either language delays or disorders. When looking at atypical language development, the three terms language delay, difficulty and disorder can be used interchangeably (Bennett et al., 2008; Geers et al., 2016). This chapter aims to introduce you to issues surrounding Speech, Language and Communication Development, the impact that this has on an individual and suggestions as to possible supporting strategies. Using evidence from research, along with case studies and questions for reflection, it aims to:

- define the terms Speech, Language and Communication

- outline two approaches in our understanding of language

- identify the differences between language delay and language disorder

- discuss examples of language delay and language disorder

- explore the social and cognitive impact of language delay and language disorder

- suggest possible supporting strategies for individuals experiencing issues with SLCN.

Speech, language and communication

The terms Speech, Language and Communication are often used interchangeably, but are in themselves, different concepts and, without any one of these, individuals may become confused and unable to communicate effectively (Blackburn and Aubrey, 2016). Speech is defined by how words and sounds are produced (McLaughlin, 2011) and includes the use of articulation, voice and fluency. A child may be able to articulate, but can still have difficulties with communication. Speech is defined as the 'ability to co-ordinate the mouth to produce the sounds that make words' (Hayden and Jordan, 2012, p. 9). Having communication skills means that people can form relationships with others through expressing their own feelings and being able to recognise those of others (Mountstephen, 2010). People are able to express their feelings through their language in the particular vocabulary and expression they use.

Language constructs the way in which people communicate and is used to describe a system of symbols that carry meaning and can be separated into two aspects: expressive and receptive language (Bogdashina, 2005). Modes of communication are generally described as either receptive language, which involves receiving and decoding or interpreting language, or expressive language, which is the encoding or production of a message. Communication can be viewed as using language for different functions, including understanding non-verbal communication, whereas the term speech simply covers the use of verbal communication (Browne, 2008; McLaughlin, 2011).

Modular or constructivist?

Modular perspectives posit that language development is controlled by specialised mechanisms, much like the olfactory system evolved to detect, learn and process airborne particles. In this perspective, language learning might be quite independent of other cognitive abilities. By contrast, constructivist and biologically based perspectives tend to emphasise the progressive, experience-dependent emergence of complex skills, including language. These theories postulate that domain-general cognitive capacities and processes are recruited to develop language. The frameworks make distinct predictions: modular theories expect language-specific learning processes and products, while constructivist approaches suggest that we construct language, knowledge and meaning from our experiences.

Fodor (1983) suggests that many psychological processes, including language, are a self-contained set of processes that are independent of other processes with a significant innate basis heavily linked with rules and language-specific processing being in evidence (Harley, 2009). For language to be a distinct module, there must be an identifiable location in the brain that is associated with it, the Broca's area being an example.

In contrast, the constructivist approaches include Piaget and Vygotsky. Vygotsky believed that cognitive processes (for example, language, thought, reasoning) develop through social interaction and that language is necessary for learning and precedes cognitive development (Bigras et al., 2017). He thought that children developed speech and language skills to serve as social skills and once these were internalised they led to higher thinking skills. Language thus has two functions: the receiving of information and the development of thought. Children have 'private' or internal speech – when they talk to themselves as they are engrossed in an activity, for instance. This private speech eventually becomes internalised (inner speech) and thought is the result of language (Shabani, Khatib and Ebadi, 2010).

 Pause for reflection

■ Thinking about the two perspectives to language described above, how would each of these theories impact how practitioners think about language issues within the classroom?

A child's cognitive development progresses by social interactions with others, the so-called social origins of mind (Hasan, 2002), which encourages development through the guidance of skilful adults. Language begins as pre-intellectual speech and gradually develops into a sophisticated form of inner speech, one of the main forces responsible for cognitive development. For Piaget, language is dependent on and springs from cognitive development (Oakley, 2004). That is, children's cognitive development determines their language development (for example, the use of words as 'bigger' or 'more' depends on children's understanding of the concepts they represent). He argued that the developing cognitive understanding is built on the interaction between the child and the things, which can be observed, touched and manipulated. Language was one of a number of symbol systems developed in childhood, rather than a separate module of the mind and can be used to represent knowledge that children have acquired through physical interaction with the environment.

Language delay or language disorder?

Speech and language delay and disorder are common developmental difficulties in childhood, existing in 10 per cent of children aged seven years and below in the UK (Law, Peacey and Radford, 2000). Wallace, Watson and Cullen (2015) identify a speech or language delay as being that a child has developed speech and language in the correct sequence, but at a slower rate than other children of their age, whereas a speech or language disorder means that a child's speech or language ability is significantly different from what is typical of children of their age (Klem et al., 2016). It may surface as a primary difficulty, where it cannot be accounted by any other condition (Stark and Tallal, 1988), or a secondary difficulty (where it can be accounted for by a primary condition such as autism, hearing impairment, behavioural or emotional difficulties or neurological conditions).

Language delay

A child with a language delay will follow the same pattern of language development as their peers but this would be at a slower rate and have a delay in reaching appropriate milestones. Language delays are less severe than language disorders and can often be caused due to issues such as hearing impairment or autism. Additionally, language delays can have a negative impact on children often disturbing their development socially, emotionally and academically (Herman et al., 2016). For example, Schoon et al. (2010) found that those who had language delays in their childhood were more likely to have mental health issues in adulthood. However, Tsybina and Eriks-Brophy (2007) argue that the long-term impact for children with language delays are not as serious as for those with language disorder and delay often occurs early on in their lives, and can be overcome with appropriate support.

Activity

- How would language delay be seen within the classroom?

- What support strategies might be beneficial for pupils with language delay?

Speech, language and communication needs

Learning to speak is one of the first ways children learn to communicate (Beuker et al., 2013). In the absence of language acquisition, communication can prove to be a challenge for the development of social skills for children with SLCN. SLCN is currently recognised in relation to communication and interaction, but not cognition and learning. The SEND Code of Practice (2015) (DfE, 2015) refers to SLCN, as primarily difficulties with communication: aspects of language that relate to how a child interacts with others. Being able to understand and use language is essential for children to be able to communicate socially and maintain friendships (Andrés-Roqueta et al., 2016) and children with SLCN are at a disadvantage where peer relationships are concerned (Craig, 1993). With regard to social relationships and difficulties in interacting with other children, those with SLCN are often seen as 'less preferred playmates than their normally developing peers' (Fujiki, Brinton and Todd, 1996, p. 195) and are often withdrawn and have difficulty in developing and maintaining friendships. As a result of challenges both socially and academically, children are often faced with academic failure and social exclusion (Marton, Abramoff and Rosenzweig, 2005), leading to a low self-esteem throughout life (Jerome et al., 2002).

Language disorders

Language disorders are more severe than language delays and can be caused by a number of reasons such as hereditary causes, and functional and environmental causes. A language disorder is characterised by impairment in the development of a child's language capabilities, which opposes their intelligence. It is also characterised by a child's inability to understand or share their own ideas or feelings because of impairment in language, speech or hearing and the ability to communicate these feelings with others; this includes both verbal and non-verbal interactions and transmissions of thoughts, messages and information.

Language disorders and conditions also include the comprehension or expression of spoken or written language, including attained and developmental disorders, a diminished ability to exchange thoughts, opinions, information or other forms of communication by means of language, reading, speech or hearing. Language disorders can be caused by receptive or expressive language issues, cognitive dysfunction, psychiatric conditions and hearing disorders, and can be due to cognitive or neurological dysfunctions, which result in issues in symbolisation or in delays in language and speech development.

Korpilahti, Kaljonen and Jansson-Verkasalo (2016) state that children begin language development at birth and through typical development most children have a basic vocabulary of 50 words by the age of 2 years. Language includes conversation with others by following shared rules of grammar, so that the language makes sense when spoken. Language includes receptive language (understanding others) and expressive language (conveying information, expressing feelings, etc.) (McLaughlin, 2011). With autism, for example, there can be difficulties in both receptive and expressive language and communication which results in language delay, yet the effective use of speech can be present.

Activity

- How would language disorders be seen within the classroom?

- What support strategies might be beneficial for pupils with language disorders?

Autism spectrum disorder

Autism Spectrum Disorder (ASD) is a diagnosed neurodevelopmental disorder that is caused when the brain does not fully develop (Landrigan, 2010). Research suggests that individuals living with autism have 'structural abnormalities' in their brains which link to and may give reason for specific social and emotional difficulties and for delays in language development and consequent social and emotional difficulties, this atypical development of the brain being the 'blooming and pruning' hypothesis (Frith and Hill, 2004, p. 4). Furthermore, many common characteristics of people on the autistic spectrum include social anxiety and difficulties in communicating (Landrigan, 2010). A very common sign of autism is difficulty communicating socially (Bellini et al., 2007), which could lead to individuals struggling with establishing and maintaining relationships, communicating their feelings, understanding those of others and being able to empathise. Children with ASD display very early signs of having a language delay before the age of two years (Guinchat et al., 2012).

Developmental language disorder

Developmental Language Disorder (DLD) is a heterogeneous language disorder that affects either expressive and/or receptive language (Ellis Weismer, 2013). DLD is diagnosed when children fail to acquire their own language for no obvious reason. This results in children who have difficulty understanding what people say to them, and struggle to articulate their ideas and feelings. Recent research has shown that, on average, two children in every class of 30 will experience DLD severe enough to hinder academic progress (Norbury et al., 2016). DLD is a condition where children have problems understanding and/or using spoken language. There is no obvious reason for these difficulties, for example, there is no hearing problem or physical disability that explains them. In the past, DLD was known as Specific Language Impairment. As with ASD, children with DLD have expressive and receptive issues (Taylor and Whitehouse, 2016). There are differences, however, such as syntax deficits (Kjelgaard and Tager-Flusberg, 2001) and that individuals with ASD have receptive language deficits that are more severe than expressive language ones (Hulme and Snowling, 2009). A key factor that differentiates ASD from DLD is that individuals living with ASD have greater semantic and social communication (SC) (pragmatic) difficulties (Maljaars et al., 2012).

Social Pragmatic Communication Disorder

DSM-V lists two neurodevelopmental deficits in SC: ASD and Social (Pragmatic) Communication Disorder (SPCD), differentiated by Repetitive and Restricted Behaviours, required for an ASD diagnosis but being absent in SPCD. This disorder is relatively new and so it is not known whether it is yet a valid diagnosis (Mandy et al., 2017). It is widely debated by some that SPCD is commonly seen in many other disorders, including ASD and that it is not plausible to yet confirm it as a completely separate diagnosis (Norbury, 2014). Those who do accept differential diagnoses suggest that it is a lack of ability to communicate both verbally and non-verbally, particularly in social situations (Swineford et al., 2014). While characteristics associated with SPCD are much like those presented in autism such as lack of SC, complication and inability to decode and understand, what is not established as well in SPCD is the ability to change tone of voice and or body language to empathise who may be speaking or listening (Baird and Norbury, 2016). They also suggest that those living with SPCD find it challenging to communicate socially, whereas those with ASD do not. In addition, characteristics such as restricted and repetitive behaviours commonly found in autism are not included in the criteria for SPCD (Norbury, 2014) and some children who do not meet the criteria for ASD present many characteristics that fit SPCD such as language disorders (Gibson et al., 2013). On the other hand, findings from Mandy et al. (2017) suggest that there is not yet evidence to completely separate SPCD from autism and suggest the same neurodevelopmental pathway (Norbury, 2014).

Aphasia

Language disorders can either be developmental or acquired. An example of an acquired language disorder is aphasia, which appears after a neurological illness or injury such as stroke or traumatic head injury. According to the DSM-V, aphasia is classified as a neurocognitive disorder (Simpson, 2014), while ICD-10 refers to aphasia as a language disorder due to damage of the areas of the brain associated with language function (ICDData, 2017). DSM-V does not single out aphasia as a language disorder but instead categorises it as a neurocognitive disorder placed on a spectrum with more severe conditions, such as dementia (Simpson, 2014). Godefroy et al. (2003), suggest that the fundamental determinant of aphasia is the location of cortical lesions in the Broca's and Wernicke's areas with individuals experiencing difficulties in language function (Kyoung Kang et al., 2010). There are subtypes of aphasia including Broca's (expressive), Wernicke's (receptive), anomic, global and semantic aphasia (Hoffman and Chen, 2013). For individuals with Broca's aphasia, fluency is poor but comprehension is good. Additionally, speech output is reduced, short utterances are exhibited and the use of vocabulary is limited. In comparison with Wernicke's aphasia, individuals can speak fluently, but experience poor comprehension and an unawareness of difficulties such as interpretation of numbers, pictures and gestures. When damage occurs to the Wernicke's area, individuals may encounter trouble with comprehension, understanding writing and reading aloud, but have no trouble with fluency (Kavanagh et al., 2010).

Difficulties associated with aphasia have detrimental effects on school achievement such as reading and writing and are usually associated with social, emotional, health and behavioural problems and could lead to depression, isolation and truancy and eventually, it may affect poor employment prospects and their quality of life in future. There has been a significant interest in reanalysing the function of Broca's area in language (Hagoort, 2005; Burns and Fahy, 2010). Damage to the Broca's area alone may not cause aphasia and Broca's aphasia is associated with large lesions extending beyond the Broca's area. Broca's aphasia requires extensive brain lesions; lesions restricted to Broca's area are associated with mild language production defects.

 Activity

- Taking one of the issues described above, what impact would this have on a pupil and their relationship with peers and adults?

- Research a specific strategy that would support this pupil in the classroom both in social skills and in the curriculum.

The social and cognitive impact of language delay and language disorder

Cognitive areas such as inhibitory control and cognitive flexibility are connected to SC skills in turn-taking, strategic attention or listening skills (Marton, Abramoff and Rosenzweig, 2005). A child who struggles with SC, expressive and receptive issues frequently struggles in making and maintaining friendships and this can have a detrimental impact on a child's social, mental and emotional well-being (Conti-Ramsden and Botting, 2008).

Language is a crucial tool in determining cognitive development, as it offers children the ability to explore their thoughts in more depth, and whether or not a child is diagnosed with autism or another disorder linked to language delay or language disorder, they may experience great difficulty in many cognitive factors including Working Memory (WM) which influences further cognitive functions (Holmes et al., 2015), including reasoning, comprehension and learning (Goswami and Bryant, 2007). WM also plays a particularly important role in supporting children learning to read and that roughly two-thirds of children who struggle with language difficulties also have trouble with reading among other obstacles (Montgomery and Hayes, 2005).

Language delay can impact children's abilities in literacy as they develop (Larney, 2002), including difficulty with decoding print, reading comprehension, phonic skills, spelling and also Maths writing (Vilenius-Tuohimaa, Aunola and Nurmi, 2008). The Bercow review in 2008 (DfE, 2008) found that children whose attainment fell below the nationally expected level in reading at the end of key stage one typically had delays in the development of communication, language and literacy. Like language delays, language disorders could have a lasting impact on cognitive and social development of children, including their ability to read and spell (Clegg et al., 2005). Furthermore, children with language disorders may struggle to develop social skills (Brownlie, Bao and Beitchman, 2016) and find it harder to socialise with their peers in school and to maintain friendships, as their ability to comprehend the feelings and thoughts of other children is at a lower level than most children of their age. Adults with language disorders also have few friends and the quality of these friendships is unsatisfactory (Durkin and Conti-Ramsden, 2007). Wallace, Watson and Cullen (2015) go further to identify risk factors including belonging to a family with a history of language disorders and low parental education, having the Y chromosome, prematurity or having a low birth weight.

Children with expressive or receptive communication issues may also have problems with social skills, affecting their ability to form relationships and friendships and can cause them to become isolated by their peers or prefer their own company. Such children may also be the target of or become bullies themselves, due to their lack of resolving things verbally. Catts, Hogan and Adlof (2005) found that many children with language disorders or delay are at risk of dyslexia and there may be a link between language disorders and ADHD, anxiety disorders and oppositional defiant disorder (ODD) and conduct disorder.

Language disorders can show to have a significant impact on the individual's language development (Siu, 2015), including heightened anxiety, difficulties with expressive and/or receptive grammar, poorer quality friendships and avoidance of social activities (Brownlie, Bao and Beitchman, 2016). Memory and executive control (executive functions) can be affected in both language delay and disorder (Beeson et al., 1993). Executive functions are needed to allow individuals to concentrate and stay focussed and include inhibition (self-control), cognitive flexibility, WM and interference control (paying attention). Diamond (2013) found that communicative success depended on the stability of executive functioning. Language and memory are interdependent and involve the need to sustain attention (Lee and Pyun, 2014) and WM.

A further issue affecting individuals with language delay and disorder is that of the Theory of Mind (ToM) involving the ability to understand others mental states. Ramachandra and Schneider (2011). found that when addressing the relation between ToM and language, results from a language test found that those with a severe language impairment, exhibited problems in ToM. A delayed ToM can also have an impact on relationships as peers or adults may assume that such an individual lack understanding, when actually struggling with effective communication (Bogdashina, 2013).

Supporting individuals experiencing issues with SLCN

Professionals such as teachers have a key role of advocating children with language and communication issues. The Bercow review (DfE, 2008) emphasised the duty for teachers to obtain training and develop their understanding and knowledge of how to adapt their curriculum and teaching practices to meet the needs of individuals with SLCN (Norbury and Broddle, 2016).

Activity

Stephen is 12 and attends mainstream secondary school.

He has the following difficulties with Speech, Language and Communication:

■ Problems understanding long or complicated sentences.

■ Difficulties learning new vocabulary, new words need to be specifically taught.

■ Difficulties understanding higher-level language such as reasoning, problem solving.

■ Difficulties putting his thoughts into words.

■ Problems knowing when he does not understand.

■ Difficulties knowing which style of language to use with both his peers and staff.

■ Behaviour difficulties associated with his SLCN, including frustration and a tendency to become angry when he feels he is struggling.

Stephen is coming into your class next term. Here are a few examples of how you might support him:

1. Use a One-Page Profile, or pen portrait to record important information about him such as what particular strengths and communication needs he has and ways of supporting these.

2. Share the lesson plan with Stephen which he can refer to.

3. Check with him and explain any of the language that he does not understand.

4. Use peer support in the form of 'buddies'.

■ Can you think of any other specific approaches you could use with Stephen?

It is useful to understand the scale of need for children with SLCN.

Table 11.1 Special educational needs in England: January 2017 State-funded primary schools

Special educational needs in England: January 2017 State-funded primary schools	*SEN support*		*Statement or EHC plan*		*All*	
	Number	*%*	*Number*	*%*	*Number*	*%*
Specific learning difficulty	58,985	10.3	2,138	3.4	61,123	9.7
Moderate learning difficulty	142,284	24.9	5,400	8.7	147,684	23.3
Severe learning difficulty	1,903	0.3	2,443	3.9	4,346	0.7
Profound and multiple learning difficulty	568	0.1	1,215	1.9	1,783	0.3
Social, emotional and mental health	92,735	16.2	6,740	10.8	99,475	15.7
Speech, language and communications needs	**168,368**	**29.5**	**15,401**	**24.7**	**183,769**	**29.0**
Hearing impairment	8,101	1.4	2,564	4.1	10,665	1.7
Visual impairment	4,721	0.8	1,183	1.9	5,904	0.9
Multi-sensory impairment	1,512	0.3	303	0.5	1,815	0.3
Physical disability	13,145	2.3	4,987	8.0	18,132	2.9
Autism spectrum disorder	25,169	4.4	17,325	27.8	42,494	6.7
Other difficulty/disability	24,063	4.2	2,538	4.1	26,601	4.2
SEN support but no specialist assessment of type of need	29,160	5.1	153	0.2	29,313	4.6
Total	**570,714**	**100.0**	**62,390**	**100.0**	**633,104**	**100.0**

Source: Gov.uk (2018).

With SEN support, pupils will be receiving special educational provision. All mainstream schools have funding to support pupils with SEN and disabilities, the notional SEN budget, and can decide how to use this to support pupils with SEN. If a pupil does not make progress at SEN support, schools should adapt the support given or consider requesting an Education Health and Care Plans (EHC P) needs assessment.

 Pause for reflection

From Table 11.1, it is clear that the percentage of primary school pupils with Speech, Language and Communications Needs is high in comparison to other categories. If you were in charge of a primary school that included a range of pupils with SEN support and a limited budget, what would your priorities be in ensuring that yours was an inclusive school? Who might you consult for support in making your decisions?

There are a range of strategies which can be used to support individuals with SLCN, below are a few examples of commonly used ones.

Makaton and Picture Exchange Communication System

Within the classroom, different pedagogical strategies can be employed to support communication including the use of visual, timetables, symbols and timers. Establishing class routines and using signing systems such as Makaton are also interventions in supporting language disorders. These strategies have shown to be effective in supporting the development of speech with Mistry and Barnes (2013) finding that Makaton produced a positive correlation with the advancement of spoken English. Another intervention for developing a child's communication is Picture Exchange Communication System (PECS), which is a useful tool for young children to communicate with others through use of exchanging symbolic cards. According to Flippin, Reszka and Watson (2010), PECS caused small to moderate gains in communication for children on the autistic spectrum. PECS provide children with SLCN a way of communicating in an alternative way to speaking (Cagliani, Ayres and Whiteside, 2017). PECS involves a child exchanging a picture with the adult supporting them to show them what they want or need (Wearmouth, 2017). Children are taught how to use PECS as a way of developing their communication skills (McDonald, Battaglia and Keane, 2015) and to encourage them to understand the functions of communication (Bondy and Frost, 2001). See Chapter 8 on Autism Spectrum Disorder.

Activity

- How could you use the PECS or MAKATON within your practice?
- What are the benefits of using such commutation systems?

Scaffolding language and modelling

Bruner believed adults should be active in the role of supporting a child's learning through the practice of scaffolding. Scaffolding refers to organised interactions, between an adult and a child, that is helpful in the aim of aiding a child reach a specific target, for example, communication. The use of verbal scaffolding such as paraphrasing, writing prompts and wait times are effective ways of supporting language disorders, with Wasik and Jacobi-Vessels (2017) recommending that scaffolding strategies such as asking questions to allow extended response is constructive for improving children's language development. Modelling language is also a way to increase expressive speech in children with ASD. It is important to model it in a way that is straightforward for them to imitate such that pronoun reversals do not occur because children with ASD do not process prosody-related tasks well (Peppé et al., 2007). This is crucial in social and play situations whereby modelling (for example, turn-taking, requesting), and adult facilitation will enable a child to experience, imitate and practice in the situation. If the child is saying a word/sentence wrongly, it is best to repeat it in the correct form rather than place emphasis on the error.

Supporting expressive language

Expressive language issues may be apparent in subjects such as Literacy where a child may struggle with their reading due to problems in syntax, word-retrieval, etc. (Hulme and Snowling, 2009). Teachers should provide the class with high-quality, differentiated teaching strategies and to have high expectations of all students, including group work, interactive computer sessions or independent reading time with the teacher or teaching assistant. The child may struggle, but it is important that they are not rushed and it also allows continuous assessment of pupils' changing abilities (McMinn, 2006). Depending on the severity, teachers could work with professionals such as the special educational needs co-ordinator (SENCO) and speech and language therapist (SLT) to provide high level of supportive interventions (Zeng, Law and Lindsay, 2012). Comprehension difficulties may be less obvious than expressive issues, and so the child should be asked to try and explain what they just read to ensure that there are no issues in a child's understanding (Maljaars et al., 2012).

Supporting receptive language

Receptive language issues can affect working memory, which may be evident, for example, in Maths lessons in which executive functions are required in organising, problem-solving and retaining data. Individuals with issues in this area can take longer to decode what has been said or seen – the time, efforts and energy this takes may result in a child falling behind as the teacher may move on to another topic (Norbury, Tomblin and Bishop, 2008). Issues within auditory-processing does not help in retaining information for enough time for it to be processed and for a child to understand. This is vital in school as pupils use their working memory on a daily basis. In Maths lessons, teachers could use simple sentences and teach one concept at a time, while continuingly checking pupils' understanding (Hulme and Snowling, 2009). Simple strategies such as reducing distractive noises by closing the door to aid focus, using visual aids and tactile cues as a multisensory approach to giving instructions or teaching in general would support children's learning (Glazzard et al., 2015). For example, using tactile objects such as cubes instead of writing down numbers or drawing apples to represent numbers can aid in semantics (McMinn, 2006).

 Activity

Anita is seven years old and attends a mainstream primary school. She is living with autism and has difficulties in receptive language, in particular understanding oral language and listening.

She has difficulties in the following areas:

- Retaining auditory information, and in following instructions and directions.

- Answering questions may be related to a limited understanding of question forms.

- Filtering out background noise and have difficulties with verbal reasoning.

- Turn-taking in conversation.

- Pragmatic difficulties such as poor understanding, poor use of tone, facial gesture and body language, and poor eye contact.

- Establishing and maintaining peer relationships.

Anita is falling behind in her work and often gets frustrated and angry. As she puts it, 'I don't get it'. The SENCO has asked you to support Anita on a one-to-one basis in class. How would you work with the class teacher to ensure that Anita does not feel isolated from her peers, or unable to access the curriculum? It might be useful to produce a support plan aimed to focus on both general issues, such as making friends, along with specific strategies such as ones targeting the concern with following instructions.

Therapies

Another way to support children with SLCN is to provide them with speech and language therapy with support from a SLT, a professional who works closely with children with SLCN and offers guidance to help them develop their language and improve their cognitive skills (Hodkinson and Vickerman, 2009). SLTs are responsible for arranging treatments, help and attention for children with SLCN and their parents while working with other practitioners within a school context. SLTs are expected to involve other professionals in the support they provide for children with SLCN in order to ensure that the child's needs are met (Lindsay et al., 2006).

There are also specific therapeutic interventions which can be effective in supporting specific disorders, for example, in the case of Childhood Apraxia of Speech (CAS), a motor speech disorder. children may have difficulties saying sounds, syllables, and words caused by an area in the brain, which has a difficulty communicating with the required muscles to move the lips, jaw and tongue needed for speech and communication. The child will mentally know what they want to say; however, their brain struggles coordinating the correct muscle movements to say the words which can be very frustrating for the child. Murray and Iuzzini-Seigel (2017) state that the aim of CAS treatments should be to increase speech production and fluency or when shown, using augmentative and alternative forms of communication, for example, sign language, gestures, voice output devices and communication board when speaking. Preston et al. (2016) found that ultrasound imagining used in conjunction with speech therapies has shown to be beneficial to people with CAS. It shows the child their tongue shapes when saying different words which may help children stabilise their motor patterns, therefore enabling more constant and accurate productions of sounds and syllables.

An intensive therapy is Rapid Syllable Transitions (ReST) and Maas et al. (2008) identified that ReST treatments are a high-intensity practice of pretend words that have different phonetic structure and lingual stress. Using these pretend words enables the children to practise motor planning and programming on actual word-like forms. Deferred low-frequency 'knowledge or result' are provided during therapy and practice at home, with the purpose of merging learning through self-evaluation.

 Pause for reflection

Revisit the two views as to how language may develop, namely the modular and constructivist approaches. From what you have read in the chapter about how individuals with SLCN could be supported, which of the approaches apply to each of the strategies outlined and why?

Activity

You are facilitating a focus group comprising a SENCO, a classroom teacher, a teaching assistant, parents of a child with SLCN and a member of the SEN Outreach Service. You will be discussing the teaching and support needs of a pupil with SLCN to enable them to remain in an inclusive primary school.

■ Research the roles that each one of them may play in the discussion.

■ Identify three themes you would wish to explore with the group.

■ Suggest a question you could put to each member of the group.

Summary

The terms Speech, Language and Communication are used interchangeably, but each has a specific definition and function. The modular and constructivist perspectives of language both have a part to play in strategies to support individuals with SLCN. Although there are differences between language delay and language disorder, both have an impact on the social and cognitive development of children and adults. There are a range of possible supporting strategies for individuals experiencing issues with SLCN, from modifying the curriculum, teaching strategies to the involvement of professionals such as SLT. The importance of communication skills cannot be underestimated, and it supports cognitive, social and emotional development and underpins all interactions between pupils and practitioners.

References

Andrés-Roqueta, C., Adrian, J.E., Clemente, R.A. and Villanueva, L. (2016). Social cognition makes an independent contribution to peer relations in children with Specific Language Impairment. *Research in Developmental Disabilities*, 49, pp. 277–290.

Baird, G. and Norbury, C.F. (2016). Social (pragmatic) communication disorders and autism spectrum disorder: Table 1. *Archives of Disease in Childhood*, 101(8), pp. 745–751.

Beeson, P.M., Bayles, K.A., Rubens, A.B. and Kaszniak, A. (1993). Memory impairment and executive control in individuals with stroke-induced aphasia. *Brain and Language*, 45, pp. 253–275.

Bellini, S., Peters, J., Benner, L. and Hopf, A. (2007). A meta-analysis of school-based social skill interventions for children with autism spectrum disorders. *Remedial and Special Education*, 28, pp. 153–162.

Bennett, T., Szatmari, P., Bryson, S., Volden, J., Zwaigenbaum, L., Vaccarella, L., Duku, E. and Boyle, M. (2008). Differentiating autism and Asperger syndrome on the basis of language delay or impairment. *Journal of Autism Development Disorder*, 38, pp. 616–625.

Beuker, K.T., Rommelse, N.N.J., Donders, R. and Buitelaar, J.K. (2013). Development of early communication skills in the first two years of life. *Infant Behavior & Development*, 36(1), pp. 71–83.

Bigras, N., Lemay, L., Bouchard, C. and Joell, E. (2017). Sustaining the support in four-year-olds in childcare services with the goal of promoting their cognitive and language development. *Early Child Development and Care*, 187(12), pp. 1987–2001.

Blackburn, C. and Aubrey, C. (2016). Policy-to-practice context to the delays and difficulties in the acquisition of speech, language and communication in the early years. *International Journal of Early Years Education*, 24(4), pp. 414–434.

Bogdashina, O. (2005). *Communication issues in autism and Asperger's syndrome*. London: Jessica Kingsley Publishers.

Bogdashina, O. (2013). Sensory theory in autism makes sense: A brief review of the past and present research. *OA Autism*, 1(1). p. 3.

Bondy, A. and Frost, L. (2001). The picture exchange communication system. *Behavior Modification*, 25(5), pp. 725–744.

Brown, C. (2008). *Developmental psychology*. 1st ed. London: SAGE.

Brownlie, Elizabeth & Bao, Lin & Beitchman, Joseph. (2016). Childhood Language Disorder and Social Anxiety in Early Adulthood. Journal of abnormal child psychology. 44. 1061–1070. 10.1007/s10802-015-0097-5.

Brownlie, E.B., Bao, L. and Beitchman, J. (2016). Childhood language disorder and social anxiety in early adulthood. *Journal of Abnormal Child Psychology*, 44(6), pp. 1061–1070.

Burns, M. and Fahy, J. (2010). Broca's area: Rethinking classical concepts from a neuroscience perspective. *Topics in Stroke Rehabilitation*, 17, pp. 401–410.

Cagliani, R.R., Ayres, K.M. and Whiteside, E. (2017). Picture exchange communication system and delay to reinforcement. *Journal of Developmental and Physical Disabilities*, 29, pp. 925–939.

Catts, H.W., Hogan, T.P. and Adlof, S.M. (2005). Developmental changes in reading and reading disabilities. In Catts, H.W. and Kamhi, A.G. (eds.), *The connections between language and reading disabilities*. Mahwah: Lawrence Erlbaum Associates Publishers, pp. 25–40.

Clegg, J., Hollis, C., Mawhood, L. and Rutter, M. (2005). Developmental language disorders - a follow-up in later adult life. Cognitive, language and psychosocial outcomes. *Journal of Child Psychology and Psychiatry*, 46(2), pp. 128–149.

Conti-Ramsden, G. and Botting, N. (2008). Emotional health in adolescents with and without a history of specific language impairment (SLI). *Journal of Child Psychology and Psychiatry*, 49, pp. 516–525.

Craig, H.K. (1993). Social skills of children with specific language impairment: Peer relationships. *Language, Speech, and Hearing Services in Schools*, 24, pp. 206–215.

Department for Education (2008). *The Bercow review*. Available online at: http://webarchive. nationalarchives.gov.uk/20130321005340/https://www.education.gov.uk/publications/ standard/publicationdetail/page1/DCSF-00632-2008 (Accessed 13/08/2018).

Department for Education (2015). *Special educational needs and disability code of practice: 0 to 25 years*. Department for Education. Available online at https://assets.publishing. service.gov.uk/government/uploads/system/uploads/attachment_data/file/398815/ SEND_Code_of_Practice_January_2015.pdf (Accessed 12/08/2018).

Diamond, A. (2013). Executive functions. *Annual Review of Psychology*, 64, pp. 135–168.

Durkin, K. and Conti-Ramsden, G. (2007). Language, social behavior, and the quality of friendships in adolescents with and without a history of Specific Language Impairment. *Child Development*, 78(5).pp 1441–1457.

Ellis Weismer, S. (2013). Developmental language disorders: Challenges and implications of cross-group comparisons. *Folia Phoniatrica Et Logopaedica: Official Organ of the International Association of Logopedics and Phoniatrics (Ialp)*, 65, pp. 68–77.

Flippin, M., Reszka, S. and Watson, L.R. (2010). Effectiveness of the Picture Exchange Communication System (PECS) on communication and speech for children with autism spectrum disorders: A meta-analysis. *Am J Speech Lang Pathol*, 19(2), pp. 178–195.

Fodor, J.A. (1983). *The modularity of mind*, Cambridge: MIT Press.

Frith, U. and Hill, E.L. (2004). *Autism: Mind and brain.* 1st ed. London: Oxford University Press.

Fujiki, M., Brinton, B. and Todd, C.M. (1996). Social skills of children with specific language impairment. *Language, Speech, and Hearing Services in Schools*, 27, pp. 195–202.

Geers, A., Tobey, E., Moog, J. and Brenner C. (2016). Persistent language delay versus late language emergence in children with early cochlear implantation. *Journal of Speech, Language and Hearing Research*, 59, pp. 155–170.

Gibson, J., Adams, C., Lockton, E. and Green, J. (2013). Social communication disorder outside autism? A diagnostic classification approach to delineating pragmatic language impairment, high functioning autism and specific language impairment. *Journal of Child Psychology and Psychiatry*, 54(11), pp. 1186–1197.

Glazzard, J., Stokoe, J., Hughes, A., Netherwood, A. and Neve, L. (2015). *Teaching & supporting children with special educational needs & disabilities in primary schools.* 2nd ed. London: Learning Matters.

Godefroy, O., Dubois, C., Debachy, B., Leclerc, M. and Kreisler, A. (2003). Vascular aphasias: Main characteristics of patients hospitalized in acute stroke units. *Stroke*, 33(3), pp. 702–705.

Goswami, U. and Bryant, P. (2007). *Children's Social Development: Peer interaction classroom learning (Primary Review Research Survey 2/1b).* Cambridge: University of Cambridge Faculty of Education.

Gov.uk (2018). *Special educational needs in England: January 2017 State funded Primary Schools.* Available online at: www.gov.uk/government/statistics/special-educational-needs-in-england-january-2017 (Accessed 01/02/2018).

Guinchat, V., Thorsen, P., Laurent, C., Cans, C., Bodeau, N. and Cohen, D. (2012). Pre-, peri- and neonatal risk factors for autism. *Acta Obstet Gynecol Scand*, 91, pp. 287–300.

Harley, T. (2009). *Talking the talk: Language, psychology and science.* London: Psychology Press.

Hasan, R. (2002). Semiotic mediation and mental development in pluralistic societies: Some implications for tomorrow's schooling. In Wells, G. and Claxton, G. (eds.), *Learning for life in the 21st century: Socio-cultural perspectives on the future of education.* Oxford: Blackwell, pp. 112–126.

Hayden, S. and Jordan, E. (2012). *Language for learning in the secondary school.* 1st ed. Abingdon: Routledge.

Herman, K.C., Cohen, D., Owens, S., Latimore, T. and Reinke, W.M. (2016). Language delays and child depressive symptoms: The role of early stimulation in the home. *Prevention Science*, 17(5), pp. 533–543.

Hodkinson, A. and Vickerman, P. (2009). *Key issues in special educational needs and inclusion.* London: SAGE, pp. 17, 166.

Holmes, J., Butterfield, S., Cormack, F., van Loenhoud, A., Ruggero, L., Kashikar, L. and Gathercole, S. (2015). Improving working memory in children with low language abilities. *Front Psychol*, 6, p. 519.

Hulme, C. and Snowling, M. (2009). *Developmental disorders of language learning and cognition.* Chichester: Wiley-Blackwell.

ICDData.com. (2017). *Aphasia.* Available online at: www.icd10data.com/ICD10CM/Codes/R00-R99/R47-R49/R47-/R47.01 (Accessed 20/11/2017).

Jerome, A.C., Fujiki, M., Brinton, B. and James, S.L. (2002). Self-esteem in children with specific language impairment. *Journal of Speech, Language, and Hearing Research*, 45, pp. 700–714.

Kang, E.K., Sohn, H.M., Han, M.K., Kim, W., Han, T.R. and Paik, N.J. (2010). Severity of post-stroke aphasia according to aphasia type and lesion location in Koreans. *Journal of Korean Medical Science*, 25, pp. 123–127.

Kavanagh, D.O., Lynam, C., Düerk, T., Casey, M. and Eustace, P.W. (2010). Variations in the presentation of aphasia in patients with closed head injuries. *Case Reports in Medicine*, *2010*, 5 p. Article ID 678060.

Kjelgaard, M.M. and Tager-Flusberg, H. (2001). An investigation of language impairment in autism: Implications for genetic subgroups. *Language and Cognitive Processes*, 16, pp. 287–308.

Klem, M., Hagtvet, B., Hulme, C. and Gustafsson, J.E. (2016). Screening for language delay: Growth trajectories of language ability in low - and high - performing children. *Journal of Speech, Language, and Hearing Research*, 59, pp. 1035–1045.

Korpilahti, P., Kaljonen, A. and Jansson-Verkasalo, E. (2016). Identification of biological and environmental risk factors for language delay: The Let's Talk STEPS study. *Infant Behavior Development*, 42, pp. 27–35.

Landrigan, P. (2010). What causes autism? Exploring the environmental contribution. *Current Opinion in Pediatrics*, 22(2), pp. 219–225.

Larney, R. (2002). The relationship between early language delay and later difficulties in literacy. *Early Child Development and Care*, 172(2), pp. 183–193.

Law, J., Peacey, N. and Radford, J. (2000). *Provision for children with speech and language needs in England and Wales: Facilitating communication between education and health services.* Research report. Great Britain: Department for Education and Employment, no. 239.

Lee, B. and Pyun, S.B. (2014). Characteristics of cognitive impairment in patients with post-stroke aphasia. *Annals of Rehabilitation Medicine*, 38(6), pp. 759–765.

Lindsay, G., Dockrell, J., Mackie, C. and Letchford, B. (2002). *Educational provision for children with specific speech and language difficulties in England and Wales.* 1st ed. Coventry: CEDAR.

Maas, E., Robin, D.A., Wright, D.L. and Ballard, K.J. (2008). Motor programming in apraxia of speech. *Brain and Language*, 106, pp. 107–118.

Maljaars, J., Noens, I., Scholte, E. and van Berckelaer-Onnes, I. (2012). Evaluation of the criterion and convergent validity of the diagnostic interview for social and communication disorders in young and low-functioning children. *Autism: The International Journal of Research and Practice*, 16, pp. 487–497.

Mandy, W., Wang, A., Lee, I. and Skuse, D. (2017). Evaluating social (pragmatic) communication disorder. *Journal of Child Psychology and Psychiatry*, 58(10), pp. 1166–1175.

Marton, K., Abramoff, B. and Rosenzweig, S. (2005). Social cognition and language in children with Specific Language Impairment (SLI). *Journal of Communication Disorders*, 38, pp. 143–162.

McDonald, M.E., Battaglia, D. and Keane, M. (2015). Using fixed interval-based prompting to increase a student's initiation of the picture exchange communication system. *Behavioral Development Bulletin*, 20(2), pp. 265–275.

McLaughlin, M.R. (2011). Speech and language delay in children. *American Academy of Family Physicians*, 83(10).

McMinn, J. (2006). *Supporting children with speech and language impairment and associated difficulties*. 2nd ed. London and New York: Continuum International.

Mistry, M. and Barnes, D. (2013). The use of Makaton for supporting talk, through play, for pupils who have English as an Additional Language (EAL) in the foundation stage. *International Journal of Primary, Elementary and Early Years Education*, 41(6), pp. 603–616.

Montgomery, J.K. and Hayes, L.L. (2005). Literacy transition strategies for upper elementary students with language disabilities. *Communication Disorders Quarterly*, 26(2), pp. 85–93.

Mountstephen, M. (2010). *Meeting special needs: A practical guide to support children with Speech, Language and Communication Needs (SLCN)*. 1st ed. London: Practical Pre-School Books.

Murray, E. and Iuzzini-Seigel, J. (2017). Efficacious treatment of children with childhood apraxia of speech according to the international classification of functioning, disability and health. *Perspectives of the ASHA Special Interest Groups*, 2, p. 61.

Norbury, C. (2014). Practitioner review: Social (pragmatic) communication disorder conceptualization, evidence and clinical implications. *Journal of Child Psychology and Psychiatry*, 55(3), pp. 204–216.

Norbury, C. and Broddle, E. (2016). Equip teachers to support children with language disorders in the classroom. Available online at: www.theguardian.com/science/head-quarters/2016/nov/01/equip-teachers-to-support-children-with-language-disorders-in-the-classroom (Accessed 12/06/2018).

Norbury, C., Tomblin, J.B. and Bishop, D.V.M. (eds.) (2008). *Understanding developmental language disorders: From theory to practice*. London: Psychology Press.

Oakley, L. (2004). *Cognitive development*. 1st ed. East Sussex: Routledge.

Peppé, S., McCann, J., Gibbon, F., O'Hare, A. and Rutherford, M. (2007). Receptive and expressive prosodic ability in children with high-functioning autism. *Journal of Speech Language and Hearing Research*, 50(4), pp. 1015–1028.

Preston, J.L., Maas, E., Whittle, J., Leece, M.C. and McCabe, P. (2016). Limited acquisition and generalisation of rhotics with ultrasound visual feedback in childhood apraxia. *Clinical Linguistics & Phonetics*, 30, pp. 363–381.

Ramachandra, V. and Schneider, E. (2011). Theory of mind reasoning in people with aphasia: The role of language and executive functions. *Procedia Social and Behavioral Sciences*, 23, pp. 207–208.

Schoon, I., Cheng, H. and Jones, E. (2010). Resilience in children's development. In Hansen, K., Joshi, H. and Dex, S. (eds.), *Children of the 21st century: The first five years*, chapter 14. Bristol: Policy Press.

Shabani, K., Khatib, M. and Ebadi, S. (2010). Vygotsky's zone of proximal development: Instructional implications and teachers' professional development. *English Language Teaching*, 3(4), pp. 237–248.

Simpson, J. (2014). *DSM-5 and neurocognitive disorders*. Available online at: www.carrieresantementale.ca/Resource%20Library/Clinical%20Mental%20Health/DSM-5%20and%20Neurocognitive%20Disorders%20-%202014-05.pdf (Accessed 20/11/2017).

Siu, A.L. (2015). Screening for speech and language delay and disorders in children aged 5 years or younger: US preventive services task force recommendation statement. *Pediatrics*, 136(2), pp. 474–481.

Stark, R.E. and Tallal, P. (1988). Language, speech, and reading disorders in children: Neuropsychological studies. In McCauley, R.J. (ed.), *Language, speech, and reading disorders in children: Neuropsychological studies*. Boston: Little, Brown and Company, pp. 1–169.

Swineford, L.B., Thurm, A., Baird, G., Wetherby, A.A. and Swedo, S. (2014). Social (pragmatic) communication disorder: A research review of this new DSM-5 diagnostic category. *Journal of Neurodevelopmental Disorders*, 6(4).

Tsybina, I. and Eriks-Brophy, A. (2007). Issues in research on children with early language delay. *Contemporary Issues in Communication Science and Disorders*, 34.

Vilenius-Tuohimaa, P.M., Aunola, K. and Nurmi, J.E. (2008). The association between mathematical word problems and reading comprehension. *Educational Psychology*, 28(4), pp. 409–426.

Wallace, I., Watson, L. and Cullen, K. (2015). *Screening for speech and language delays and disorders in children age 5 years or younger*. Available online at: www.ncbi.nlm.nih.gov/books/NBK305674/n (Accessed 8/12/2017).

Wasik, B.A. and Jacobi-Vessels, J.L. (2017). Word play: Scaffolding language development through child-directed play. *Early Childhood Education Journal*, 45(6), pp. 769–776.

Wearmouth, J. (2017). *Special educational needs and disabilities in schools*. London: Bloomsbury.

Zeng, B., Law, J. and Lindsay, G. (2012). Characterizing optimal intervention intensity: The relationship between dosage and effect size in interventions for children with developmental speech and language difficulties. *International Journal of Speech–Language Pathology*, 14, pp. 471–477.

12 Chromosomal and gestational diversity

Introduction

Some types of chromosomal conditions such as Fragile X syndrome (FXS) are inherited, while most such as Down's syndrome and Turner's syndrome are not passed from one generation to the next. There is a great deal of literature and research into strategies to support individuals living with issues such as autism, Attention Deficit Hyperactivity Disorder (ADHD) and dyslexia. The numbers of pupils seen in inclusive classrooms with chromosomal and gestational issues have risen in inclusive classrooms over the past few years. This chapter examines the causes, characteristics and strategies to support individuals with FXS, Down's syndrome, Cri du chat syndrome and foetal alcohol syndrome (FAS). It aims to:

▨ describe the causes of the following chromosomal and gestational diversities: FXS, Down's syndrome, Cri du chat syndrome and FAS

▨ identify the features of such diversities

▨ discuss the similarities and differences between FXS and Autism Spectrum Disorder (ASD)

▨ discuss the moral and ethical dilemma associated with prenatal testing for Down's syndrome (DS)

▨ outline classroom support strategies for pupils living with FXS, Down's syndrome Cri du chat syndrome and FAS.

Chromosomal conditions can be caused by:

Changes in the number of chromosomes. These changes are not inherited but occur as random events during the formation of reproductive cells (eggs and sperm, an error in cell division results in reproductive cells with an abnormal number of chromosomes), for example, a reproductive cell may accidentally gain or lose one copy of a chromosome. If one of these atypical reproductive cells contributes to the genetic makeup of a child, the child will have an extra or missing chromosome in each of the body's cells.

Changes in chromosome structure can also cause chromosomal disorders. Some changes in chromosome structure can be inherited, while others occur as random accidents during the formation of reproductive cells or in early foetal development and the inheritance of these changes can be complex.

Fragile X syndrome

FXS is the most prevalent cause of inherited intellectual disability in males (Green, 2003; Fisher, Morling and Murray, 2004; Roberts et al., 2016) and is also a significant cause of intellectual disability in females. When viewing characteristics, the ICD-10 defines FXS as a spectrum, with the learning disability of the individual spanning mild to severe (ICD Codes, 2018), which causes specific behavioural, physical and cognitive attributes (Green, 2003). It affects approximately 1 in 4,000 males and 1 in 8,000 females. A UK screening study in 2003 estimated an overall prevalence of FXS in the general population of 2.3/10,000 (or 1 in 4,425). Other estimates suggest that it is present in 1 in 4,000 males and 1 in 8,000 females, but that this may be an underestimation and it occurs in all racial and ethnic groups with as many females as males carrying the gene abnormality. It can cause a wide range of difficulties with learning, as well as social, language, attentional, emotional and behavioural problems. In addition, approximately 1 in 250 females and 1 in 600 males are carriers of the Fragile X pre-mutation.

A condition is considered X-linked if the mutated gene that causes the disorder is located on the X chromosome, one of the two sex chromosomes. The inheritance is dominant if one copy of the altered gene in each cell is sufficient to cause the condition. In most cases, males experience more severe symptoms of the disorder than females. A striking characteristic of X-linked inheritance is that fathers cannot pass X-linked traits to their sons (National Human Genome Research Institute, 2018). Nearly all cases of FXS are caused by an alteration (mutation) in the FMR1 gene where a DNA segment, known as the CGG triplet repeat, is expanded. Normally, this DNA segment is repeated from 5 to approximately 40 times.

This additional DNA prevents normal coiling, which interferes with the production of the Fragile X protein, thought to be important for normal brain development. In people with FXS, however, the CGG segment is repeated more than 200 times. The abnormally expanded CGG segment inactivates (silences) the FMR1 gene, which prevents the gene from producing a protein called Fragile X mental retardation protein. Loss of this protein leads to the signs and symptoms of FXS. Both boys and girls can be affected, but because boys have only one X chromosome, a single Fragile X is likely to affect them more severely. Thus, FXS is caused by a gene on the long arm in the X chromosome (Hayward et al., 2016) and identified through DNA tests (Fernández Carvajal and Aldridge, 2011).

Features of FXS

Children with FXS display a range of characteristics typical in other conditions such as ASD and ADHD. The main three visual features of FXS are large ears which often protrude, elongated face and macroorchidism (enlarged testes) in males (Charalsawadi, 2017).

Physical characteristics of FXS can be subtle or not present at all but they can include low muscle tone and loose joints, long narrow face and prominent ears and in some cases a heart murmur. They can also have difficulties in sensory processing, this can result in hypo- or hypersensitivity to certain sounds, tastes, smells or textures. However, some characteristics can have a positive effect on an individual with FXS including possessing a good vocabulary, good imitation skills, curiosity and long-term memories comprehension and using single-word vocabulary. Individuals with FXS have been described as having likeable personalities and good sense of humour (Howlin, Charman and Ghaziuddin, 2011).

In addition to mental impairment, hyperactivity, emotional and behavioural problems, anxiety and mood swings, people with FXS also show what doctors call 'tactile defensiveness', which means they do not make eye contact and do not like physical contact and are hypersensitive to touch and sound. Also, they show language delays, muddled thinking, concentration and difficulties with abstract concepts. Physical problems that have been seen include eye, orthopaedic, heart and skin problems. Girls who have the full FMR1 mutation have mild intellectual disability. Other features common to both boys and girls include eye problems (squint, strabismus), ear infections, social anxiety and obsessions along with sensory sensitivity.

A typical trait within a child or young person with FXS is a delay in their speech and language development, as well as exhibiting sensory processing difficulties. This includes hypo- or hypersensitivity to: visual processing, auditory processing, taste, smell and touch sensitivity (Tomchek and Dunn, 2007). Emotional, social and communication, difficulties also arise, especially in girls, which can include anxiety and oversensitivity to certain environments (East and Evans, 2001). Cognitive characteristics may involve issues in spatial memory, visual motor coordination, short-term memory and symbolic language.

FXS and autism

FXS is recognised as the most common genetic cause of intellectual disability and autism spectrum disorder (ASD). FXS is often mistaken for ASD as individuals with FXS often show characteristics of ASD. ASD is a behavioural diagnosis, whereas FXS is a medical, genetic diagnosis. Originally, it was thought that there were just behavioural similarities, although researchers have found that it might also include genetic and biological components. One of the main differences which separate the two is that FXS causes a range of functions across all areas, ASD, on the other hand, is recognised by a cluster of symptoms rather than one particular condition.

When looking at the diagnosis from the DSM-V (Diagnostic Statistic Manual), individuals with FXS have to accommodate the diagnostic criteria for ASD before acquiring the label, 'associated with FXS' (Deweerdt, 2011). The comparisons between the brain activities that distinguishes a child with FXS to a child with ASD may lead to earlier interventions and diagnosis (Devitt et al., 2015), therefore suggesting the importance of the co-morbidity. Budimirovic (2017) found that it was more common for a child to be diagnosed with ASD and then later receive an extra diagnosis of FXS.

As well as learning disabilities, common behavioural features include short attention span, distractibility, impulsiveness, restlessness, over activity and sensory problems. Girls with or without learning disabilities may show concentration problems and social, emotional and communication Many children and adults with FXS show autistic like features, including avoiding eye contact, anxiety in social situations, insistence on familiar routines and hand flapping or hand biting. Although many people with FXS relate well to others, anxiety in unfamiliar or unpredictable situations may cause them to act in this way. A substantial minority of individuals with FXS will show greater problems relating to others and may receive a dual-diagnosis of autism and speech and language are usually delayed.

Characteristics that have been found to differ between the FXS behavioural phenotype and ASD include:

- The frequency of intellectual disability is higher in FXS than in ASD. Most males and about a third of females with FXS have intellectual disability, while only approximately 40 per cent of individuals with ASD have intellectual disability.

- Motor coordination deficits are worse in FXS than in ASD.

- Individuals with ASD are more likely to show worse receptive language than expressive language, while individuals with FXS tend to show the opposite pattern.

- Interest in socialising is higher in FXS in general than ASD (although limited by anxiety and avoidance).

- Imitation skills are better in FXS than in ASD when the level of intellectual impairment is controlled.

Activity

Read Chapter 8 on ASD.

■ There are two pupils in your class, one of whom has a diagnosis of ASD and another has a diagnosis of FXS. Identify a teaching or support strategy aimed at including both of these children in a group task for a specific curriculum area.

Classroom support

There are a number of strategies which can be used to support a pupil with FXS. These include: giving small chunks of information at a time; avoid using or requiring too much eye contact; whole picture learning and the use of visual aids; short achievable tasks to experience success and predictable and structured routine.

Reducing anxiety and distraction

One of the characteristics that individuals with FXS have, which can become a barrier in the classroom, is social anxiety and shyness. Once an individual becomes anxious, they can tend to have maladaptive behaviours such as tantrums, screaming, panic and trying to flee the situation. This is because their brains and bodies are going into a fight-or-flight stage when a triggering event happens. A strategy to reduce anxiety is 'side-on teaching', where when working 1-2-1 with the individual instead of facing them, the teacher sits next to them, reducing eye contact. To help reduce anxiety, avoid direct pressures including the setting of time limits, questions in front of the class and insistence on joining in. This results in less chance of the individual to become anxious and maladaptive behaviours (Dew-Hughes, 2003).

Another strategy which can help avoid the individual with FXS to not become anxious is to create and uphold a consistent routine and know what to expect day-to-day. They also know what is required and allows them to keep organised. Teaching individuals' ways of coping and self-regulation is also useful, by using methods such as breathing techniques.

As individuals with Fragile X can become distracted within a classroom setting due to certain stimuli and their oversensitivity within their senses, one way to overcome this would be to place the individuals towards the front or side of the class. This would reduce the area of which a distracting stimulus would occur (National Fragile X Foundation, 2004).

Maths and English

Another characteristic that individuals with FXS have is an intellectual delay. This can make them feel behind compared to their classmates as they take longer to complete tasks, such as in Maths and English. A strategy to help the individual with writing is trying to find an alternative way of recording, such as the use of a computer and modifying worksheets to require less writing and still retain the information needed. Also, support can be provided when verbal instructions are accompanied with visuals or a practical demonstration. Individuals with FXS are very visual learners, so using visual representations in Maths is useful, as it is the use of tactile real-life examples. It also helps to present tasks as a whole, rather than explaining them step by step. This is because individuals FXS find it better to process information all at the same time as they find it difficult to link different information together.

Use of board games

Introducing board games to learning has major benefits for individuals with FXS, as they can help with different delays and skills at the same time. But it is also a 'fun' way of learning. They can promote a number of skills such as:

- turn taking

- communication and social interaction

- fine motor skills and hand-eye coordination

 Activity

The National Fragile X Foundation publishes a comprehensive guide, which provides practical information that includes:

1. A background on FXS.

2. Descriptions of behaviour and learning styles.

3. A discussion of educational and community resources.

4. Sample lesson plans for children with FXS at a variety of developmental levels.

5. Strategies to facilitate the inclusion of children with FXS.

This can be accessed via the (National Fragile X Foundation, 2017) website.

- From the checklist entitled: Key Educational Strategies for Children with Fragile X a Summary Checklist p20, identify how any of these strategies could be used within your practice.

Down's syndrome

DS is a congenital condition caused by chromosomal disorder in which an error in cell division results in an extra copy of chromosome 21 in the baby's cell (Selikowitz, 2008). There are normally 46 chromosomes in each cell, with 23 inherited from each parent. However, in a child with DS, there are 47 chromosomes because there are three instead of two copies of chromosome 21, coining the medical diagnosis of Trisomy 21. This additional genetic material in the cell alters the typical development of the body and brain, causing the characteristics associated with DS. As such, children with DS have distinctive facial features and physique, may possess a degree of intellectual disability and experience delayed development in language and cognition which varies greatly across individuals.

There are three different types of DS, with Trisomy 21 being the most common, accounting for 95 per cent of DS cases. In 4 per cent of DS cases, the extra chromosome 21 or a portion of it attaches to another chromosome (usually chromosome 14), producing the formation of Translocation Trisomy 21. The third and rarest form is called Mosaic Trisomy 21, whereby the baby has a combination of two types of cells, some containing 46 chromosomes and some containing 47. With the prevalence of 1 in 1,000 births in the UK, DS is the most common chromosomal cause of intellectual disability (Wu and Morris, 2013). It occurs randomly in people of all races and economic levels and thus far, no behavioural activity of parents or environmental factors is known to explain the aberrant cell division. However, a history of research shows that the maternal age of 35 or greater and/or having had a child with DS would increase the risk of the baby having DS (Parker et al., 2010).

The moral and ethical dilemma of prenatal testing

Prenatal testing and the consequences of a positive result for DS is a much-debated topic. While some feel that prenatal testing is a means for parents to obtain information about their baby prior to birth such as health and developmental problems, others dispute that prenatal testing will lead to more terminations of babies with or without DS (Kazemi, Salehi and Kherollahi, 2016). Iceland law permits abortion after 16 weeks if the foetus has a deformity and is close to eradicating DS births. With ethical and medical concerns arising from this issue, Goodley and Runswich-Cole (2016) put forth the idea that screening out genetic abnormality is devaluing the lives of people living with disabilities because it focusses on the ableism ambitions of normalisations and therefore questions the meaning of disability studies. They argue that it would be more constructive and reduce resources to focus on early medical support and developmental intervention initiations during childhood to increase the life expectancy and quality of life of children with DS.

Activity

Read the following articles.

▓ What are the arguments for and against such a proposal?

The Independent: *New Down's syndrome screening process hailed as 'transformational' But campaigners fear test becoming more common in the NHS without ethical debate on screening out condition.*

This article can be accessed via the website (Independent, 2017).

The Guardian: *Do we really want a world without Down's syndrome? A new Prenatal test could eradicate Down's syndrome. Actress Sally Phillips, who has a child with the condition, explains why that would make the world a poorer place.*

This article can be accessed via the website (Guardian, 2016).

Features of Down's syndrome

DS affects multiple organ systems, which give rise to many health and sensory issues which affects learning and may become prominent as they get older. It is estimated that around half of babies with DS have congenital heart disease which is the main cause of death in babyhood though some may be treated with medications and/or surgery (Sanaa, Abdenasser and Ayoub, 2016). Poor cardiac functions also lead to sleep apnoea which affects memory, concentration, attention and lethargy level that is often misinterpreted as hyperactivity behaviour (Bull, 2011).

They generally have low immune systems, which make them susceptible to infections such as pneumonia and leukaemia, and it takes longer than others to recover (Khan, Malinge and Crispino, 2011). In addition, they are more inclined to struggle with weight gain and inactivity because of hypothyroidism, in which there is a lack of hormones to regulate temperature and energy. Although these medical issues may not seem directly related to learning, they are likely to lead to exhaustion and increased vulnerability to minor infections which are common in school settings. Chronic health problems can take a toll on their bodies which could possibly lead to poor school attendance and fewer opportunities to learn.

Another primary feature of children with DS is having low muscle tone, termed as hypotonia. It contributes to delays in physical development such as crawling and walking, in which problems with posture, mobility, breathing, speech and reflexes ensue as they grow older (Buckley, 2003). This impedes their development in gross and fine motor skills, and everyday self-care routines such as eating, dressing may be impaired. Physical activities may be challenging for them which may result in avoidance or unwillingness to attempt. In addition, around two-thirds of children with DS have some form of hearing impairment. They experience fluctuating hearing loss caused by middle ear fluid, suggesting that speech sounds may not be consistently and easily heard, on top of the noise level in a typical classroom (Bull, 2011). Therefore, they may not be able to process auditory information which hinders their ability to communicate effectively and follow instructions in class.

It is also reported that 70 per cent of children with DS experience visual difficulties in manifold, ranging from near/farsightedness, cataracts, eye squint, cross eyes, rapid involuntary eye movements and more (Woodhouse, 2005). Like any other children with visual impairment, this could affect speed of working, reading and writing skills, spatial awareness and social interactions due to the reduced ability to recognise body language and facial expressions. There may be difficulty in both comprehending language and producing language, due to low muscle tone, for example, pupils may have difficulty articulating and producing sounds and forget the order of sounds and syllables (Stoel-Gammon, 2001). It is also probable that poor intelligibility leads to unusual conversation styles that can impact communication negatively.

With respect to cognitive difficulties, recent studies have shown that children with DS have a general executive deficit which makes it difficult for them to co-ordinate two tasks at the same time (Lanfranchi et al., 2010). In addition, they have weak short-term memory skills that make processing verbal information difficult for them, which is important for learning to speak, understanding language and reading progress (Gathercole and Alloway, 2006). Ceblua, Moore and Wishart (2009) suggest that children with DS may have difficulty with social-perceptual abilities such as interpreting the thoughts, emotions and intentions of others, affecting social behaviour and interaction (Ceblua, Moore and Wishart, 2009) and lead to rejection, bullying and even isolation (Delano and Snell, 2006).

Classroom support

With varying degrees of support and accommodation, children with DS are able to achieve academic success and research has found that inclusive education helps children with DS gain academic, social and behavioural advantages (Wolpert, 2001).

Fine motor skills

To support their motor issues, teachers can provide increased opportunities for practising fine motor skills which will benefit muscle development as it requires repetitive training (Jobling and Mon-Williams, 2000). Using multi-sensory activities and materials that are attractive and motivating to practise with and being open and creative to finding suitable tools for tasks to enable participation and success will be helpful. For example, using marker pens to write instead of thin pencils and using paint to colour instead of colouring pencils.

Communication

Placing the child with DS at the front of the class enables them to hear and see from a closer distance and pick up non-verbal communication and cues. To support attention rephrasing, repeating and keeping sentences short and brief is an instructional method that is effective and widely used today (Muijs and Reynolds, 2001). Providing cues and visual materials to support spoken language will prevent the child from being disengaged just because he/she missed an instruction. Therefore, prints used should be in large print with good contrast, and pictures used should be clear and colourful. Having a timetable or checklist may help them to keep on task and is also a useful habit for independence.

Capitalising on their strong visual learning modalities is a way to counter their poor auditory processing and working memory abilities. Visual demonstrations, pictures and illustrations are effective in providing instruction and understanding (Copeland and Keefe, 2007). Gibbs and Carswell (2010) also highlight that written, visual and sign language modes compensate for their weakness in auditory learning and encourage total communication. To encourage retention of learning, it is recommended to review concepts frequently using a range of information sources such as videos, activities and mind maps. Tasks broken down into smaller and manageable components, so that skills are well-targeted and well-challenged to optimise learning opportunities, are also effective (Szidon and Franzone, 2009). Studies have shown that children with DS have strong imitative behaviour so modelling is essential to teach social skills (Silverstein et al., 1979).

 Activity

The Down's Syndrome Association, UK, has produced two educational support packs, one aimed at primary schools and the other aimed at secondary schools.

They can be accessed via the website (Downs Syndrome Association, 2018).

The Primary Education Support Pack contains ten units with information about the specific learning profile associated with having DS, legislation and guidance, effective strategies for inclusion, developing language skills, accessing the curriculum, teaching reading, developing writing skills, learning mathematics and numeracy skills, promoting positive behaviour and social skills, successful transitions and using computers in learning.

The Secondary Education Support Pack units describe the learning profile associated with having DS, legislation and guidance, strategies for inclusion, developing language skills, accessing the curriculum, teaching reading, developing writing skills, acquiring mathematics and numeracy skills, promoting positive behaviour and social skills, transition to secondary school, 14+ transition and onto Further Education, alternative accreditation at Key Stage 4 and computers as an aid to learning, with a unit dedicated to encouraging meaningful relationships and sex and relationships education. The 14+ transition planning unit includes a guide to Person Centred Planning and explains how to prepare for student centred transition reviews.

- Locate one of the units from the support pack which is most relevant to your practice and identify how you could use this within your context.

Cri du chat syndrome

Cri du chat syndrome (CCS) is a chromosome problem caused by a missing piece of chromosome 5. The syndrome is called Cri du chat (French for 'cry of the cat') because affected babies often have a high-pitched cry. It is a rare genetic disorder with an estimated incidence between 1:20,000 and 1:50,000 births (Wu et al., 2005) and is associated with a partial deletion on the short arm of chromosome 5. The missing piece of the chromosome is the short (called 'p') arm of chromosome 5. Therefore, it is said to be caused by deletion of chromosome 5p. Most cases are thought to occur as a result of damage to the chromosome during the development of the egg or sperm.

The clinical features of CCS include a high-pitched cry in infancy and childhood (Sohner and Mitchell, 1991), malocclusion, hyper- and hypotonia, delayed motor development (Carlin, 1990), microcephaly (Niebuhr, 1978), mild-to-profound intellectual disability (Cornish, Munir and Cross, 1999), a short attention span, hyperactivity, and a stereotypical, aggressive and self-injurious behaviour pattern (Collins and Cornish, 2002).

Those affected with CCS experience delayed speech and language development. According to the literature, a substantial share of individuals with CCS (reports vary from 23 per cent to 50 per cent) do not develop spoken language at all (Carlin, 1990; Cornish and Pigram, 1996). When those affected by CCS do develop spoken language, however, receptive language has been found to be significantly better than expressive language.

Features of CCS

Not all babies with a missing short arm of chromosome 5 will develop CCS. Some will have only very mild abnormal features or have no abnormal features at all. There are a number of features, which include:

- The baby has a cry which is high-pitched and has been described as sounding like a cat. The mewing cry becomes less obvious with the increasing age.
- Sucking and feeding problems are common in the first year of life.
- Features in the baby's head may include a small head (microcephaly), small jaw (micrognathia) and wide-set eyes.

■ Abnormal features in the face also include downward slant to the eyes, low or abnormally shaped ears and skin tags in front of the ear. There may be an extra fold of skin over the inner corner of the eye (epicanthic fold).

■ Abnormal features in the hands and feet include partial webbing or joining together (fusing) of the fingers or toes. There may be a single line (crease) in the palm of the hand (there are normally two skin creases).

■ The affected newborn baby may be small and grow slowly. The affected child may have learning difficulties. There may be slow development of motor skills (for example, a delay in walking) and of speech and language.

■ Other features may include a hernia in the groin and separation of the muscles in the tummy. There is also an increased risk of heart defects and abnormalities in the brain, kidneys or bowel.

Classroom support

Children may show hyperactivity and inattentiveness, alongside a poor concept of danger. However, it is important to note that pupils with CCS do possess good memory for faces and places, have an enjoyment of books and music, are generally happy, sociable and enthusiastic.

Perhaps because of its relatively low prevalence, CCS has received relatively little attention from special education researchers and professionals. Still, as Ohr (1998) noted, the prevalence of Cri du chat among people with mental retardation may be as high as 1 in every 350 individuals. Thus, it would not be uncommon for special education professionals to encounter children with CCS during their career.

Descriptive accounts of the developmental and behavioural characteristics associated with CCS have identified significant deficits in these children's learning abilities, language development, academic achievement and overall adaptive behaviour functioning. Many children with CCS also present with severe behaviour problems, such as self-injury, aggressive behaviour and stereotyped movement disorder (Cornish and Bramble, 2002).

 Pause for reflection

Pituch et al. (2010) conducted a survey which listed 54 skills/behaviours (for example, toileting, expresses wants and needs, and tantrums) representing a number of adaptive behaviour domains (for example, self-care, communication and problem behaviour). Parents rated their child's current level of ability/performance with respect to each skill/behaviour and indicated the extent and identified nine high priority skills/behaviours:

1. Personal safety

2. Toileting

3. Describing events and feelings

4. Following directions

5. Responding appropriately to questions

6. Listening to the teacher

7. Asking for information

8. Pedestrian safety skills

9. Expressing wants and needs.

■ Why do you think that parents identified these particular skills as high priority?

Support for specific areas might include:

Social and emotional development

■ Support children's social development by recognising and positively reinforcing successful social interactions.

■ Focus on what the child can do and provide opportunities for the child to engage in experiences that interest them.

■ Maintain a calm environment that promotes emotional security through consistency.

■ Planned relaxation and quiet activities can assist children in maintaining a calm state.

Physical development

■ Provide opportunities for children to challenge themselves and expend excess energy.

■ Experiences that enhance visual motor integration such as fine motor tasks including pre-writing skills.

■ Use strategies such as playing soft music or redirecting to a quiet activity when the child becomes overactive.

Language and communication development

- Provide a plan for the daily events/routine and discuss this with the child so they know what comes next.

- Provide a structured and predictable routine.

- Provide visual cues to accompany the routine so that child with Cri du chat can anticipate what comes next. Establish a routine for transitions, that is, when indoor play is about to finish, give the children a warning by playing music for them to tidy up, etc.

- Use clear and simple instructions, ensuring instructions have been understood before giving more.

- Incorporate activities to increase desire to communicate such as music sport or play activities.

- Utilise ICT to aid communication.

- Employ techniques to facilitate receptive language.

Cognitive development

- Set achievable goals and tasks for the child that they are capable of achieving.

- Ensure experiences provided are within the child's capacity for maintaining attention.

- Remind children of routines regularly.

- Reinforce learning with concrete examples, such as in the case of maths.

 Activity

Taking Fragile X, Foetal Alcohol Spectrum Disorder (FASD) and Cri du chat together:

1. What pedagogic responses are recommended for all three diversities?

2. What pedagogic responses are distinctive to only one of the diversities?

3. In the list for (2) are there any pedagogic responses that could or should be listed for all three diversities?

4. In the list for (2) are there any pedagogic responses that seem to be completely specific, different or specialised?

5. Which pedagogic responses could arguably be relevant to all children (including those without SEND)?

Foetal alcohol spectrum disorder

Foetal Alcohol Syndrome Disorder is an umbrella term for the array of different impairments an infant is likely to develop as a result of being exposed to alcohol during pregnancy, such as facial abnormalities and cognitive delay. The full range of prenatal alcohol damage varies from mild to severe and encompasses a broad array of physical defects and cognitive, behavioural and emotional deficits. FASD is a result of alcohol consumption during pregnancy. Alcohol is a teratogen – a substance that interferes with the development of the embryo or foetus. When a pregnant woman drinks, the alcohol in her blood passes freely through the placenta into the foetus's blood. Because the foetus does not have a fully developed liver, it cannot filter out the toxins from the alcohol as the mother can. Instead, the alcohol circulates in the foetus's blood system killing brain cells and damaging the nervous system of the foetus throughout pregnancy, but prenatal exposure to alcohol is a preventable cause of disability (Whitehurst, 2012). The consumption of alcohol during pregnancy may be the result of an array of multiple factors, such as the lack of education, poor maternal mental health and the lack of employment prospects (Van Vuuren and Learmonth, 2013).FASD includes:

1. FAS

2. partial foetal alcohol syndrome (pFAS)

3. foetal alcohol effects (FAE)

4. alcohol-related birth defects (ARBD)

5. alcohol-related neurodevelopmental disorder.

FAS is recognised as the most common identifiable cause of acquired mental intellectual development disorder. The true prevalence of FAS is not known, but International studies and the World Health Organization (2017) indicate that 1 in 100 children are born with FASD worldwide. With the high level of binge-drinking in the UK, it is possible that this number may well be underestimated. In 2012–2013, there were 252 diagnoses of the syndrome, which can leave victims severely mentally and physically impaired, compared with 89 in 1997–1998. Cases are up 37 per cent since 2009–2010. It is feared that those so far diagnosed are the tip of the iceberg. There is often no physical sign of the condition, but victims are left with learning difficulties and an inability to connect emotionally with their peers. Without diagnosis, they are often not helped during their time at school and become isolated as adults.

Susan Fleisher, chief executive of the National Organisation for Foetal Alcohol Syndrome, speaking to the Guardian in 2014 suggested that studies in Italy and the USA show that between 2 per cent and 5 per cent of the population is affected and that in the UK we are closer to 5 per cent, although we cannot say that for sure because it is under-diagnosed and difficult to diagnose with only 20 per cent having the physical signs of this condition such as small, wide-set eye openings, flattened philtrum, thin upper lip, lower ears and different creases in the hands.

FAS was first described in 1973 (Jones and Smith, 1973) and is caused by maternal alcohol consumption during pregnancy. Alcohol is a teratogen that easily crosses the placenta and thus can have devastating effects on the developing embryo and foetus. The brain is particularly vulnerable to prenatal alcohol exposure Streissguth (2007) and the most profound effects are on brain development and on cognitive and behavioural outcomes. There is no safe lower limit for alcohol consumption during pregnancy and the absolute amount of alcohol and prenatal exposure to alcohol can disrupt foetal brain development at any point during pregnancy (Clarke and Gibbard, 2003).

Features of foetal alcohol syndrome

The features of FAS can include:

- distinctive facial features;

- growth deficits such as low birth weight;

- brain damage, such as small skull at birth, structural defects and neurological signs;

- physical problems such as heart, lung and kidney defects;

- behavioural or cognitive deficits – may include cognitive delays, learning disabilities, attention deficits, hyperactivity, poor impulse control, social problems, language deficits and memory problems;

- several neurocognitive features often associated with FAS are learning disabilities, speech and language delays, problems with reasoning and judgement, impairments in abstract thinking, diminished impulse control, volatile emotions, poor social skills and vulnerability to peer pressure.

FAS is the most clinically recognisable form of FASD. It is diagnosed based on the presence of a characteristic set of facial features, combined with growth and neurocognitive defects. The characteristic facial features may include a thin upper lip, a flat nasal bridge, an upturned nose, small wide-set eyes and a smooth philtrum (the vertical groove between the upper lip and nose). The clinical features of other forms of FASD are less well defined and more complex to diagnose. The diagnostic criteria for FAS rely on anomalies in three distinct areas: pre- and/or postnatal growth deficiency; central nervous system dysfunction and characteristic facial anomalies (Riley, Infante and Warren, 2011). FAS is the only diagnosis from the four types of FASD according to the International Classification of Diseases

(ICD-10; code Q86.0). In DSM-V, it is categorised under Neurobehavioral Disorder Associated with Pre-natal Alcohol Exposure (ND-PAE).

In addition to brain injury, individuals with FAS will have characteristic facial features. The facial features are easiest to identify in children between 3 and 14 years of age. As children with FAS grow older, the facial features may change, making FAS more difficult to recognise. Along with brain injury and facial features, children with an FAS may experience stiffness in their joints, gross and fine motor delays and seizures. These students may need additional assistance in the cafeteria, on the playground and in the classroom. Providing an appropriate education is important for all students including children with prenatal alcohol exposure. Children with prenatal alcohol exposure do not always exhibit obvious physical differences from their peers, so they are often expected to act and learn as other children do.

Brain dysfunction in children with FAS often leads to primary disabilities such as poor adaptive functioning, language deficits, attention difficulties and reasoning and memory deficits (Clarke and Gibbard, 2003). The neuropsychological and neurobehavioural problems often stem from early childhood, during adolescence and into adulthood. Secondary disabilities that arise after birth as a result of the primary disabilities include psychiatric disorders, disrupted school and employment experiences, alcohol abuse/illicit drug use, trouble with the law and inappropriate sexual behaviour (Streissguth et al., 2003). A Swedish research group found that adults who were diagnosed with FAS in childhood revealed impaired psychosocial outcomes, decreased cognitive and executive functions and impaired social cognition. Furthermore, individuals with FAS often have problems with their daily planning and living an independent life (Rangmar et al., 2015).

The effects of FASD can be mild or severe, ranging from reduced intellectual ability and attention deficit disorder to heart problems and even death. Many children experience serious behavioural and social difficulties that last a lifetime. Prenatal alcohol consumption is associated with poor educational outcomes. Streissguth, Randels and Smith (1991) identified that the average IQ of adolescents and adults with FAS is 68. The study concluded that individuals with FAS are less likely to experience positive educational outcomes due to the learning impairments associated with their disability.

Classroom support

There are a number of invisible FASD characteristics, which may include: attention deficits; memory deficits; difficulty with abstract concepts (for example, maths, time and money) and poor problem-solving skills. There are five keys to working successfully with students with an FASD: structure, consistency, variety, brevity and persistence. It is important to understand that students with an FASD can lack internal structure, so there is a need to provide an external structure as much as possible. Practitioners should be consistent in their responses and in the daily routine, so that the pupil has a sense that their surroundings are predictable. Students with an FASD have difficulty maintaining attention, so it is important that teachers and support staff are to be brief in their explanations and directions.

 Activity

The British Columbia Ministry of Education in Canada has published a comprehensive learning resource for teachers working with pupils living with FAS.

It can be accessed via the website (British Columbia Ministry of Education, 2018).

■ Taking any of the following subheadings, identify how these strategies could be used within your context.

1. Attentional Difficulties

2. Cause and Effect Thinking

3. Social Skills

4. Personal Skills

5. The Physical Environment of the Classroom

6. Planning the Day: Maximise Structure and Routine

7. Memory Skills

8. Language Development

9. Reading and Writing

10. Motor Skills

11. Mathematical Skills

12. Money Concepts

13. Science Skills

14. Fine Arts.

Summary

'Some of them even go to school these days'.

As we move towards a more inclusive agenda for schools in the UK, it is important that teachers and support staff working in the area of SEND are conversant with the aetiology, features and pedagogic responses to well-documented and researched areas such as ADHD, ASD and dyslexia, for example. However, it is also important to acknowledge other conditions which are becoming increasingly frequent in classrooms and have an impact on children, young people and their families. As such, it is equally important that educational practitioners understand chromosomal and gestational issues such as the ones outlined in this chapter also.

References

British Columbia Ministry of Education (2018). *Teaching students with fetal alcohol syndrome/ Effects*. Available online at: www2.gov.bc.ca/assets/gov/education/kindergarten-to-grade-12/ teach/teaching-tools/inclusive/fetal-alcohol-syndrome.pdf (Accessed 12/02/2018).

Buckley, S. (2003). Literacy and language. In Rondal, J. and Buckley, S. (eds.), *Speech and language intervention in Down syndrome*. London: Whurr Publishers Ltd, 132–153.

Budimirovic, D. (2017). *Fragile X Syndrome and autism spectrum disorder: Similarities and differences*. National Fragile X Foundation. Available online 2018 at: https://fragilex. org/2014/support-and-resources/fragile-x-syndrome-and-autism-spectrum-disorder-similarities-and-differences/ (Accessed 03/03/2018).

Bull, M.J. (2011). Health supervision for children with Down Syndrome. *Journal of Pediatrics*, 128(2), pp. 393–406.

Carlin, M.E. (1990). The improved prognosis in cri du chat (5p-) syndrome. In Fraser, I.W. (ed.), *Key issues in mental retardation research*. London: Routledge.

Charalsawadi, C. (2017). Common clinical characteristics and rare medical problems of Fragile X Syndrome in Thai patients and review of the literature. *International Journal of Paediatrics*, 2017(4), pp. 1–11.

Clarke, M.E. and Gibbard, W.B. (2003). Overview of fetal alcohol spectrum disorders for mental health professionals. *The Canadian Child and Adolescence Psychiatry Review*, 12(3), pp. 57–63.

Copeland, S.R. and Keefe, E.B. (2007). *Effective literacy instruction*. Baltimore: Paul H. Brookes.

Cornish, K.M. and Bramble, D. (2002). Cri du chat: Genotype-phenotype correlations and recommendations for clinical management. *Developmental Medicine and Child Neurology*, 44(7), pp. 494–497.

Cornish, K.M., Munir, F. and Cross, G. (1999). Spatial cognition in males with fragile-X syn- drome: Evidence for a neuropsychological phenotype. *Cortex*, 35(2), 263–271.

Cornish, K.M. and Pigram, J. (1996). Developmental and behavioural characteristics of Cri-du-Chat syndrome. *Archives of Disease in Childhood*, 75, pp. 448–450.

Delano, M. and Snell, M.E. (2006). The effects of social stories on the social engagement of children with Autism. *Journal of Positive Behaviour Interventions*, 8(1), 29–42.

Dew-Hughes, D. (2003). *Educating children with Fragile X*. London: Routledge Falmer.

Deweerdt, S. (2011). 'Reclassification of Rett syndrome diagnosis stirs concerns'. Spectrum News. Available online at: https://spectrumnews.org/news/reclassification-of-rett-syndrome-diagnosis-stirs-concerns/ (Accessed 12/08/2018).

Downs Syndrome Association (2018). *For families and carers: Education support packs*. Available online at: www.downs-syndrome.org.uk/for-families-and-carers/education/ education-support-packs/ (Accessed 12/02/2018).

East, V. and Evans, L. (2001). *At a glance - a practical guide to children's special needs*. New York: Continuum International Publishing Group.

Fernández Carvajal, I. and Aldridge, D. (2011). *Understanding Fragile X Syndrome*. 1st ed. London: Jessica Kingsley Publishers.

Fisher, J., Morling, E. and Murray, F. (2004). *Supporting children with Fragile X Syndrome*. Hull: David Fulton Publishers.

Gathercole, S.E. and Alloway, T.P. (2006). Practitioner review: Short-term and working memory impairments in neurodevelopmental disorders: Diagnosis and remedial support. *Journal of Child Psychology and Psychiatry*, 47(1), pp. 4–15.

Gibbs, E.D. and Carswell, L.E. (2010). Using total communication with young children with Down syndrome: Aliterature review and case study. *Journal of Early Education and Development*, 2(4), pp. 306–320.

Guardian (2014). *Sharp rise in babies born with foetal alcohol syndrome*. Available online at: www.theguardian.com/society/2014/jun/21/pregnant-women-alcohol-abuse (Accessed 10/01/2018).

Guardian (2016). *A new prenatal test could eradicate Down's syndrome. Actress Sally Phillips, who has a child with the condition, explains why that would make the world a poorer place*. Available online at: www.theguardian.com/lifeandstyle/2016/oct/01/do-we-really-want-a-world-without-downs-syndrome-ds-prenatal-test (Accessed 12/01/2018).

Goodley, D. and Runswick-Cole, K. (2016). Becoming dishuman: Thinking about the human through disability. *Discourse: Studies in Cultural Politics of Education*, 37(1), pp. 1–15.

Green (2003). *Educating children with Fragile X Syndrome: Amulti-professional view*. London: Routledge and Taylor & Francis.

Hayward, B.E., Zhou, Y., Kumari, D. and Usdin, K. (2016). A set of assays for the comprehensive analysis of fMR1 alleles in the Fragile X-related disorders. *Journal of Molecular Diagnostics*, 18, pp. 762–774.

Howlin, P., Charman, T. and Ghaziuddin, M. (2011). *The SAGE handbook of developmental disorders*. London: SAGE Publication.

ICD Codes (2018). *ICD-10-CM Code Q99.2: Fragile X chromosome*. Available online at: https://icd.codes/icd10cm/Q992 (Accessed 14/05/2018).

Independent (2017). *New Down's syndrome screening process hailed as 'transformational'*. Available online at: www.independent.co.uk/news/health/downs-syndrome-screening-nhs-new-latest-blood-tests-a8044846.html (Accessed 12/01/2018).

Jobling, M.A. and Mon-Williams, M. (2000). Motor development in Down syndrome: A longitudinal perspective. In Elliot, D., Weeks, D. and Chua, R. (eds.), *Perceptual-motor behaviour in Down syndrome*. Champaign, IL: Human Kinetics

Jones, K.L. and Smith, D.W. (1973). Recognition of the fetal alcohol syndrome in early infancy. *Lancet*, 2, pp. 999–1001.

Kazemi, M., Salehi, M. and Kheirolahi, M. (2016). Down syndrome: Current status, challenges and future perspectives. *International Journal of Molecular and Cellular Medicine*, 5(3), pp. 125–133.

Khan, I., Malinge, S. and Crispino, J.D. (2011). Myeloid Lukemia in Down syndrome. *Critical Reviews in Oncogenesis*, 16(1–2), pp. 25–36.

Lanfranchi, S., Jerman, O., Pont, E. D., Alberti, A. and Vianello, R. (2010). Executive function in adolescents with Down syndrome. *Journal of Intellectual Disability*, 54, pp. 308–319.

Muijs, R.D. and Reynolds, D. (2001). *Effective teaching. Evidence and Practice.* 1st ed. London: Paul Chapman Publishing.

National Fragile X Foundation (2004). *Lesson planning guide for students with Fragile X Syndrome.* Available online at: https://fragilex.org/wp-content/uploads/2012/01/Lesson-Planning-Guide-for-Students-with-FXS.pdf (Accessed 06/07/2018).

National Fragile X Foundation (2017). *A practical approach for the classroom.* Available online at: https://fragilex.org/2017/education/lesson-planning-guide/ (Accessed 06/07/2018).

National Human Genome Research Institute (2018). *Learning about Fragile X Syndrome.* Available online at: www.genome.gov/19518828/learning-about-fragile-x-syndrome/ (Accessed 12/02/2018).

Ohr, P.S. (1998). *Cri-du-Chat syndrome. Health-related disorders in children and adolescents: A guidebook for understanding and educating.* Washington: American Psychological Association.

Parker, S.E., Mai, C.T., Canfield, M.A., Rickard, R., Wang, Y. and Meyer, R.E. (2010). Updated national birth prevalence estimates for selected birth defects in the United States, 2004–2006. Birth Defects Research. Part A. *Clinical and Molecular Teratology*, 88(12), pp. 1008–1016.

Pituch, K.A., Green, V.A., Didden, R., Whittle, L., O'Reilly, M.F. and Lancioni, G.E. (2010). Educational priorities for children with cri-du-chat syndrome. *Journal of Developmental and Physical Disabilities*, 22, pp. 65–81.

Rangmar, J., Sandberg, A.D., Aronson, M. and Fahlke, C. (2015). Cognitive and executive functions, social cognition and sense of coherence in adults with fetal alcohol syndrome. *Nordic Journal of Psychiatry*, 2, pp. 472–478.

Riley, E.P., Infante, M.A. and Warren, K.R. (2011). Fetal alcohol spectrum disorders: An overview. *Neuropsychology Review*, 21(2), pp. 73–80.

Roberts, J.E.; Tonnsen, B.L.; McCary, L.M.; Caravella, K.E. and Shinkareva, S.V. (2016). Brief report: Autism symptoms in infants with Fragile X Syndrome. *Autism and Developmental Disorders*, 46(12), pp. 3830–3837.

Sanaa, B., Abdenasser, D. and Ayoub, E.H. (2016). Congenital heart disease and Down syndrome: Various aspects of a confirmed association. *Cardiovascular Journal of Africa*, 27(5), pp. 287–290.

Selikowitz, M. (2008). *Down syndrome.* Oxford: Oxford University Press.

Silverstein, A.B, Aguilar, B.F., Jacobs, L.J., Levy, J.E. and Rubenstein, D.M. (1979). Imitative behaviour by Down's syndrome persons. *American Journal of Mental Deficiency*, 83(4), pp. 409–411.

Sohner, L. and Mitchell, P. (1991). Phonatory and phonetic characteristics of prelinguistic vocal development in cri du chat syndrome. *Journal of Communication Disorders*, 24(1), pp. 13–20.

Stoel-Gammon, C. (2001). Down syndrome phonology: Developmental patterns and intervention strategies. *Down Syndrome Research and Practice*, 7(3), pp. 93–100.

Streissguth, A.P. (2007). Offspring effects of prenatal alcohol exposure from birth to 25 years: The Seattle prospective longitudinal study. *Journal of Clinical Psychology in Medical Settings*, 14(2), pp. 81–101.

Streissguth, A.P., Randels, S.P. and Smith, D.F. (1991). A test retest study of intelligence in patients with fetal alcohol syndrome: Implications for care. *Journal of the American Academy of Child and Adolescent Psychiatry*, 30(4), pp. 584–587.

Szidon, K. and Franzone, E. (2009). *Task analysis*. Madison: National Professional Development Center on Autism Spectrum Disorders, Waisman Center, University of Wisconsin.

Tomchek and Dunn (2007). Sensory processing in children with and without autism: Acomparative study using the short sensory profile. *The American Journal of Occupational Therapy*, 61(2), pp. 190–200.

Van Vuuren A.J. and Learmonth, D. (2013). Spirit(ed) away: Preventing foetal alcohol syndrome with motivational interviewing and cognitive behavioural therapy. *South African Family Practice*, 55(1), pp. 59–64.

Whitehurst, T. (2012). Raising a child with foetal alcohol syndrome: Hearing the parent voice. *British Journal of Learning Disabilities*, 40, pp. 187–193.

Wolpert, G. (2001). What general educators have to say about successfully including students with Down syndrome in their classes. *Journal of Research in Childhood Education*, 16(1), pp. 28–38.

Woodhouse, J. (2005). Vision in children with Down syndrome: Aresearch update. *Down Syndrome News and Update*, 4(3), pp. 87–89.

World Health Organization (2017). Counting the costs of drinking alcohol during pregnancy. *Bulletin of the World Health Organization*, 9, pp. 320–332. Available online at: www.who.int/bulletin/volumes/95/5/17-030517/en/ (Accessed 12/06/2108).

Wu, J. and Morris, J.K. (2013). The population prevalence of Down's syndrome in England and Wales in 2011. *European Journal of Human Genetics*, 21(9), pp. 1016–1019.

Wu, Q., Niebuhr, E., Yang, H. and Hansen, L. (2005). Determination of the 'critical region' for cat-like cry of Cri-du-chat syndrome and analysis of candidate genes by quantitative PCR. *European Journal of Human Genetics*, 13, pp. 475–485.

Index

attachment disorder (AD), reactive
attachment disorder (RAD) 100–2;
classroom support 102; dissociation 102;
genetics 100–2; neurology 102; social
factors 102

attachment theory 98, 102, 132, 164;
ambivalent attachment 99; avoidant
attachment 99; disorganised attachment
99; secure attachment 99

attention disorders (attention deficit
hyperactivity disorder (ADHD),
attention deficit disorder (ADD)) 81,
95, 152–67; cognitive explanations
162–3; diagnosis and classification
(DSM-V, ICD10, ICD11) 153–6;
dopamine 158–9; environmental and
risk factors 161–2; genetic factors
156–8; managing hyperactivity 165;
managing impulsivity 166; managing
inattention 165; Moderate Brain
Arousal Theory 159; myths surrounding
ADHD/ADD 156; neuroanatomy 160–1;
pharmacotherapy 159–60; as a social
construct 163–4

autism spectrum disorder (ASD) 131–50,
158–9, 195, 200, 228; Comic Strip
Conversations 149; definition of 133;
DSM-V 133–4; executive dysfunction
138, 158–9, 228; genetics of 134–5;
ICD11 133–4; monotropism 139–40;
power cards 148–9; refrigerator mothers
132; risk factors 137–8; Schools Autism
Standards 145; social stories 148;
structural abnormalities in the brain
135–7; support in the classroom 143–8;
theory of mind 138–40, 149, 200; token
economy strategies 147–8; triad and
dyad of impairment 133–4; weak central
coherence 139

biopsychosocial model of disability 76, 86,
141

Bruner, J. 110–11; modes of representation
110; scaffolding 110–12, 203

Care Act (2014) 43

Centre for Studies on Inclusive Education
(CSIE) 78

child and adolescent mental health services
(CAMHS) 34, 43, 48

Children Act (1989) 36

Children and Families Act (2014) 15, 61–2

cognitive impact of language delay and
language disorder 199–200

Council for Disabled Children 22, 51

Cri du chat syndrome (CCS) 222–5;
classroom support 223–5; features 222–3

critical incidences 66

developmental milestones 96–8, 111, 127,
164, 194

dilemma of difference 88

discourses 7, 45, 55, 63, 76–93, 141, 181, 188

Down's syndrome (DS) 218–22; classroom
support 220–5; communication 221–2;
features of 219–20; fine motor skills 220;
genetics of 218; prenatal testing 218–19

dyslexia 91, 96, 170–88; cerebellar
theory 179; characteristics of 172–3;
classification and diagnosis 173–4;
classroom strategies 182–8; cognitive
explanations of dyslexia 181; debate
surrounding 180–1; definitions of 175–6;
difference/deficit 174; dyscalculia 173;
dysgraphia 173; environmental and
risk factors 181–2; genetics of 176;
insula-disconnection syndrome 179;
magnocellular theory 179; metacognition
and 186–7; neurobiological factors

177–8; neurodiversity 171; orthographic dyslexia 173; phonological dyslexia 173; phonological theory 178; rapid auditory processing theory 178; visual theory 178

Early Years Foundation Stage (EYFS) Framework 63
Education Act (1981) 8
Education Act (1996) 9
Education, Health and Care Plans (EHCP) 6, 11, 65
Education Select Committee report on SEN (2006) 10
Elliott, J. G. 180–1
Equality Act (2010) 29
Erikson, E. 102–5; adolescence 105; identity formation 105; life stages 102–4
Every Child Matters (2003) 34, 42
expressive language and communication 193, 196, 197, 198, 209

families 11, 12, 16, 21, 31, 33, 34, 42, 45–7, 52, 56, 60–73; ADHD 157, 164; autism 134–5, 145; dyslexia 176, 187
foetal alcohol spectrum disorder (FASD): classroom support 228–9; foetal alcohol syndrome (FAS) 226–30
Fragile X syndrome (FXS) 212–17; and autism 214–15; classroom support for 216–17; features of 214; genetics of 213–14

Gibbs S. 180–1
graduated response 18, 20–1, 50, 51; Assess Plan Do Review 12, 13, 16–20
Green Paper: Excellence for all Children Meeting SEN (1997) 9
Green Paper: Support and Aspiration (2011) 11

hard-to reach parents 68–9
home-school partnerships 69

impairment 115–19, 126–8, 141, 200, 214, 220; ADHD 153, 156, 163; autism 133, 135, 138, 139; disability and impairment 96, 97; dyslexia 170, 173–4; language 90, 194–5, 201; medical model 84; social model 85, 89
inclusion 8, 10, 17, 23, 41, 47, 55, 58, 66, 71–81, 89, 92, 108, 126, 217, 221; inclusive teachers 80–1; index for 80
integration 77

labels 84, 88, 89
Lamb Inquiry (2009) 25, 61, 62, 72
Laming Report (2003) 42

language development 193–5; constructivist perspective 193–4; language delay 194–5; modular perspective 193
language disorders 195–8; aphasia 198; Developmental Language Disorder (DLD) 197; Social Pragmatic Communication Disorder (SPCD) 197
learning difficulty 8, 9, 11, 12, 70, 85, 90, 91, 96, 115, 117–21, 141, 170–8, 186, 190, 195, 199, 201
Lewis, A. (general differences and unique differences) 142
local authorities (LAs) (local education authorities (LEAs)) 15, 16, 17, 26, 37, 43, 53, 120
local offer 16, 17, 43, 73

mainstream 7, 8, 9, 10, 17, 23, 54–5, 59, 76–9, 90, 92, 98, 115, 143–5, 200, 202, 204; classroom 76, 143, 144, 202; education 7, 8, 9, 10, 17, 23, 54, 55; schools 7, 8, 9, 10, 17, 23, 54, 55, 202
medical model of disability 22, 55, 63, 76, 83–6, 89, 90–2, 116, 141
models of working with families 71–2; empowerment model 71; negotiating model 72; parent as consumer 71; transplant model 71
multi-agency working 33–48; information sharing and the multi-agency approach 33–5; models 47–8; Multi-Agency Safeguarding Hub (MASH) 48; multi-agency team (MAT) 43–8; practice 49–50

National Award for SEN Co-ordination 52
National Health Service (NHS) 14, 15, 43, 48, 122, 219
National Workforce Agreement (2003) 54
nature nurture debate 90, 95; Dweck, C. 95; fixed IQ 90, 95; untapped potential 95
Norwich, B. (general differences and unique differences) 142

Ofsted 55, 79, 88; Common Inspection Framework (2016) 32; framework for SEND 12–14; safeguarding 32–3
outcomes of disabled pupils and those who have SEN 14

parent partnerships 52, 62–4, 68–9, 72–3
Piaget, J. 106–7, 193–4; play 107, 110; stages of cognitive development 106–7, 121
Plowden Report (1967) 61
power relationships (French, J. and Raven, B.) 67
prevent strategy 36

profound and multiple learning difficulties
(PMLD) 115–28; aetiology 122–3;
conception 122; definitions 117–19;
historical perspective of 116–17; IQ and
PMLD 119; P scales, Rochford Review
124; pregnancy, labour and after birth
123; Quest for Learning 126–7; Rett
syndrome 121; Routes for Learning
125–6; SMART and SCRUFFY targets 125

Quality Care Commission 14, 43
Quality First Teaching 81–2, 185; waves
model of intervention 82–3

receptive language and communication
199, 203–6, 228
Removing Barriers to Achievement (2004) 9

Safeguarding and Child Protection 25–37;
appropriate training for all staff 30–1;
Designated Safeguarding Lead (DSL)
27; Keeping children Safe in Education
(2016) 26, 29, 32; Keeping Children
Safe in Education (2018) 29; Local
Safeguarding Children Boards (LSCBs)
26; What to do if you're Worried a Child
is Being abused (2015) 27; whole-school
culture 30
segregation 7–8, 85, 89, 96
SEN Co-ordinator (SENCO) 50–2, 203–6;
graduated response 19–20, 23
SEND Code of Practice (1994) 8, 23
SEND Code of Practice 0–25 (2015) 12,
14–15; areas of SEN and support 117;
dyslexia 175; graduated response 18–20;
multi-agency 34, 43–4, 48; P scales 127;
parents 69; Quality First Teaching 81,
185; safeguarding 36; SENCO 50–1; SLCN
195; teaching assistants 53, 55
SEN statements 7, 8, 10, 11, 23
Snowling, M. 180–1
social model of disability 55, 63, 83–6, 90,
91, 96, 117, 118

Special Educational Needs and Disability
Act (2001) 9
special schools 7–10, 15, 23, 79, 92, 115
speech, language and communication needs
(SLCN) 195
Support and Aspiration: A New Approach
to SEN and Disability (2016) 62
supporting individuals with speech,
language and communication needs
(SLCN) 200–6; Makaton 144, 202;
modelling 203; One-Page Profile 12, 126,
201; Picture Exchange Communication
System (PECS) 202–3; scaffolding
language 203; speech and language
therapies 205–6; supporting expressive
language 203; supporting receptive
language 204

teaching assistants (TAs) 20, 41, 52, 56, 79,
82–3, 111, 203; Deployment and Impact
of Support Staff project (2003–2009)
54; Higher Level Teaching Assistants
(HLTAs) 53
Teacher's Standards (2011) 31

UN Convention on the Rights of a Child
(1989) 77

voice of the child 23, 35–7, 62–3, 73, 193;
safeguarding 35–6
Vygotsky, L. 106, 108–11, 193; peer
mediated learning 108–9; zone of
proximal development 108–10

Warnock Report (1978) 7–8, 61, 63, 71, 92,
116
Working Group on Child Protection and
Disability in England (2003) 28
Working Together to Safeguard Children
(2015) 26, 27, 34, 35, 43

Youth Inclusion and Support Panel
(YISP) 47

Printed in Great Britain
by Amazon

85721589R00140